Rebecca was born in Australia and now lives in London with her husband and dogs and any combination of her three children (depending on who has decided to move in this week.) Rebecca spends her non-writing time singing, sailing, swimming, or walking the dogs. The rest of the time is spent sorting the family archives finding more inspiration for stories about every day, interesting people.

This book is dedicated to Richard Arnold Clarke and to his son Arnold Richard Clarke and to his son James Richard Clarke and to his son Seamus Matthew Clarke.

Rebecca Clarke

A BARE CHRONICLE OF EXISTENCE

Stories and Letters from Internment in
Norway During WW1

AUSTIN MACAULEY PUBLISHERS™
LONDON • CAMBRIDGE • NEW YORK • SHARJAH

A CIP catalogue record for this title is available from the British Library.

ISBN 9781398456464 (Paperback)
ISBN 9781398456471 (ePub e-book)

www.austinmacauley.com

First Published 2022
Austin Macauley Publishers Ltd®
1 Canada Square
Canary Wharf
London
E14 5AA

Table of Contents

Prologue 11

Richard Arnold Clarke – "But Procrastination and Delay
Are My Only Portion in this World." 15

HMS India – "She is a Good Sea Boat." 33

Sinking of HMS India— "Submarine on Starboard Bow" 52

What to Do with the Sunken Sailors? 86

The First Few Months—"Well, News is Scarce." 100

First Half of 1916 – "Hopes, Ambitions and Ideals have Gone." 125

Second Half of 1916 – "Not Letters but a Bare Chronicle of
 Existence." 139

First Half of 1917 – "The News Is Forced." 176

Second Half of 1917 – "I Regret My Letters Often Get
Left Unwritten Nowadays." 190

First Half of 1918 – "London Seems a Long Way Off." 211

Second Half of 1918— "I Am in No Wise over Brimming
 with Cheerfulness." 241

A Caricaturist's View – "A Great Humourist Has Obviously
 Not Let this Opportunity Go." 260

What Next? What Are the Stories of and What Happened
 to some of the HMS India Crew? 275

Rogues Gallery   **309**

The Rest of Arnold's Life   **321**

Epilogue   **327**

References   **331**

Appendix   **337**

The Clarke Family   *337*

Hms India Casualitites   *341*

HMS India Gotaland Survivors   *349*

HMS India Gotaland Survivors   *349*

nearly

collapsed outwards & the whole train sank
into the earth. If the Recording Angel
takes down all our words - well my
pages wont read wholesome. If Paradise
is one half the place we make it out to
be, I often wonder there's not a bigger
rush for the early doors.

I grow to _____

more & more every day. I
do wish the war would stop. We all
sigh for the moon. A good dose of
strychnine would relieve all, but one is
too afraid. Well for the time being

yrs a

24.

POSTAL CENSORSHIP.

The British Censorship
is not responsible for the
mutilation of this letter.

Prologue

I came to learn of R Arnold Clarke and his sisters soon after I began a teenage romance with his grandson. Arnold was dead by then but his presence and that of his sisters, was not. My husband, James, grew up in a leafy Eastern suburb of Melbourne, Australia with his family and had a holiday house in the seaside town I grew up in. His father, Richard, was from Northern Ireland but had settled in Melbourne upon marriage.

When first visiting their house, I remember being impressed by all the antique furniture. The living room had a large leather topped desk and above it, a portrait of a man with a huge moustache and small eyeglasses. Whilst it was a formal portrait, the man in question had a twinkle in his eye and I got the feeling that he was a gentle soul. The house was filled with furniture, art works, photos and mementos like this portrait and I learnt that they all came from Henbury. Henbury was the extended family home in New Milton, a large village in the New Forest in Hampshire. The home of Richard's maiden aunts.

As I became a part of the family, I came to know more of the family history and the vast amounts of memorabilia stored in antique dressers, boxes, old shipping trunks and files. I had never seen one family with so much in the way of diaries, letters, photographs and I was to learn that what I was seeing in these early days was just scratching the surface.

The treasure trove that made up the family archive had been inherited by Richard. He and his sister Christine were the only descendants from a large family of five sisters and two brothers and were responsible for the managing of the estates of not only their parents but their aunts as well. Richard had moved to Australia after falling in love with Margaret but got the chance to return to England in the mid-1970s for work and was able to bring his young family with him.

The two years spent in London gave Richard the opportunity to share his wife Margaret, daughter Kate and son James with his aunt Edith and briefly with

Aunt Anne (Queenie) in the New Forest and with his father in Belfast. Richard's aunts were in or nearing their nineties at this stage but still lived together in Henbury, the house that their father had moved to in 1918.

Sadly, the other aunt, Winifred, had died in late April 1977 and Richard and family arriving in June the same year just missed seeing her again. Only five months after arriving in England, Aunt Anne (as Richard called her) died and on the very same day Arnold, in Belfast, had a stroke.

The Clarke family returned to Melbourne in 1978 and settled into a more stable life. In 1984, Aunt Edith passed away at the impressive age of 98. The issue of clearing Henbury then fell to Richard and his sister, Christine. To say that the aunts had held on to everything is putting it mildly. I have found receipts and hotel brochures from the post war era and multiple boxes of photographs of people we will never be able to identify.

Richard and Christine had to work out what would happen to a house full of antique furniture (much of it from their aunt's childhood house in High Street, Gravesend) as well as books and letters, diaries and stamps, photos and paintings. What would happen was to pack most of it up, put it in a container and sail it across the seas to Australia where the drawers were repacked with the saved memorabilia and many boxes were stored without even being opened. The job of sorting through them was such a big one and there was little free time to dedicate to it amid busy family life.

In the early 1990s a portion of the letters began to be read by new eyes with a friend of the family deciding to include Edith and Winifred's writings in a PHD. The discussions at this time piqued my interest and about fifteen years later, when Richard and Margaret retired and moved to a new house, I was only too happy to become custodian to the boxes of letters, diaries and photographs.

Clearing a space in a wardrobe in the study and I piled up the boxes and dragged them out every now and then to try to sort through and make sense of them. They were certainly fuel for the imagination—diaries dating back to 1898 telling of a holiday taken by a twelve-year-old girl on a three masted steam yacht owned by a rich aunt and of family holidays to the Victorian and Edwardian fashionable seaside resorts of England and train journeys to Scotland to spend more time with the rich aunt in huge houses nestled in the Scottish Highlands. Letters from Newnham College, Cambridge where one of the aunts studied in the first decade of the 20th century. Photos of girls performing drills and exercises at a college for physical education set up just for young women.

It was such fascinating stuff and I knew I wanted to do something with it—to bring it out into the world. Lurking behind the wealth of material written and collected by the aunts was the story of the youngest child, Richard Arnold Clarke, and the time he had spent as a Prisoner of War in Norway in the First World War.

Time passed quickly and my time was taken by the seemingly never-ending commitment of child raising and teaching and running a house whilst my husband worked away. In 2013, we were offered the opportunity to live in London for a year. We grasped the opportunity with eager hands, packed up three children, billeted out 2 dogs and set off. The year quickly turned into two years and before we knew it, we had bought a house and moved the contents of our storage facility into our new West London residence—the contents including 6 boxes of diaries and letters.

By this time, I was only home educating one child, the other two having made their way to tertiary education and I found myself with more time. It was exciting to open these boxes and start the adventure of sorting and discovering again. I dove headlong into transcribing the diaries and letters of Edith, Anne and Winifred and starting planning how I might bring these stories to life, but Arnold kept lurking in the background. Mentioned in letters but hard to find in the census and official documentation. He intrigued me.

I visited the National Archives in search of background information on the aunts and was reminded of the files I had looked at with my father-in-law some years back. The files dealing with the ship Arnold had been on during WW1 and the subsequent torpedo attack and internment of its crew. I decided I would come back another day and have a better look. Around the same time, I stumbled across a few letters from Arnold to his sister Queenie (Anne Victoria but known as Annie or Queenie).

The letters were written from Norway and painted a portrait of a sad, lonely and at times desperate young man. I was also intrigued by the story of my father-in-law finding several letters of Arnold's being sold online through eBay. Why would anyone else be interested in the letters of a World War One Engine Room Artificer?

A trip back to Australia and the news that my parents-in-law were downsizing to a retirement unit led me to help with sorting and packing and the discovery of a larger pile of letters from Norway kept in Arnold's metal sea going box along with photos and the war medals my husband thought he had lost as a child. Reading the letters compelled me to shelve my work on his elder sisters and decide to focus on Arnold and his story. His letters provide a way into a part of World War One that is seldom spoken of and little known, but it is a story that needs to be told.

However, before I get Arnold to tell his story, I would like to introduce him by telling a little of his childhood and how he ended up aboard a ship in North Sea in August 1915.

Richard Arnold Clarke –
"But Procrastination and Delay Are My
Only Portion in this World."

Richard Arnold Clarke was the youngest of the six living children of Richard Feaver (I will refer to him as R Feaver as this is how he signed his name) and Rebecca Clarke. He was the youngest of a close knit, lively, well-educated, and loving family. Born in 1893, he had four surviving elder sisters—Dorothy (b. 1884), Edith (b.1886), Anne or Queenie (b. 1887) and Winifred (b. 1889). He also had one elder brother, Wilfrid, who was two years older than him.

His sisters had all been educated at primary and secondary school and then two of them attained university degrees (not that they were awarded as women were not allowed to be awarded their degrees at this stage). Arnold and his brother were the babies of the family but shared a love of cricket and games with their sisters and photographs show happy smiles and a family who happily spent time with each other.

Of all the Clarke siblings I have found Arnold's early life the most difficult to research. The first port of call for all family research are the census records. Being born in 1893, he does not feature in the 1891 census and then I could not find him in the 1901 or 1911 census either, so I was reliant upon family documents or what little was available online.

It may have been reasonable to think that because there were two living descendants (his children Richard and Christine) that there would be anecdotal evidence but Arnold never spoke of his early life to his children and so it was a matter of wringing the most information out of the slimmest pickings.

Travel diaries and photos written and kept by his sisters show Arnold enjoying family holidays in the seaside resorts of Worthing and Gorleston and Herne Bay in the summers of 1899 and 1900 and 1905, respectively. He is only referred to directly once in the Worthing diary on 18 August, a Friday, *Margaret,*

Winnie and Arnold had a goat chaise—apparently there were not enough donkeys to go around.

He gets two direct mentions in the Gorleston holiday diary—13 August, *Father, Dorothy and Arnold went into Yarmouth* and 14 August, *Mrs Starbuck, Arnold and Leslie went by a brabe to the Lake (Fritton)* and then he is lumped together with his siblings on 15 August, *Father and Mother took the three youngest into Yarmouth.*

It is hardly surprising that the activities of a 7 or8-year-old boy do not feature highly or frequently in the diaries of his teenage sisters. Wilfrid is similarly ignored. However, there are a few seaside photos from Herne Bay with all the family included and the boys involved in rowing and playing on the sands.

Even six years later, when Queenie, Winnie, Wilfrid and Arnold head to Scotland to spend time with Aunt Di after the death of their mother, the boys get very few mentions and when they are they always mentioned together— 24 August, *In the afternoon the boys went for a row* and 28 August, *the boys bathed before breakfast.* In this later diary, though, all the activities "we" partook include "the boys" as opposed to the earlier diaries where there is a feeling that Edith, the author, would have been happy for the "youngest" to be kept away!

Sorting through postcards and letters brought up little in the way of mail to or from Arnold, but one piece raised more questions than answers. A postcard with cricketer G.H Hirst on the front is addressed "Master A Clarke. c/o Miss Bennett, Steyne School, Worthing, Sussex" with a date stamp of 9 p.m., Sp 14, 03, Gravesend and a green half penny stamp. The brief message reads—*Hope you arrived safely. I am sending you the cricketer you wished for and will try and grab some more. With much love, Winnie.*

Sorry! Worthing? I had always been under the impression that he was educated in Gravesend like his sisters and brother were until they attended secondary school. Why would you send a ten-year-old to a different county to be educated? I had knowledge through creating a family tree that Aunt Harriet (Rebecca's sister) lived in Worthing with her haberdasher husband, Robert and their nine children but it still did not really make sense that young Arnold would be sent away from home.

I finally made inroads with the census by looking for Arnold Clarke not Richard Arnold Clarke and bingo, there he was in 1901 a boarder/pupil at 13 The Steyne, Worthing. So, he was there from the age of eight. He was still a baby.

From the Steyne School in Worthing, Arnold (with his brother Wilfrid who had been at Gravesend Municipal Day School) went to St. Lawrence School in Ramsgate. They both started at the school in 1904. Arnold wrote to Edith soon after arriving, *We arrived quite safely at the school and it will be alright after a week or we get into the way of the school. I am in third form and we have to learn Greek or German, would you ask mother which I have to. We have not begun football yet. We can see the seniors played easily and can talk to them but are not allowed to speak. We went to our own little chapel this morning for church. Arnold.*

There is a handful of postcards send to and from Wilfrid and Arnold to their sisters. They are often of cricketers as a passion for cricket was something that all siblings shared and they enjoyed hunting out certain cricketers to send to each other whilst also keeping up with each other's news. Queenie seems to have been the best at writing and keeps her brothers updated with her studies at Cambridge.

Wilfrid left Ramsgate in 1908 and Arnold in 1909. Wilfrid went straight to Vickers in Erith on an engineering apprenticeship and Arnold went all the way to Glasgow to a shipping firm called Yarrow and Sons. Arnold also commenced an apprenticeship as an engineer.

To understand why Arnold might have gone as far away as Glasgow, one needs to understand a bit about the family history. Arnold's rich Aunt Dinah (his mother, Rebecca's, eldest sister) was the widow of Sir William Pearce, 1st Baronet. Dinah and William married in Gillingham, near to Gravesend and after supervising the building of HMS "Achilles" (the first ironclad warship) in Chatham, William moved to Glasgow to become a partner in a shipping firm before eventually becoming the sole owner of Fairfield Shipping and Engineering Company.

He became an incredibly wealthy man and had many family members employed in his business, including one of his brother-in-law's, Dinah's sister Ann's husband. Even though Sir William had been dead a long time when Arnold moved up there, many family members, both close and distant, remained in the area and Dinah visited frequently having property in Scotland. With all these connections it is not surprising that Arnold was able to find work up there.

The first indication we have of Arnold living in Glasgow is a mention made in one of Edith's travel diaries from 1909. Edith had travelled to Glasgow to meet with Aunt Di for a motor trip through the Lakes District. Before setting off, she spent a few days in Glasgow with her aunt meeting with family members.

She writes on 20 September 1909, *Very soon after Arnold came in and stayed to dinner and I thought already he seemed older in his ways. We had a very nice, if somewhat short chat, until he had to leave.* It is hard to know when Edith had last seen Arnold, but one imagines that he would have returned to Gravesend after leaving St Lawrence's after the school year had concluded, so she had probably seen him quite recently.

She catches up with him again on the 22, *I stayed and chatted until it was time for me to go to Scotsburn (sic) (probably means Scotstoun). Arnold was not in when I arrived but he and Lennie Shute soon came up. What a difference there was between the two. Arnold so tall and broad, Lennie so very small in height and breadth. We had tea downstairs as A's table would have been too small for two. We then wandered down towards the river and I saw Farrow's (sic— probably means Yarrow's) works from—side but it was too late to go over them.*

We then set off for the Pearce Institute. A introduced me to the Glasgow tribe which is rather extraordinary after the London ones. We found Auntie and Miss Prescott at the club and we all went down to the hall for music and singing concert by the girls of the club of WCA and to hear an address. Left soon after 9 o'clock, we to motor home to the hotel, A to wander back to his lodgings.

Three days later she sends a postcard to Queenie to update her on Arnold— *I went to tea with the Shute's and then onto A's for another. His house is a dear wee one and his landlady very nice I should imagine but only judging from her sister. I saw Yarrows buildings and the shop where A works, but it was absolutely dark. He wants some larger waistcoats (I am bringing two home), some kid gloves to hide his hands on a Sunday and a third thing I have forgotten but will substitute on my own—letters.*

After this, Arnold falls off the records until January 1911 when a letter is sent from him to Queenie. It is a light-hearted letter full of inside jokes which makes it quite difficult to understand but the sentiment and the affection between siblings is clear. As are Arnold's sketching skills which we are introduced to for the first time.

The confusing thing about this letter is the address on the top of the first page. There are no records of Arnold visiting Lincoln and, to my knowledge, no one of any significance in Lincoln to visit. The postmark on the front of the envelope, however, is for Scotstoun, where he lived in Glasgow so maybe it was a part of the inside joke—hard to know.

Start Of WW1

After this there is no remaining communication between Arnold and the rest of the family until 1914. A reference in Wilfrid's obituary refers to Wilfrid and Arnold signing up for duty for WW1, unbeknownst to each other, on the same day. Arnold's Admiralty records have this day as the 5 September 1914, 39 days after the war started.

His address is given as Whiteinch, Glasgow and family anecdotes have him still working at Yarrow's engineering at this point but upon enrolling he went into training and admiralty records have him stationed firstly at HMS Pembroke 1. HMS Pembroke was a shore-based training facility in Chatham, not far from the family home in Gravesend.

It was a facility used to train engineers and engine room artificers— "As warships became more complex the Navy had to introduce training courses especially for engineers and artificers. Also, stokers serving the boilers in the engine rooms and this 'school' was one of the first buildings to appear on St. Mary's Island beside Number 2 basin."[1]

St. Mary's Island was a part of the Chatham Dockyards and was a part of the shore facility Arnold trained at. December 1914 saw him return to Scotland but this time he was in Edinburgh at another training facility—Granton.

Referred to as Columbine in his official documents, the training base near Edinburgh was in the harbour at Granton where trawlers and yachts, used for patrol work and minesweeping, were based. This was training in the very work Arnold would be involved in once he went to sea in April 1915. The one surviving letter, written 22 January 1915 and a postcard from 26 December 1914 are the only personal recollections of this time.

The postcard has Arnold on the front with two unnamed, uniformed men and is sent to Queenie and he writes, *This wasn't faked. It was pouring hard and we just walked into the shop and had them taken.* It is our first view of Arnold in his RNVR uniform, if hidden under a large coat.

The letter gives the impression he did not particularly enjoy his time in Granton—*Ever since getting my so called hook my luck has deserted me and I wish I had never seen Granton and I shall be heartily glad when I can safely put E.R.A RN after my name, but procrastination and delay are my only portion in this world and a brain running to seed.*

---

[1] http://www.stmarysislandhistorygroup.co.uk/1914-to-1920/4587963795

This sense of impatience speaks of a man ready to get to move on from training and get to work however there were three more months of training, most of them done back in London at HMS Pembroke II before Arnold signed on to duty at the Royal Docks on *HMS India* on 13 August 1915.

Arnold and Wilfred approximately 1904

Arnold and Winnie with mother approximately 1903/4

Arnold and Wilfred as babies, 1894

Family holiday in Herne Bay, 1905. Queenie, Father,
Winnie and Arnold's foot

RAC   WSC   WRC

Arnold, Winnie, and Wilfred. I do not think Winnie is happy with
the way Arnold is holding the cat!

Taken on the tennis court at Daneholme. Arnold, Winnie, and Queenie seated
on the ground. Aunt Harriet, Father, and Uncle Robert

From left Wilfrid, Arnold, Rebecca, a friend, and Winnie at the back of 21 High Street——the pharmacy and home until 1906.

Arnold and Nurse at Daneholme.

A formal photo of Lady Dinah Pearce or Aunt Di as she was known to the Clarke children. Rebecca's stepsister who was older than her by fifteen years.

Arnold back row right with hockey team at St Lawrence School, Ramsgate

WSC ERC AVC ARC
Old High St garden

G. H. Hirst
Hope you arrived safely. I am sending you
the cricketer you wished for, and will
try and get some more. With much love Winnie

Post card sent to Arnold at Steyne School, Worthing

Daneholme, Pelham Road, Gravesend. The family moved after mother died in 1906.

Father reading (unsure as to where this was taken)

Photo from the Herne Bay Holiday in 1905.

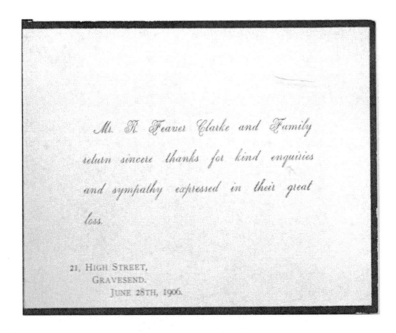

Mr. R. Feaver Clarke and Family
return sincere thanks for kind enquiries
and sympathy expressed in their great
loss.

21, HIGH STREET,
GRAVESEND.
JUNE 28TH, 1906.

The black edged mourning card issued by the family after the untimely death of
Rebecca in 1906.

*Father asleep in a chair—a male Clarke family trait that
continues to this day!*

Winnie, Father, maybe Dorothy, and Wilfrid at Daneholme

Rebecca Clarke née Sowter

Winifred Sowter Clarke

Postcard sent to Arnold at Steyne School, Worthing

Family photo without Dorothy taken whilst on holiday in Herne Bay in 1905. I love the caption— "The sulks". Wilfrid is struggling to stay looking sulky.

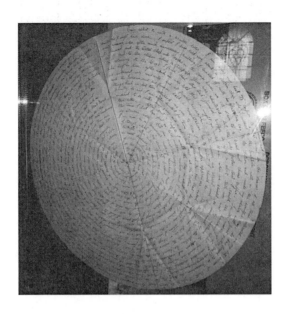

A photo of the front side of Wilfrid's circular letter. The letters written to the family were often sent from one member to another so that 5 or 6 versions did not need to be written. Soon after moving to Erith to start his apprenticeship with Vickers Wilfrid was asked for write a circular letter for the family—he took the instructions quite literally. It is a work of Art!

Arnold in a running race at what would be St Lawrence's, Ramsgate

Arnold's letter to Queenie dated 1912 (on the envelope). He is in a light-hearted and jovial mood.

HMS India –
"She is a Good Sea Boat."

I would like to spend time looking at *HMS India*, her history, and the role she played, ever so briefly, in the First World War. My research and connecting with chatrooms and interested parties has shown me that the story of the ship and its crew appeals to people on many diverse levels. For some, the family history side of things is what is interesting; for others, it is to do with the letters and philately bent and then there are those who come solely from the side of the history of WW1. This chapter is for them!

Steamer SS India was launched on 15 April 1896. Built by Caird and Co of Greenock, she was the largest boat of the P & O fleet at the time she started sailing for them. Her first trips were between Britain and India and in 1898, she set sail for Australia for the first time and in 1900 was the first ship to use P & O's new harbour facilities in Fremantle.

She was a large passenger steamer who, in peace time, carried up to 314 first class and 212 second class passengers as well as four hundred crew. She had twin funnels and weighed about 8,000 tons and even though she was only a single-screw ship (meaning that she had a single propellor), she was still relatively fast, capable of 18 knots on a regular basis and going as fast as 19 and a half knots on one recorded occasion.

After war was declared in July 1914, the Admiralty commandeered around half the fleet of P & O's ships for use in the new conflict. The ships were to be either used as Merchant Navy ships for the carrying of troops and supplies or as Armed Merchant Cruisers. The Merchant Navy were unarmed but vital to the war effort as they imported food and raw materials and provided passage for troops in and out of war zones. Britain had the largest merchant fleet in the First World War.

Armed Merchant Cruisers were, as their name implies, armed and used in a more confrontational mode in the war. There were a detailed and specific checklist ships had to meet before being considered for conversion to an Armed Merchant Cruiser. That list included, amongst other things, conditions such as being able to stay at sea for at least 50 days at a cruising speed of 10 knots, being able to be divided into watertight compartments, good protection of coal and the ability to be quickly taken away from its usual purpose.

Seven of P & O's ships were converted into Armed Merchant Cruisers—the *Himalaya, India, Macedonia, Mantua, Moldovia, Marmora, Morea and Berrima.* The conversion, whilst complicated, was often completed in the swiftest of time margins. Guns were added to the ships, rangefinders were placed on the bridge, holds were refitted as magazines, steel plating was placed on the hulls to assist in protecting the engines and steering mechanisms.

Items like glass and furniture were removed to make the ship safer in the event of an attack and to provide more room for the troops and sailors onboard. There was also a need to add operating theatres and sick bays as the ships would be at sea for extended periods and would not be able to return to land due to illness or injury in the crew. One of the fastest conversions of a merchant ship to an Armed Merchant Cruiser happened in just nine days.

SS India was converted from passenger ship to armed cruiser in April 1915 at Silley Weir's Wharf in Blackwall, East London. The first entry of the Ship's Log, written on the 12 April 1915 states that "Ship at Messrs. Silley Weir's Wharf; men employed as requisite for mounting guns and refitting ship during whole of day."[2]

The next five days sees the ship complete its transformation with the log commenting at various times that the hands have been "Ammunitioning ship" and "taking in ammunition." Time was also spent "cleaning and sweeping boat deck, taking in stores" as well as coaling the ship and evaluating its stability. Stability could be an issue with Armed Merchant Cruisers as they usually relied heavily on cargo and luggage for ballast and this was not provided when the ships were at war and the ships had been made more unstable by the addition of guns and armoury on board.

On Sunday the 18 April 1915, the now *HMS India* "Received draft of forty men from HMS Pembroke", in addition to those already on board and then at

---

[2] *HMS India* Copy of Log. National Archives ADM 53/44825

2:10 p.m. "Cast off hawsers and proceeded down the river." This once elegant international cruiser was now a war ship.

10th Cruiser Squadron

HMS India had been earmarked to become a part of the 10th Cruiser Squadron. A squadron under the command of Rear Admiral Dudley de Chair that was integral to the success of the Blockade of Germany. The 10th Cruiser Squadron had been in operation since the beginning of the war but was struggling due to the stress being put on the aging and inappropriate ships being used.

The nine Edgar class cruisers that had primarily made up the squadron were over twenty years old, a similar age to some of the P & O ships but the Edgar class were not cut out for the work they were expected to do. Their role was to intercept, board and capture German warships and merchant vessels as well as intercepting all ships headed to German ports. They covered around 220,000 miles of sea in all weathers. There were simply not enough ships and most were ill equipped for the demands placed upon them and they started to struggle with the workload.

Towards the end of November 1914, the Edgar class cruisers were deemed unfit for purpose and retired from the 10th Cruiser Squadron. It was decided to use Armed Merchant Cruisers to the make up the greater part of the squadron. They were fast, nimble, and accustomed to high, challenging seas but even they still found the constant work in the North Sea a challenging affair with harsh weather (far worse than had been anticipated) and high, treacherous seas. One boat, *HMS Alcantara* reported 12 days (in July 1915) of almost continuous fog and mist.

When the fleet was at its largest, there were twenty-four ships and over 7,000 men in the squadron all working at the same time to defend the Blockade of Germany. Over the course of the war 41-Armed Merchant Cruisers served the 10th Cruiser Squadron. The men serving on these ships were a mix of merchant sailors who had sailed on the ships as passenger vessels and Royal Navy Reserves (RNR), Royal Naval Volunteer Reserves (RNVR) and other trained sailors. The crews were nicknamed the "Muckle Flugga Hussars" after the Muckle Flugga Island and lighthouse situated at the very top of the Shetland Islands. Arnold uses this term in one of his letters in 1916.

The Blockade of Germany commenced in August 1914 and involved one of the largest sea offensives that had ever taken place. The aim of the British

Government was to blockade the entire length of the English Channel – from the seas between the Northwest of Scotland and Greenland and Iceland and down to the seas at the beginning of the Dover Straits.

The aim was simple—seal both entrances to the North Sea and intercept any suspicious marine traffic whilst dodging enemy submarines. It was the most protracted naval operation of the First World War lasting for over three years and was anything but simple. There were a great many ships to intercept for instance, in 1915 there were 3,098 ships chased, intercepted and examined and 743 of them were found to be carrying contraband and were sent into port to be examined further.

The British Government was hoping to control the amount of contraband being shipped to German ports by German and neutral ships. It was a controversial move and made difficult as the British government kept changing their mind as to what was defined as contraband. In the beginning, it was anything that was clearly for use in war but as the war continued items such as rubber, iron, copper, wool and various food items were added to the list. It was hard for the ships captains and boarding crews to keep up.

By the time the squadron was disbanded at the end of 1917 the 10th Cruiser Squadron had intercepted and boarded 12,979 vessels, had intimidated 2,039 vessels to hand themselves in to British ports for examination and had only failed to intercept a mere 642 ships in over 3 years of patrolling. A real success story for the British Government and the war effort.

Conducting Inspections of Suspicious Ships

The main task of the 10th Cruiser Squadron was to attempt to limit if not completely stop the shipping of contraband by neutral ships. There was a strict code of conduct in place for ascertaining if ships had contraband and how they might be inspected. The suspicious ship would be intercepted by one of the cruisers and a red pennant would be hoisted indicating the request for the neutral ship to stop.

All ships were suspicious until proven otherwise, so guns were made ready and blank shots were fired after the squadron ship had raised their white ensign. Boarding a suspect ship was a complicated and dangerous process that relied on the small boats called cutters or whalers being lowered into the sea with at least one officer, an armed guard, and a searching party aboard. This would be done day or night (under searchlight), in calm or rough seas—it did not matter.

The small boats used were not particularly easily manoeuvrable or particularly agile. Whilst it was difficult to launch these boats, it was potentially even more difficult to come alongside a suspect ship that might not be happy about being inspected. These ships might not offer any help and might just drop a ladder. Dangerous does not even begin to describe it. Once the search party was on board, the officer would give the captain of the suspect ship an opportunity to reveal what was on board and have a look through the ships papers before sending his search party to look for contraband.

If contraband was found, there were a couple of options. If there was not a great amount, it would be destroyed with the captain's permission and the ship would continue its journey. If a more substantial quantity was discovered, then the ship would be sent with an armed guard to Kirkwall (and sometimes an accompanying trawler) where it was held captive. The boarding process could take as long as two hours and the squadron ship would be circling out of firing range the whole time, keeping an eye on proceedings.

10th Cruiser Squadron Crew

The majority of crew on the 10th Cruiser Squadron boats were a combination of the Royal Naval Reserves (RNR), the Royal Naval Volunteer Reserves (RNVR) and the Mercantile Marine Reserve (MMR) as well as a small amount of Royal Navy and Coastguard and Infantry. The RNR were the Navy volunteer force of professional civilian sailors who were primarily made up of merchant mariners and fisherman.

The RNVR "was formed of individuals who were not seafarers in civilian life, but who undertook Naval training and volunteered to serve ashore or afloat."[3] The MMR dealt with the "shortfall in manpower" by getting "a number of officers and men of the Merchant Marine to agree to serve with the Royal Navy under certain terms, which made them subject to Naval discipline while generally retaining their Merchant Marine rates of pay and other conditions."[4]

Submarine Warfare

The British government and Admiralty entered the war aware of Germany's development of the submarine as a weapon but were sure that it was not yet up

---

[3] Barnettmaritime.co.uk

[4] Barnettmaritime.co.uk

to being a threat and would only be used for surveillance duties. The war did not need to progress far before they began to realise how very wrong, they were. The Germans had been developing *Untersee-boats* in the years leading up to the war and their impact quickly became worryingly obvious.

In September 1914, the force of the U-Boats and the devastation they could wreak was seen when one U-Boat alone sunk three British cruisers in just over an hour. The Royal Navy was shocked and they figured out that they were dealing with far more serious a threat than they had anticipated. The Germans were incensed by the changing of contraband lists by the British and on 18 February 1915, they issued a statement declaring that any hostile merchant ships encountered in British or Irish waters would be destroyed without regard for crew or passengers.

This statement totally defied the rules set out in the Declaration of London and shocked not just the British and the Triple Entente but also the USA. The entire world joined in this shock when the Germans announced that they would fire indiscriminately upon all hostile merchant ships regardless of their position. Until this point, the U-Boats had risen to the surface to give the crews of belligerent ships time to abandon the ship before it was sunk by deck guns or explosives or, a last and expensive option, a torpedo.

From February 1915, they would fire when submerged and without warning upon any enemy vessel – there were no neutral vessels, everyone who was not Germany or the Triple Alliance was an enemy. This included passenger ships like the Lusitania who was famously torpedoed in May of 1915.

HMS India

HMS India had her first introduction to the Blockade of Germany at the beginning of May 1915. She had sailed from London to Sheerness where the guns were tested and then it was up to the Northern Patrol region. Her job was to patrol the Northern border of the blockade keeping watch for ships that might be carrying contraband. The ships log mentions all boats that were sighted, contacted and those who were boarded.

The Danish *SS Jens Bang* was challenged and boarded by members of the *HMS India* and found to be loaded with grain from Boston, it was sent to Kirkwall. As were the *SS Nordland* and the *SS Volrath Tham*, who were also found to be loaded with contraband and sent off for further inspection.

On 18 May 1915, *HMS India* was back in Glasgow loading up with more coal. Six days were spent in loading coal and supplies before another three weeks at sea in what sound to be challenging sailing conditions with reports of snow and "pitching heavily: high NWly sea". One more stint in Glasgow "coaling" and "party of 5 new men joined up" and after sending of men to hospital for treatment they could not get onboard and on the 27 June 1915, *HMS India* steamed back up to Northern Patrol for what would be her last period of active duty. It was an eventful start to the journey with major engine issues the day after they left port. The log reads

"28/06

3:20 p.m.: Stopped: main feed pump given out

4:25 p.m.: Engine repairs finished

5:15 p.m.: Steering engine broke down

5:25 p.m.: Put hand steering gear in use

6:30 p.m.: Steam steering gear connected up"[5]

Not the smoothest start to a patrol.

The last entry in the logbook at the National Archives is made at the end of June 1915 and from that point we are reliant upon the recollections of her crew as to what happened in the month leading up to the tragic day of 8 August 1915.

One of the most intimate of recollections is that of Sub-Lieutenant Ernest McKeag RNR who wrote a detailed journal of his time on *HMS India* and this diary now sits in the library of the Imperial War Museum. McKeag was an ex-Merchant Navy Officer and served as a midshipman on *India* which was a low-ranking officer role. He writes about the time leading up to August 1915.

On the Norwegian coast off the mouth of Vest fjord (the fjord well north of the Arctic Circle leading into Narvik) was a very busy one and we had the use of two armed trawlers to assist us by acting as scouts. Two German merchant ships were known to be in Narvik waiting their chance to make a dash and we were eagerly waiting for them.

They made their dash and although one got through by running into territorial waters on the approach of our trawler the Tenby Castle. But it was at great expense of her (the German's) steering gear, which was smashed by a well-directed shot from the trawler, before the German could cross into safety. The other German, the Freidrich Arp, was sunk by the Tenby Castle and the

[5] *HMS India* Copy of Log. National Archives ADM 53/44825

prisoners, to the number of thirteen, who had been allowed to clear off the ship before the trawler opened fire were handed over to us for safe keeping.[6]

He makes mention of sightings of U-boats and of a *couple of occasions when the India was lucky enough to evade being torpedoed. "It happened to be exactly 10 o'clock at night and as we altered course to zigzag every ten minutes, we were on the swing when he fired and the torpedo went harmlessly on a parallel course to us".*

The 10th Cruiser Squadron employed several tactics to try and avoid being struck by torpedoes. As well as having rudimentary radars and men on look out, the boats would often sail in zig-zag patterns, changing course as often as every ten minutes to make their course harder to track and predict, they would also regularly alter their speed to make their movements more unpredictable. *HMS India* regularly adopted these tactics as described by men on the ship and one who witnessed it from a U-boat.

So, Where Does Arnold Fit In?

After training at HMS Pembroke 1 and at HMS Columbine in Granton, Arnold returned to London to complete his training at HMS Pembroke 2. Arnold was using his engineering training to assist him in his war training to become an Engine Room Artificer (ERA). The work of an ERA was down in the engine rooms but as opposed to stokers, ERAs were educated men who could read and write and were able to use arithmetic. They had knowledge of the way engines and boilers worked and were able to maintain and fix them. The Pembroke offshore facilities both trained ERA's. They were skilled mechanics. His records have him at Pembroke II from 2 February to the 12 April 1915 and then aboard *HMS India* from 13 April 1915. Maybe he got one night at home in 9 The Avenue, Gravesend with father and Dorothy before joining the ship—considering what was to happen four months later, I very much hope so.

The first stop *India* made after leaving Silley's Weir in London was Gravesend. The log from the 18 April reads "5:15 p.m.: Reached Gravesend and changed pilots". I like to imagine that Father, Nurse, Dorothy, and any of the other sisters who may have been home walked down to the pier at Gravesend to

---

[6] Thompson, J. Imperial War Museum Book of the War at Sea 1914-1918. Pan Macmillan, London. 2011

watch their brothers ship pause and then move on, them waving not knowing if or when they might see Arnold again.

There are two pieces of mail in existence from the time that Arnold was aboard *HMS India*. The first is a postcard written on the 26 April when the boat was on route to its first Northern Patrol. The card is marked *HMS India* (armed liner) c/o GPO London. He writes a welcome back to term Queenie and informs her that *weather changed now, a bit squally and wet*.

At this stage he has only been on board thirteen days so there does not seem to be too much to report. He does note, however, that the workload is relentless stating *"Sunday has not brought the general slack—about in best suit"*.

The second postcard is not dated but was written to Winifred when she was living in and teaching London and looks to be dated towards the end of the summer term— perhaps July. It has a "censored on board" marking and Arnold also refers to being aboard the cruiser.

He writes, *Have had a pretty good time out lately, fine weather as well. I hope you have had similar. No bathing (at least not voluntary) but have tennis and cricket going. Thanking you in anticipation when the mail comes aboard.* All was going well for him at this stage although there is what is to become a familiar sense of loneliness and homesickness from his letters with a yearning for contact with home.

A photo from the collection of Seaman Robert Charles Maynard. In the family album it was annotated "Loading guns"

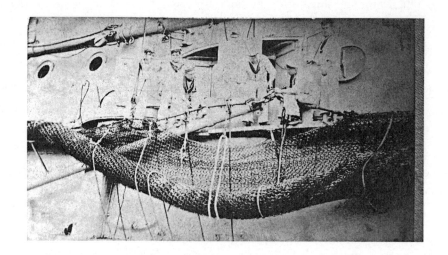

From the collection of Fireman William Tilley, this looks as though it might have been taken in docks whilst the ship was being prepared to join the 10th Cruiser Squadron.

SS India, probably before she was transformed into an Armed Merchant Cruiser.

A couple of official portraits of Commander William G A Kennedy in his navy uniform.

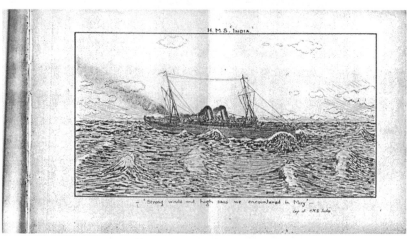

Two of Arnold's etchings HMS India, at least one of these was completed whilst he was on patrol "and not petrol" as he notes!

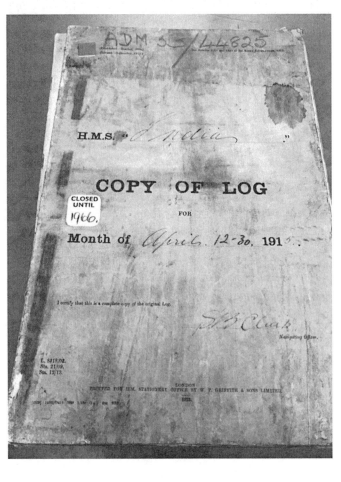

ADM 5.../44825

H.M.S. "*India*"

COPY OF LOG

FOR

Month of *April. 12-30*, 191*5*

I certify that this is a complete copy of the original Log.

J.B. Clark
Navigating Officer.

L. 5318/02.
Sta. 21/09.
Sta. 12/13.

LONDON
PRINTED FOR HM. STATIONERY OFFICE BY W. P. GRIFFITH & SONS LIMITED.
1923.

~ *H. M. S. India* ~

~ *On patrol* ~
and not petrol

The logbook of the HMS India that dates until the end of June. The later logbook probably went down with the ship.

Above is a photo of U22, the U-boat that was responsible for the torpedo of HMS India. And below some of the crew and officers having a drink on U22.

The Log of the H. M. S. India

(The origins of this poem are unknown but have been shared amongst descendants of *HMS India* survivors)

When Britain on Germany war did declare,
The H. M. S. "India" wanted to share.
In slaying detestable pirates and Huns,
So she had her decks strengthened and mounted some guns.

Ri-toorai i-ooral ri-tay.
She looked very fine in her orthodox grey,
With a fifty-knot bow-wave to lead foes astray.
Ri-tooral—etc.

We steamed down the Thames and at Sheerness we lay.
We tested our guns and I'm sorry to say,
They strewed broken windows all over the deck,
And the Midshipmen's cabins did terribly wreck.
Ri-tooral—etc.

We were likely to be in pretty bad way.
For the steam-steering gear also carried away.
Ri-tooral—etc.

In order to clear up this horrible mess,
We put ship about and ran in for Sheerness.
And after some trouble in anchoring there,
We worked up to daylight our ship to repair.
Ri-tooral—etc.
We cleared out of Sheernees the very next day,
With destroyers to keep all the tin-fish at bay.
Ri-tooral—etc.

We steamed through the Downs and we all thought it fine.
Till the look-out man suddenly sighted a mine,
We circled around it and sent it to pot
By filling its jacket with 303 shot.
Ri-tooral—etc.
We entered the Channel by Folkestone Gateway
And soon lost the land for we stood well away
Ri-tooral—etc.

Off Ireland we sighted a submarine top,
So we blazed off our guns and we gave it her hot,
But the tin-fish she dived and sank under the wave

And thought herself lucky her skin so to save.
Ri-tooral—etc.
If we'd had some luck the I venture to say,
In Davy Jones' locker her ribs now would lay.
Ri-tooral—etc.

A heron blown out from the land in a gale,
Fagged out by his flight perched himself on our rail.
We fed him on fish which we stole from the cook,
Till he finally choked with a large piece he took.
Ri-tooral—etc.
A least that's the yarn that has come up our way.
If you ask my opinion about it, I say
Ri-tooral—etc.

Strong winds and high seas we encountered in May.
The gallant old ship soaked itself with the spray
But in spite of her wetting she heavily scored,
For divil a green sea did she take aboard.
Ri-tooral—etc.
She gave all the others a splendid display,
As she crashed through the billows that rose in her way.
Ri-tooral—etc.

In June we waylaid the steamship "Gøtaland,"
Up in the North Sea full goods contraband.
We had her hove to in a couple of ticks,
And soon put an end to her pro-German tricks.
Ri-tooral—etc.
Our six-pounder warning she had to obey,
And we sent her to Kirkwall without much delay.
Ri-tooral—etc.

At three in the morning a strange light was shewn,
Away out to sea so the bugle was blown,
To stations we tumbled as quick as could be

And primed all the guns to receive enemy.
Ri-tooral—etc.
It's all very well on a bright sunny day,
But in isn't much cop in your night-dress array.
Ri-tooral—etc.

We signalled a large Yankee barque to heave to.
Her skipper used language both flowery and blue
And held on his course so we fired a blank shot
To show him we'd not stand American rot.
Ri-tooral—etc.
On boarding we found that discretion held sway,
So we looked at his papers and bade him good-day.
Ri-tooral—etc.

On June the fourteenth the Swede "Malmland" we caught
For four hours we chased her with coal running short,
Then had to release her Jove we felt sore,
But we captured two ships full of magnetic ore.
Ri-tooral—etc.
The "Nordland" and "Volrath Tham" fell as out prey.
Though the "Malmland" escaped us she gave them away.
Ri-tooral—etc.

Then we turned to the South and harbour we sought,
Till we ran up the Clyde and made Glasgow our port.
The city's not bad while the weather is bright
And the girls bless their hearts are a bit of all right.
Ri-tooral—etc.
We all made the most of our all too brief stay,
And very successfully spent all our pay,
Ri-tooral—etc.

Then off up to Norway once more we did go,
Where the sun shines all night on the mountains of snow,
And whales and porpoises gambol and heave,

Till disturbed by the ship when they hurriedly leave.
Ri-tooral—etc.
We captured two ships in the course of the day,
The "Frederik the Eighth" and the "Renteria".
Ri-tooral—etc.

On July the tenth we were Zig-zagging wide
When a torpedo missed us and skimmed past our side.
If our paint had been a few inches more thick,
That submarine shell would have finished the trick.
Ri-tooral—etc.
We cut in for port without any delay,
And raced in the armed Merchantman "Patia."
Ri-tooral—etc.

On another encounter I also must dwell.
Namely, how we took captive "Sire Ernest Cassel."
When she stoked all she knew in the limit to get,
But how we got inside her and stayed there you bet.
Ri-tooral—etc.
We turned her head round and well out of the bay,
And sent her to Kirkwall to make a brief stay.
Ri-tooral—etc.

But on August the eighth in the Western Fjord,
Came an end of our ship and of many aboard.
A torpedo struck her a terrible blow
By number three gun and soon sent her below.
Ri-tooral—etc.
A hundred and twenty the Germans did slay,
But the "Saxon" and "Götland" saved us. Hurray!
Ri-tooral—etc.

Source: Marie Barltrop

51

Sinking of HMS India—
"Submarine on Starboard Bow"

8 August 1915 was the fateful day that everything changed for *HMS India* and her crew. The day had started off quite predictably.

Early morning—the India sighted its first ship of the day and following procedures of contacting all vessels, belligerent or not, contact was made and the course was altered to intercept *S.S Gloria*, a Swedish ship. Two armed trawlers, HMS Saxon and HMS Newland accompanied India.

Gloria was boarded and searched over an almost two-hour period and allowed to proceed at about 10 a.m. Commander Kennedy subsequently radioed his superior on HMS Virginian informing of the contents of the *Gloria*. The India started to make her way back to the patrol line, zig zagging as commanded and making a speed of about 14 knots.

11:00—another ship was spotted heading towards Taen Island, inside the territorial limit and India followed in order to check her identification. Once again, India left her position on the patrol line. The ship was identified as another Swedish steamer, *S.S Atland*. She was cleared to sail on and India changed course again to attempt to re-join the patrol line.

12:00—*HMS India* receives an urgent message from *HMS Virginian* to find *S.S Gloria* and send her to Kirkwall as it has been decided that her contents need further examination. *India* alters course again and increases her speed.

14:00—*HMS India* reports that she cannot find *S.S Gloria.*

15:00—*HMS India* observes a steamer inshore and alters her course.

16:00—contact is made with the steamer but by this stage it is inside the territorial limit so India cannot do anything. On radio contact the steamer states that she is the *S.S Hillhouse* and is under ballast and traveling from South Shields to Archangel in ballast and she hoists the red ensign indicating that she is friendly ship.

Commander Kennedy is reported to be instantly suspicious but is unable to do anything and after sighting and signalling the *Saxon* the course is altered once more to head back to the patrol line. On course another steamer is sighted and the course changes to go and meet the new ship. Commander Kennedy leaves the bridge to go to the wireless room to make contact leaving Sub-Lieutenant Alltree RNR in charge.

16:40—alarm is sounded.

The story of the sinking of *HMS India* is best told in the words of the men who were there. The most dramatic telling comes from the private papers of Sub-Lieutenant Ernest Lionel McKeag. McKeag had joined the Mercantile Marines in 1913 with the aim of traveling the world, which he did until WW1 broke out and he joined the RNR.

Having joined as a midshipman and then after surviving the sinking of *HMS India*, McKeag went back to sea on *HMS Orotavia* and rose to the rank of a full Lieutenant. It is hardly surprising his account reads so dramatically as after WW1 he became a journalist and then a writer of comic book style novels. Of course, they also read dramatically as surviving the torpedoing of a ship is a dramatic event in any person's life!

Suddenly we were all startled by a shout from the starboard look out, 'Submarine on the port bow.' Lt Clark ran to the starboard wing of the bridge, shouting 'submarine, submarine,' followed by 'she's fired a torpedo at us.' I looked over the bridge dodger and saw the wake of a torpedo. It seemed to be coming directly for our foremost magazine, and I braced myself for a terrible explosion. I froze, and looking over the dodger again, saw the torpedo apparently alter course and strike about ten yards abaft the after magazine. The ship shuddered terribly at the shock.

The commander gave the orders for boats to be got away. I made my way to my boat, number 3. A number of men got into the boat, and Lt Nelson, the officer in charge, stayed to lower after the fall, while a seaman manned the forward one, and they started to lower away. As we reached the hurricane deck, a few men jumped in, but most waited for the boat to hit the water when they would slide down the falls into it. The ship had taken a list to port, so the boat caught on every projection on the ship's side, taking a long time to lower, and damaging the gunwale. Because there was still way on the ship, so sooner had our boat touched water, than it was carried half under the whaler behind us. We could not cast off or cut the falls, and one man was pinned under the whaler. He was eventually pulled out, but with a smashed arm and shoulder; he died subsequently in hospital.

The ship was sinking so quickly that now the after well deck was awash and we found ourselves on a level with the boat deck, with tremendous volumes of water dashing over us. Men were being washed in and out of the boat and seeing that it would be dragged down with the ship, I jumped.

I went down, and down, and still down, it seemed to me that I would never stop. Then little by little I felt the grip of water relax and I struck out upwards. I came to the surface, seizes a breath, and went down again. This time it seemed as though I would never come up. All sorts of thoughts flashed through my mind. I remember feeling glad I had my best uniform on. Then my hands closed on a piece of wood, and I thought I was saved. But it was only about 9 inches long. Feeling as if I could not hold my breath an instant longer, I gave up hope for the first time. Wondering how my people would receive the news I was lost, I opened my mouth with the idea of getting it over quickly, and at that moment saw a faint glimmer of light through the water. Hope burnt within me. Shutting my mouth, I struck upwards and reached the surface, to find a mast from one of the boats. Holding on, I looked in the direction of the India, to see the foremast quiver, and fall over the starboard side, followed by an explosion in or near the boiler room. I went under for the third time, but hanging on to the mast, I surfaced quickly. Looking around, the ship had gone, and all round me were men, some half naked, some fully clothed, hanging onto pieces of wreckage of which there seemed to be plenty.

Ahead of me was a waterlogged boat, with three men standing on it, and one hanging onto the bow. On one side of me was a man whose face was covered in blood. I swung myself up on the mast and shouted to the men in the boat to bale it out. But that proved impossible, as the boat went gunwales under as the swell passed. Everyone around me was in the best of spirits. I heard the strains of 'Tipperary', and light-hearted badinage (sic). I secured a boats water breaker which was floating past, under my arm to stop me rolling over.

The only person near me who showed signs of giving in was the Captain's writer. I shouted words of encouragement and told him to swim to my mast. But he drifted away and was lost, poor fellow.

I drifted a good deal, and hearing my name called, saw the electrician, Mr Johnson, holding out a flask for me to drink from. Not wanting to leave my mast,

54

I drifted past and that was the last I saw of him alive. Looking round I saw a door floating near. Still keeping hold of my mast, I leaned my weight on the door. I drifted into a mass of wreckage, large pieces of wood banged on my back. I was feeling bitterly cold and my boots were doing their best to take me to the bottom. A slight swell was running and I was borne up the sloping hills of water, I got my head dipped under. On the top of the swell, I saw the boat from Gotaland (Swedish steamer) had been lowered but whether I should be picked up in time or not I could not tell. I was fearfully cold and feeling sleepy. I rested my chin on the door and knew no more.

When I came to I was in the bottom of a boat alongside the Gotaland.[7]

McKeag was taken briefly to Norway and then allowed to return to Britain where he re-joined the war effort on *HMS Orotava*, another Armed Cruiser in the 10th Cruiser Squadron.

Whilst conducting online research I came across another personal report of the traumatic event on a blog called "after work 101" where the writer, Helen Ward, tells of her grandfather's experience on the day the India sunk.

On the afternoon of 8 August 1915, my grandfather was taking a bath on board the merchant cruiser HMS India, which was stationed just off the Norwegian coast where it was tasked with intercepting ships supplying iron ore to Germany.

At 5:40 p.m., torpedo tracks were sighted and the alarm was sounded. Before the development of underwater detection technologies, submarines were the sea-monsters of the industrial age: patrolling freely and attacking at will. Many British sailors of this period suffered from "sub-itis"—a terror of being attacked by submarines—and would often sleep on deck rather than risk sudden death at the hands of an undetected U boat.

My grandfather, however, was a professional sailor with 12 years' service in the Royal Navy behind him and, in the finest traditions of the service, kept his head and finished his bath. After drying himself and getting dressed, he headed to the lifeboats, pausing only to collect an axe.

Although the lifeboats were quickly manned and lowered, they remained connected by rope to the rapidly sinking ship. Each time the movement of the ship tightened the connecting rope, my grandfather swung at it with his axe and

---

[7] Thompson, J. Imperial War Museum Book of the War at Sea 1914-1918. Pan MacMillan, London. 2011

in this way eventually cut the rope, enabling crew to row clear. Other boats remained attached and were crushed or sunk.

Some war stories are repeated many times; as far as I know, my grandfather only told the story of the sinking of the India once—it was simply too painful to bear repetition.[8]

Deborah Callaghan tells the story of her grandfather, Lieutenant Charles Nelson who survived the sinking, but a medical report written over four years later tells of the lasting scars. She wrote to me— "Amongst the papers is a 'Certificate of Wounds and Hurts.' It describes how Charles Nelson was:

'Injured on 8 August 1915, by being torpedoed by enemy submarines, the ship being sunk.

Dived overboard and centre of leg was struck by wreckage whilst in the water, causing traumatic periostitis (script difficult to read) from which subsequently developed an osteoma of tibia.

He was sober at the time (comforting to know that!).

Granted at hospital at Gosport 19 August 1919.' Signed by Surgeon Commander RN George T Bishop.

Deborah continues that "the story that I have inherited is that there were too many men for the life raft. My grandfather, being a strong swimmer, elected to swim alongside the raft for as long as he could. It was within the Arctic Circle, so survival time in the water would have been limited. Whilst swimming he received the blow to his leg from flotsam.

The rescue came shortly after the injury. I do not know the timescale, but I assume, it was minutes rather than hours. For the duration of his internment a large egg-shaped lump grew on his leg and at times the pain was very acute. On his return to England, he was sent to Lady Whittaker's Private Hospital (Pylewell House) near Lymington, Hampshire, where he had his leg amputated as it had become gangrenous. Hence the certificate of wounds and hurts."

Archibald Hurd wrote in his collection *The Merchant Navy*:

"Of the number saved, namely 189 officers and men, no less than 19 officers and 138 men had all dived into the sea, or gone down with the ship. As the vessel sank in less than five minutes after the explosion, all efforts to get the rafts out were unavailing. Commander Kennedy went down with his ship, and eventually floated up amongst the wreckage. Throughout the trying ordeal, discipline was

---

[8] Afterwork101.wordpress.com>my-grandfathers-bath

splendidly maintained. "I wish to place on record," Commander Kennedy stated in his report, "my admiration of the magnificent behaviour of the officers and men; notwithstanding the appalling swiftness of the catastrophe, the most perfect discipline prevailed until the end."[9]

Whilst Hurd is accurate on many things, he fails to realise that two rafts were successfully launched as mentioned in the formal reports.

The other three detailed reports of the sinking were formal reports requested by the Admiralty and Foreign Office and they can be found in the files being kept at the National Archives, Kew, London.[10] The reports were given by two officers and an assistant engineer and tell of the sinking of the ship and the rescue of a small number of men on the ships rescue boats. All reports also tell of the terrifying sight of a periscope from a submarine, whilst they were rowing their rescue craft the seven or eight miles to the nearest land.

Report by Sub-Lieut. Alltree R.N.R, Jørstadmoen, 11 October 1915

In accordance with your orders I beg to make an additional report of the sinking of H.M.S "India" and the arrival of survivors at Helligvaer Island. On 8 August H.M.S "India" was steaming at 56 revolutions, 14 knots, heading about SSW to head off Swedish Steamer. Lookout on foc'sle reported "Submarine on starboard bow".

Looking in the direction indicated I saw track of torpedo about 300 yards distant: at the same time Commander Kennedy ran on the bridge and ordered "hard sport" "full speed ahead", which orders were immediately carried out by Navigator and myself. I also sounded war alarm. Torpedo struck the ship below No. 3 starboard gun. Orders were given by Commander to send messages for assistance, as vessel had heeled over to port about 10 degrees and was going down by the stern.

Commander gave the order to "Abandon ship". I went into No. 2 cutter and found her ready for lowering and apparently full. I then got into the boat which was lowered by Chief Gunner Byrne and a seaman; great difficulty was experienced in getting away from the ship as she was still going through the

---

[9] Hurd, A. The Merchant Navy Volume 1. John Murray, London. 1921
[10] The National Archives ADM 1/8429/227

water at about 10 knots, all other boats in port side with exception of port whaler capsizing in water.

"India" was sinking rapidly by the stern, bow being lifted right out of the water and guns on foc'sle carrying away, vessel then broke in two by after well deck and sank rapidly. Torpedo had struck ship at about 5:41 p.m. and she disappeared at about 5:46 p.m.

On No. 2 cutter I went to edge of wreckage and saw all hands near us hanging on to spars, wreckage or rafts, whom we left for Swedish steamer, which was about 2 miles distant proceeding to assistance, to pick up, considering it not advisable to enter field of wreckage on account of capsizing, having 35 hands in cutter at the time. Port whaler left the ship with 10 hands, picking up 3 more out of the water, she being deep in the water owing to water shipped when leaving ship.

I headed for Swedish steamer but afterwards headed for the land, Helligvær bearing about Se distant 7 or 8 miles. We also saw trawler "Saxon" steaming to assistance of those in the water.

When about 2 miles from scene of disaster we sighted submarine submerged all but periscope distant about half a mile heading towards us, she diving when only about 30 yards distant.

When about halfway to land we met three motorboats one of which lowered a rowing boat which piloted us to Helligvær; we requested the motorboats which had come out to help us to land, to go to the scene of the disaster. At 8:30 p.m., we arrived at Helligvær, where we were well received, served with support and allotted rooms for the night. 9 p.m. roll call, 48 hands all told.

9 August at 3:00 a.m. Three bodies, identified as Private L Marks R M L I, Petty Officer Prior and Wm Dent, Greaser, were brought ashore by motorboat. Considerable wreckage was also brought ashore and inspected, no confidential books or papers being amongst it, with the exception of charts of coast of Scotland which I burnt. At 6 a.m., I left Helligvær with postmaster on SS "Bodin" for Bodø to report to Consul.

10 a.m. arrived Bodø and reported to Vice-Consul who communicated with Narvik and Christiania. I was then sent on Norwegian gunboat "Andenes" Lieut. Johannessen in command to Helligvær and brought men, bodies and boats to Bodø. On arrival at Bodø bodies were placed in coffins and we followed them to the mortuary. I also took a doctor to Helligvær on that journey to see Seaman Keats, who was injured in back and out hospital on arrival at Bodø.

Under directions of Consul, we were allotted hotel accommodation. 10 August at 10 a.m., I inspected No.1 starboard cutter which had been brought into Bodø. She was holed below waterline in 2 planks, the hole being only about 6" square, also stern board partially carried away, this boat with number 2 cutter and port whaler I left in care of Vice-Consul.

Funeral arrangements were made with Vice-Consul. The service being our own service was read by a Norwegian Chaplain in Norwegian. I had previously without success searched several shops and inquired of Vice-Consul for a book of Prayer in English.

The Norwegian Navy supplied a guard of six sailors, a Petty Officer and a Warrant Officer. Amongst the mourners being the British Vice-Consul, Lieut. Arentz Norwegian Navy and Lieut Johannessen Norwegian Navy. The coffins were covered with flags picked up from H.M.S "India," white ensign, Union Jack and red ensign. There were also very many floral tributes, amongst them being wreaths from the British Vice-Consul, the Norwegian Navy and the survivors of H.M.S "India".

At 3:30 p.m., we left Bodø for Bjerkvik in Gunboat "Andenes" arriving there and being turned over to the military authorities at 4 a.m., when we were encamped with the remaining survivors.

Whilst in Helligvær and Bodø, we had every kindness shown to us by the Norwegian people.

(signed) E.W Alltree Act Sub-Lieut. R.N.R

Statement by Assistant Engineer Patmore

10 October 1915

Dear Sir,

Having been informed that you require from me a written report as to how I landed on Norwegian soil from the wrecked H.M.S "India," I herewith respectfully comply with your request.

After the H.M.S "India" had been torpedoed and was sinking very rapidly, I went to my Boat Station to No.2 Cutter and found it being lowered, full of men and with Mr Alltree and Mr Jenkins, two deck officers, in it. So, I slid down a rope and jumped in myself. About two or three minutes after that the ship disappeared.

After which, we rowed round the wreckage and finding we could not assist anyone out of the water through our boat being full, the Officer in charge, Mr

Alltree, allowed the men to pull for the shore, which we could see about 6 or 7 miles off, with the idea, I believed, to land our party and come back for those clinging to wreckage, whose boats had unfortunately overturned or fouled the davits. But almost before we had left the spot where H.M.S "India" went down, a big Swedish steamer that was close by, steamed to the scene of the disaster and began the rescue work.

We also saw from our boat, No. 2 cutter, the English trawler "Saxon" in the distance, steaming full speed and making for the same spot. When we were about two-thirds of our way from the shore, the Periscope of the Submarine was sighted, bearing hard down upon us, but when she got within 20 or 30 yards of us, she dived and we did not see her again.

Halfway from the land we met three Norwegian motorboats, going full speed to the rescue work and also two small rowing boats, one of which piloted us to a place called Helligvær, where we eventually landed, about three hours after the wreck.

Trusting the above report will meet with your requirements.

I am, etc.

(Signed) F.W Patmore R.N.R

Statement by Midshipman H.R Jenkins R.N.R

10 October 1915

I have the honour to submit the following report from memory of what occurred from the time of leaving the torpedoed H.M.S "India" on August 8th in the WestFjord to our arrival at Helligvær.

After clearing the ship's side, we pulled away from the ship to avoid swamping. A few minutes after, H.M.S "India" sank rapidly by the stern and disappeared. The boat I was in, the 2nd cutter, contained Sub-Lieutenant Alltree in charge, Eng Sub Lieut Patmore, myself and 32 ratings.

The boat being full we were unable to pick up any men who were in the water, where there was a large quantity of wreckage. We saw only one other boat clear the ship which we afterwards found to be the port whaler containing 13 men. We observed a Swedish steamer and the British armed trawler "Saxon" steaming towards the scene of the disaster and we soon after proceeded towards the nearest point of land, the whaler being some distance astern and following us.

About halfway to the shore we sighted the periscope of a submarine, approximately 200 yards distant on our port bow coming towards us. When within about 30 yards of us, she stopped and having taken a look round, submerged. We had seen no identification marks on her. When about 3 miles from land we sighted 5 boats coming towards us, 3 were motorboats one of which flew the pilot flag, one small sailing boat and a rowing boat with 2 fishermen in it.

They hailed us in Norwegian which none of us understood. Four proceeded to the scene of the disaster whilst the fifth, the rowing boat, turned towards the beach indicating that she was going to show us the way in and keeping a few yards ahead of us. About an hour after we arrived at the Island of Helligvær in company with the whaler and landed at the jetty.

(Signed) H R Jenkins. R.N.R

Another interesting report is one given by a sailor onboard the U-Boat that torpedoed the *India*. I had knowledge that there was such a report, but it was not until I put out a request for any details on *HMS India* and her crew on an Internet forum called Great War Forum that I was able to get the full details. A fellow member of the forum alerted me to the fact that there was a book entitled *U-Boats Westward! by* Ernst Hashagen.

Ernst Hashagen, also known as in later life Captain Hashagen, was a sailor aboard the U-Boat and he wrote about the day leading up to and the eventual successful torpedoing of the *India*. He also explains why the survivors on the *India* rescue boats recall seeing the periscope after the sinking. Ernst Hashagen was promoted to Captain in April of 1916 and is credited on U-Boat.net with having been responsible for the sinking of 53 ships and 2 warships as well as damaging a further 5 ships and taking 2 as prizes.

This all occurred between April 1916 and the end of World War 1. I have decided to include the complete passage regarding *HMS India* below as it makes very compelling reading.

We worked in the Irish Sea over the next few days with doubled strength, angry because we had had no success picking up the prisoner.

In August we received a new task. This time we went up to the Lofoten islands, far up over the Arctic Circle. Precisely this journey proved strikingly that with a correct and purposeful planning an enterprise and the use of surprise, success was inevitable.

A whole week we steered along the Norwegian coast. Fresh wind from the east. Bright and transparent air. Long days. Northward! Gradually, the land moves closer, and an archipelago emerges from the sea. In the white light of the midnight sun shines the Svartisen glacier to the right. In front as a backdrop is the deep shadow of a steep black rocky coast. The ocean breathes calmly and smoothly. Like distant music its murmur sounds as the waves break on the cliffs and spent themselves far back in the dark bays and fjords. A deep peace. Even the wind is silent and weakly carries the plaintive cry of a seagull to our ears. Nothing bothers the majesty of nature, this image of an almost supernatural beauty and silence.

Hours pass, and the land ahead of us in the north emerges out higher.

"There's something among the islands," said the petty officer of the watch, "one point, now just under the second hilltop from the left," and a thick leather arm slides in front of my face pointing forward with outstretched fingers.

All glasses jerk up. The "subject" is examined more closely. Now we see some smoke, like a fine veil.

"A fishing trawler," says a sailor. In the meantime, I have the item in my glasses too; it does not seem to me that; rather, it looks like two medium-sized steamers. At the same moment, the "something" melts together back into one by the refraction of the rays.

"A big steamer with two funnels," says another, "I see it very clearly." But before I can position the glasses again everything contracts again to a dot and then disappears.

It is two o'clock in the morning and almost as bright as day. Softly the heart begins to beat. The islands in front of us were Lofoten. Should "he" already be there, right on the first evening of our arrival up here, the Englishman we should "pick up"? Already for months there had been repeated reports that an English auxiliary cruiser was operating in the Lofoten Islands and disrupted German ore shipping from Narvik. We should put an end to this bustle and attack and sink the ship.

Suddenly the dot reappears and quickly becomes visible and larger. We dive as fast as possible so that the refraction of the rays does not prematurely betray us and conjure up a gigantic gray submarine over the horizon.

We are beginning to recognize a large English auxiliary cruiser with two masts and two funnels. It was great luck that he ran into our arms! We close to almost 3000 meters. Then the ship changes course again and quickly disappears inside Vest fjord.

So be patient and wait!

Soon the last wisp of smoke is gone. We surface again and, carefully and anxiously, follow the lookout into the fjord. Above us, the jagged mountains of Lofoten tower into the clear northern sky. Snowfields stretch down deep.

Long before the war we cruised once with a whole squadron of battleships in Sognefjord. They appeared like toys under the overpowering Norwegian fjord walls. But a submarine became downright nothing, overwhelmed by the gigantic forms of nature. The rugged Lofoten faced the fjord like giants and looked far beyond us into the northern sea.

Finally, at 3 o'clock in the afternoon something comes back in sight. With the very clear air and the excessive visibility in these high latitudes, we are cautious enough to dive immediately with "alarm" at the first detection of the mast tops. We hover with the "eye" just over the surface and see the ship slowly approaching. Soon we realize that "he" is back, joyfully the message runs through the boat. Hopefully, we will be successful this time!

From the commands coming from the tower, one can make about a picture of what is happening above. Engine and rudder commands change frequently. Then the auxiliary cruiser seems to change its course more often. Already the torpedo tube is flooded; finally, we seem to be on it. Our engines are at their max output. But after a few minutes the machine telegraph falls back on a slow speed. Once again, our opponent moves past 2000 meters in front. We have to be patient and wait for a certain shooting opportunity.

Meanwhile the Englishman stops a steamer entering the fjord, examines his papers and then comes closer. Suddenly he changes course again, exactly to the point where we lurk, waiting. Now is the opportunity! The final commands come; the distance decreases quickly. At 1100 meters our shot is fired. Seconds pass. The torpedo has twice broken through the surface in the beginning of his journey, as the commander can see through the periscope, but then runs well. After about a minute, a dull detonation makes the boat tremble. "Hit in the stern, the enemy sinks quickly," the message comes through the mouthpiece.

The commander lets me take a look through the periscope. The ship sinks so rapidly that hardly any boats are launched. After four minutes, the whole stern section is already under water. Another three minutes, the mast tops disappear in the sea after the whole mighty ship once again rises high out of the water. Countless debris, life preservers, boats crowded with people drift on the site of the sinking. With the speed of the disaster many will be pulled down.

We go underwater to 20 meters and after about two hours we return to the wreckage to fish for life preservers or other pieces of wreckage that tell us the name of the ship we do not even know. As we approach, we still see boats drifting around, as well as a Norwegian and an armed English steamer intervening to pick up the survivors. We therefore give up our plan and run off submerged again.

Upon return, we learned that the destroyed ship had been the English auxiliary cruiser "India" (1896, 7940 Br.R.T., 340-man crew, P. & O line). 160 men were killed. The ship sank near the island Engelvär in water 240 meters deep.

Then we moved north along the outer side of the Lofoten, out into the Arctic Ocean, where the sun did not set over the sea. It was getting lonely up here. Once we met an English steamer who wanted to bring supplies to the Russians in Arkhangelsk. We sank it and were alone again. Alone with the sky and water and the midnight sun which ran a pale hand over the waves. "[11]

This more poetic version is corroborated by the logbook report from the actual U-22. This was passed on to me by Bill Kennedy, the grandson of Commander Kennedy. Even my amateur attempts at translating the German text using trusty Google translate were able to reveal the avaricious nature of the attack.

The logbook reads like a predatory animal stalking its prey and then coming back later to confirm that they did the job properly. I did find the direct translation of *Aujgetaucht* to "popped up" as quite incongruous. Such a trivial translation of the action of a torpedo laden U-boat breaching the surface to check for enemy craft to attack.

8.VIII.15 WestFjord

12h25m V—Popped up.

1h05m—Vehicle with 2 chimneys in sight. Submerged quickly. It is an English auxiliary cruiser of around 10,000t that patrols the sea changing course continuously. Tried to attack.

---

[11] Hashagen, E. (translated by Celestino Corraliza) U-Boats Westward! My Voyages to England 1914-1918 (Great War at Sea). Trident Publishing. 2019.

3h25m—lost sight of Auxiliary cruiser in the south. She is seen again later, but only at a great distance, in North east. Didn't spot it after this. At times I dove to 20m.

9h15m—A 700t steamer with a Swedish badge and heading N.O. Due to the insignificance of the object, our presence is not revealed.

11h40m—Wind N.N.O, 2-3—Resurfaced, entered the Westfjord at a low speed and loaded.

13h25m—The auxiliary cruiser is in sight. Attacks attempted.

14h45m—Auxiliary cruiser stops a merchant steamer, the course for Narvik hoisting the British war ensign for a while. No further details can be made out.

16h20m—There is an opportunity to attack.

16h35m—G.D torpedo, shot clear from the bow. Distance about 1200m. Torpedo jumps on the water and breaks through the surface another two times. Cutting angle 90°. Could not confirm what was hit by the torpedo as the periscope was submerged at the time. Detonation was dull and very violent, as it was probably a boiler-room or some ammunition that was hit.

The auxiliary cruiser immediately sagged aft, discharged a lot of fumes and sank 7 minutes after the hit, stern first, while the bow vertically stretched from the water. At the wreck site I saw people drifting who were picked up by 5 heavily loaded boats. An empty steamer with Swedish badges joined the boats.

Wreck site 67°29 'N. 13°31' 0 at 26 n depth after docking and bearing. (a handwritten acknowledgment of a sighting of the Gotaland added to the log at this point.)

18h—Went down to 20 m, kept some distance from the wreck and approached it again to find out the identity of the auxiliary cruiser from drifting wreckage.

18h30m—Panorama.

At the site of the wreck, the boats looking for floating things, the Swedish steamer and an armed fine steamer. Went down 20 metres.

18h40m—Popped up. With the help of beacons and bearings we determine the position of the wreck to be correct. (handwritten acknowledgement of F. Sansom which may be another boat that was in the vicinity of the wreck.)

Bill Anstead's research confirmed that the U-boat that sunk *HMS India* was U22 captained by Lt Commander Hoppe. Built in 1912, it was one of the smaller U-boats. Bill writes that in 1915 "it had been involved in a notorious incident off the Dutch coast when it challenged another submarine in fog and receiving no response, believed it to be enemy and sank it by torpedo. In fact, it was sister U Boat U7 captained by Hoppe's best friend and only one person survived. U22 was transferred to duties in the Baltic and North Sea soon after." After the war, U22 was surrendered to the Allies.

READ ALL ABOUT IT—what did the papers say?

Back home in Britain word of the sinking of *HMS India* reached the papers on the 13 August, five days after the event. The Northern Whig, Western Evening Herald, and Birmingham Gazette, amongst most other major papers made the announcement under the heading H.M.S India Sunk. The announcement was followed by brief text explaining that the vessel had been "Torpedoed in the North Sea while on Patrol duty."

The Manchester Courier and Lancashire General Advertiser, amongst others, included a longer article—one example of the article listed under Latest War News by Private Wires, it reads:

"H.M.S India victims

Exhausted Men in a Raft Sing "Tipperary"

Under date Tuesday, the correspondent of the "Daily Mail" at Christiania telegraphs:

With regard to the sinking of the British Auxiliary Cruiser India, I learn that large crowds assembled on the quay at the port when the survivors and dead were landed.

The dead bodies were laid in coffins covered with the British flag and were followed by hundreds of people to the mortuary chapel. They will be buried tomorrow.

In two boats were about 80 men. These were towed to land by motorboats. The saving of the other men was difficult. They were much exhausted and most of them had to be hoisted on board the rescuing boats. Some were standing on a kind of raft singing "Tipperary"."

The following day news was shared regarding the potential for the internment of the survivors and the protest the torpedoing. The Western Daily Press and Irish Independent reported:

"H.M.S India

Sunk in Norwegian Waters

Protect to Germany

(Press Association War Special)

It is officially announced that just as the Norwegian Government previously insisted, in face of contrary contention of the British Government, that the WestFjord in its entirety was a Norwegian territorial water, the Norwegian Government now, on the occasion of the torpedoing of the British Auxiliary Cruiser India has informed the German Government that the WestFjord has from time immemorial been regarded as belonging to the Norwegian Sea territory.

This is specifically the fact with respect to the part of the Fjord where India was attacked.

The funeral of 12 more English sailors from the India took place yesterday with full military honours. There were many wreaths on the coffins, including offerings from the Norwegian Navy and the British Legation. A company of Norwegian soldiers paid the last honours by the graveside."

The Yorkshire Post and Leeds Intelligencer add more detail to this story

Three British blue jackets belonging to the India were buried yesterday. The obsequies were the most imposing of their kind ever given to foreigners. The coffin and graves in which the three men were interred were covered with flowers. Lovely wreaths were sent by the British Consul and the Norwegian Naval minister. The naval squadron from the Norwegian inspection ship formed a guard of honour. At the graveside solemn anthems were rendered by members of the Choral Union. Flags were flown at half-mast.

Lieut. Allfree (sic), a British Lieutenant, who was moved to tears by the solemnity of the proceedings, on behalf of his comrades returned thanks for the great honour shown his dead compatriots."[12]

What Happened to Arnold?

It took me months of research to work out what happened to Arnold. I knew, of course, that he survived as I was married to his grandson who had met him as a child! If he had been on duty at the time the torpedo struck, then he would have been down in the engine rooms and would have had to make his way to the decks before trying to get into a life raft, but I have no way of knowing what he was doing when the torpedo hit.

I had not seen any lists of how the men were rescued when I was researching in the National Archives and then a worldwide pandemic hit and all research facilities were shut so I was unable to return to check if I had missed something.

---

[12] All newspaper quotes come from britishnewspaperarchive.co.uk.

I continued all other forms of research, contacting philatelists in Denmark, Norway and the US who were all interested in the envelopes and the censor markings on Arnold's letters.

Whilst doing this I contacted a gentleman who had authored a book which had a chapter dedicated to what happened to the survivors of *HMS India.* I started corresponding with him and he kindly offered to send me the copies of his research. I excitedly waited for the package from Denmark and when it arrived was thrilled to see letters that I had not seen before and pictures and articles and then the one thing that I had been hoping to see—lists of how the survivors had been taken to safety.

There were three options—to be picked up the *Gotaland,* to be rescued by the rescue boats from the *Saxon* or to have made it into one of the *India's* rescue boats. I was confident that he had not been in the *Gotaland* as those men could return to Britain (more on that in the next chapter), so it was one of the two other options. I really hoped that he had been in one of the two rescue craft from the *India* as whilst they had a long row to safety, they were not in the freezing waters of the North Sea waiting to be rescued.

The package full of information from Denmark confirmed that, unfortunately, Arnold had indeed been one of the men who missed out in getting a place on a rescue craft and was rescued from the sea by the rescue boats from the *Saxon.* We have no idea how long he was in the water for, but reports have stated that men were in the water for up to three hours. It must have been a terrifying experience although there are reports of the men singing to keep their spirits up.

Other reports speak of the men being almost naked when rescued, I can only assume that they got rid of their heavy boots and clothes to stop them dragging them down.

Of the approximately 350 men who were aboard the *HMS India* when it sunk, tragically about 160 of them did not survive the torpedo attack and of those, about 145 were never given a proper burial and were buried at sea. There is a memorial to them in Bodø, the township on the mainland where some of the survivors and dead were taken and there have been efforts to commemorate them in recent years.

I was also informed by a relative of one of the deceased (Steven Filmer is the great nephew of Lieutenant Robert Nelson) that the names of some of the deceased are on the Chatham Naval Memorial, which is situated near to where many of the men would have trained before heading off on the ill-fated *HMS India*. I have yet to be able to visit due to national lockdown restrictions. There are also names on the Portsmouth and Plymouth Naval Memorials, amongst others.

One of the descendants of one of the deceased crew set up an email friendship with me and was happy to share the research he had done on his great uncle, Trimmer Walter James Farrier. The Farrier story is a particularly sad one as the Farrier family lost not only Walter but also his brothers Thomas Frederic and Albert Edward and two stepbrothers. Surviving brother, Percy, came home but lost an arm in the fighting. You do hear of multiple members of the one family being killed but it is incredibly sad to lose so many men from the one family.

The men who lost their lives on 8 August 1915 in the North Sea after the torpedoing of *HMS India*.

A, Petty Officer 2c (Coast Guard), 151369 (Ch).

AERS, Frank E, Able Seaman (Coast Guard), 142921 (Po).

ALLISON, Thomas, Greaser, MMR, 781351.

ANTHONY, Thomas R, Storekeeper, MMR, 243701.

BARRELL, James W, Leading Signalman, 237068 (Ch).

BARRETT, Charles R, Private, RMLI, 19075 (Ch).

BARRY, James, Trimmer, MMR, (no service number listed).

BETHELL, Edwin, Ty/Chief Engineer, RNR.

BOYLE, William, Trimmer, MMR, (no service number listed).

BROOKS, Albert E, Able Seaman (RFR B 9669), 210160 (Ch).

BROOMAN, William, Leading Seaman (Coast Guard), 138931 (Po).

BROWN, John, Steward, MMR, (no service number listed).

BUNGARD, William A, Steward, MMR, 796977.

BUTLER, William, Stoker 1c (RFR B 5517), SS 107934 (Dev).

CAIRNS, John, Fireman, MMR, (no service number listed).

CAREY, Herbert, Able Seaman (RFR B 5028), 212125 (Ch).

CHANDLER, William R, Leading Seaman, RNVR, London 10/2698.

CHARLES, William A, Fireman, MMR, (no service number listed).

CHURCH, Frederick, Donkeyman, MMR, (no service number listed).

CLARK, Sydney B, Act/Lieutenant, RNR.

CLARKE, Charles W, Trimmer, MMR, (no service number listed).

CLARKE, Felix W, Able Seaman (RFR B 5010), 184591 (Ch).

COOK, George, Able Seaman (RFR B 4789), 178504 (Ch).

COTTON, William, Fireman, MMR, (no service number listed).

CROWLEY, Desmond J, Able Seaman, RNVR, London 4/2958.

CULHANE, Patrick, Petty Officer 1c (Pens, RFR A 2041), 146034 (Ch).

DAUBNEY, Lionel H, Steward, MMR, (no service number listed).

DAVIES, Norrie, Fireman, MMR, 794323.

DENNISON, James, Fireman, MMR, 681183.

DENT, Walter, Greaser, MMR, (no service number listed).

DEVINE, John, Fireman, MMR, (no service number listed).

DICKSON, Andrew F, Ty/Sub Lieutenant, RNR.

DIPPLE, Henry, Fireman, MMR, 747471.

DIVINE, William M, Seaman, RNR, A 7913.

DOGGETT, Michael, Greaser, MMR, 398917.

DUNCAN, James, Donkeyman, MMR, (no service number listed).

DUNN, Robert, Fireman, MMR, (no service number listed).

FARRIER, Walter J, Trimmer, MMR, 801188.

FISHER, John H L, Trimmer, MMR, 790066.

FLEGG, Joseph, Trimmer, MMR, 679132.

FREEMAN, Thomas, Fireman, MMR, (no service number listed).

FRY, Thomas, Fireman, MMR, (no service number listed).

FRYER, Henry W J, Able Seaman (RFR B 10823), SS 2901 (Ch).

GALLAGHER, Neal, Fireman, MMR, (no service number listed).

GIBSON, Charles, Private, RMLI, 19088 (Ch).

GIBSON, William, Greaser, MMR, (no service number listed).

GILBERT, John, Stoker 1c (RFR B 167), 174381 (Dev).

GLADWELL, Charles, Fireman, MMR, (no service number listed).

GOODWIN, Charles W, Able Seaman (RFR B 10072), 206685 (Ch).

GUNN, William, Private, RMLI, 14409 (Ch).

HAGGERTY, George, Trimmer, MMR, (no service number listed).

HAIGH, Louis, Fireman, MMR, 47850.

HALLIDAY, George, Fireman, MMR, (no service number listed).

HARDING, Samuel A, Boy 1c, J 34328.

HAWKES, Albert E, Private, RMLI, 19204 (Ch).

HODGES, Cyril S, Seaman, RNR, A 8400.

HOLLOWAY, Leonard, Able Seaman (RFR B 3753), 183337 (Ch).

JAMES, Albert M, Petty Officer 1c (Coast Guard), 156090 (Po).

JELLIS, Charles W, Private, RMLI (RFR A 553), 14274 (Ch).

JENNINGS, Stanley J, Steward, MMR, (no service number listed).

JONES, Herbert O, Ty/Assistant Paymaster, RNR.

KINGDON, James J, Petty Officer (NS, Coast Guard), 128972 (Po).

LEACH, Dick, Steward, MMR, (no service number listed).

LOGIE, Daniel, Trimmer, MMR, 787247.

LOVETT, Frederick J, Ty/Warrant Telegraphist, RNR.

MALONEY, Maurice, Trimmer, MMR, (no service number listed).

MARKS, Lewis, Private, RMLI, 5339 (Ch).

MATHEWS, Henry J, Head Steward, MMR, (no service number listed).

MCCARTY, James, Boatswain, MMR, (no service number listed).

MCKAY, Duncan, Fireman, MMR, (no service number listed).

MCKEEVER, Thomas, Fireman, MMR, (no service number listed).

MCRITCHIE, Roderick, Leading Seaman, RNR, B 3398.

MOFFATT, Frederick J, Able Seaman (RFR B 3972), 194815 (Ch).

NEILL, William, Fireman, MMR, 559895.

NELSON, Robert, Act/Lieutenant, RNR.

NIGHTINGALE, William, Fireman, MMR, (no service number listed).

NOBLE, Edward J, Carpenter, MMR, (no service number listed).

OILLER, William R, Leading Seaman (Coast Guard), 219400 (Po).

OSBORNE, Henry W, Able Seaman (RFR B 4981), 218175 (Ch).

PATTERSON, John, Able Seaman (RFR B 3697), 165672 (Ch).

PATTISON, Thomas, Able Seaman (RFR B 4678), 172668 (Ch).

PEACOCK, John W, Able Seaman (RFR B 357), 178585 (Ch).

PENGELLY, James, Leading Seaman (Coast Guard), 205236 (Po).

POLLARD, Charles E L, Fireman, MMR, (no service number listed).

POTTER, Percival B, Ty/Midshipman, RNR.

PRIOR, John H, Petty Officer 1c (Coast Guard) (RFR A 1532), 137246 (Ch).

RADLEY, William, Fireman, MMR, 724798.

RAYNER, Alfred H, Able Seaman (RFR B 4385), 196193 (Ch).

REVELEY, Frank, Able Seaman (RFR B 5501), 204690 (Ch).

RING, Andrew, Fireman, MMR, 767662.

ROBBINS, Edward W, Fireman, MMR, 624597.

ROBERTS, Henry, Fireman, MMR, (no service number listed).

ROBINSON, Sidney, Able Seaman (RFR B 5098), 205032 (Ch).

ROUSE, Bert, Fireman, MMR, 731142.

SALTER, Edwin C, Able Seaman (RFR B 3837), 187300 (Ch).

SAUNDERS, Wilfred A, Corporal, RMLI, 17005 (Ch).

SCOTT, Charles H, Trimmer, MMR, (no service number listed).

SEDDON, William C J, Leading Seaman, RNVR, London Z 453.

SHACKELL, Frederick, Butcher's Mate, MMR, (no service number listed).

SIMMENDINGER, William, Able Seaman (RFR B 6100), 188747 (Ch).

SMITH, Harold G, Able Seaman (RFR B 4388), 192680 (Ch).

STAMPTON, Henry, Chief Petty Officer (RFR A 1556), 143378 (Ch).

STANLEY, Robert, Able Seaman (RFR B 3583), 190580 (Ch).

STAPLES, Thomas, Leading Seaman, RNVR, London Z 62.

STENSON, Joseph, Fireman, MMR, (no service number listed).

STONE, Robert B, Engine Room Artificer, RNR, EC 121.

SULLIVAN, Patrick, Fireman, MMR, (no service number listed).

THACKARA, Roy A, Ty/Assistant Engineer, RNR.

TOWNROW, Wilfred J, Canteen Steward, 682556.

TROUNSON, Samuel P, Ty/Assistant Engineer, RNR.

WALSH, James P, Fireman, MMR, 397759.

WARD, Henry A, Fireman, MMR, (no service number listed).

WEST, Arthur H, Able Seaman (RFR B 6070), 181486 (Ch).

WHATLEY, Frank, Stoker 1c (RFR B 5974), 300924 (Dev).

WHITE, James, Writer, MMR, (no service number listed).

WIGLEY, Albert P, Trimmer, MMR, (no service number listed).

WOOD, George D H, Ty/Midshipman, RNR.

WOODSTOCK, Robert J, Refrigerating Mechanic, MMR, (no service number listed).

WOOLDRIDGE, Walter, Private, RMLI, 19097 (Ch).

WREN, Ernest F, Private, RMLI, 19259 (Ch).

Photographs from the Australian War memorial site of bodies being unloaded from the Trawler Saxon and of the funeral service held in Narvik for twelve of the deceased sailors from HMS India.

AUSTRALIAN WAR MEMORIAL   H05430

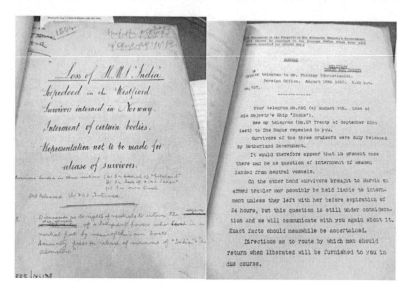

Selected pages from the files at the National Archives in London. The pages cover details of deceased and detained men as well as letters and telegrams from the Foreign Office, the Admiralty, and the British Legation in Kristiania.

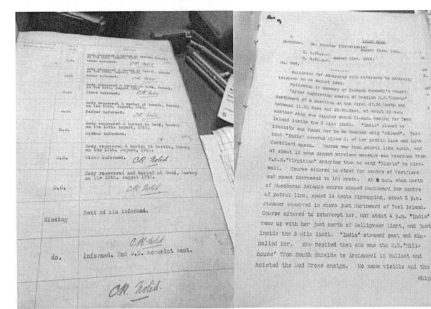

December. Mr. Finlay (Christiania)
August 31st, 1915.
R. 9.50 p.m.
R. 9.50 p.m. August 31st, 1915.
No. 999.

Following for Admiralty with reference to Admiralty telegram to me August 24th:

Following is summary of Captain Kennedy's report:

'After completing search of Swedish S.S. "Gloria" Northward of a position on the first 67.56 North and between 11.30 East and 13.30 East, at about 10 a.m. another ship was sighted about 11 a.m. making for Tana Island inside the 3 mile limit. "India" closed to identify and found her to be Swedish ship "Island". India took "India" several miles N. of her patrol line and into Vestfiord again. Course was then patrol line again, and at about 12 noon urgent wireless message was received from H.M.S. "Virginian" ordering them to send "Gloria" to Kirkwall. Course altered to steer for centre of Vestfiord and speed increased to 16½ knots. At 2 p.m. when North of Musebaran Islands course shaped Southward for centre of patrol line, speed 14 knots zigzagging, about 3 p.m. steamer observed in shore just Northward of Toel Island. Course altered to intercept her, and about 4 p.m. "India" came up with her just north of Malligvaer Light, and just inside the 3 mile limit. "India" steamed past and signalled her. She replied that she was the S.C. "Millhouse" from South Shields to Archangel in ballast and hoisted the Red Cross ensign. No name visible and the ship

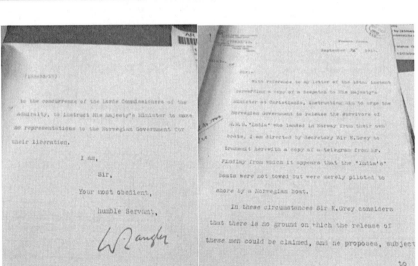

(enclosure)

... the concurrence of the Lords Commissioners of the Admiralty, to instruct His Majesty's Minister to make no representations to the Norwegian Government for their liberation.

I AM,

Sir,

Your most obedient,

humble Servant,

W. Langley

September 26th 1915.

Sir,

With reference to my letter of the 18th instant forwarding a copy of a telegram to His Majesty's Minister at Christiania, instructing him to urge the Norwegian Government to release the survivors of H.M.S. "India" who landed in Norway from their own boats, I am directed by Secretary Sir E. Grey to transmit herewith a copy of a telegram from Mr. Finlay from which it appears that the "India's" boats were not towed but were merely piloted to shore by a Norwegian boat.

In these circumstances Sir E. Grey considers that there is no ground on which the release of these men could be claimed, and he proposes, subject to

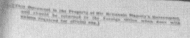

NORWAY.

NO COPY.
TO BE KEPT SECRET.

(106311/15).

Decode. Mr. Findlay (Christiania)
                                    August 9th. 1915.

        D. 4.5.p.m.

        R. 6.15.p.m. August 9th. 1915.

Urgent.

No. 881.

        In continuation of previous telegrams, British
Vice Consul at Trondhjem reports following telephonic
communication received from Vice Consul at Narvik:-
        "'India' torpedoed August 8th. 5.45.p.m.
Swedish steamer 'Götaland' brought 10 Officers, 72 men,
and 4 dead to Narvik. Captain Kennedy with 7 other
Officers, 52 men and 7 dead, 3 of whom were Officers
arrived Narvik on armed trawler 'Gannon'. Captain
Kennedy refused to go ashore and said trawler would
go out again. Two boats with 48 men and 3 dead arrived
Helligver".

        Please inform Admiralty.

The Attack Beginning.

Ten Minutes Afterwards.

H.M.S "India" and the Survivors of Death
August 8th 1915.

STRUCK!

The five previous sketches were sent to me by Bill Kennedy and I believe they were drawn by Private Reginald A Parsons—they are signed RAP and this is the only name on record to fit these initials. Parsons was a career sailor who had enrolled early in 1913. He was granted leave in 1917 to return to Lewisham to marry Dora Fuller.

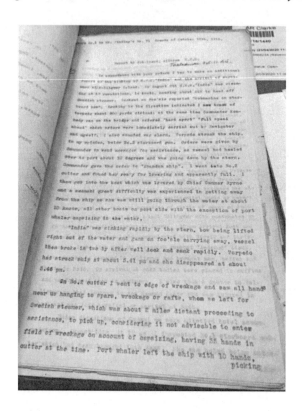

Lieutenant Alltree's Official report for the Admiralty.

NORWEGIAN PROTEST.

THE INDIA TORPEDOED IN TERRITORIAL WATERS.

(FROM OUR CORRESPONDENT.)

CHRISTIANIA, Aug. 12.

The Norwegian Government to-day informed Germany that the India was torpedoed in what has always been maintained to be Norwegian territorial waters.

The question of the internment of the seamen rescued from the India is not yet settled. Twelve have died and were buried to-day in the presence of large crowds.

CHRISTIANIA, Aug. 13.

It is officially announced that just as the Norwegian Government previously insisted, in face of the contrary contention of the British Government, that the West Fjord in its entirety was a Norwegian territorial water, the Norwegian Government now, on the occasion of the torpedoing of the British auxiliary cruiser India, has informed the German Government that the West Fjord has from time immemorial been regarded as belonging to Norwegian sea territory. This is specifically the fact with the part of the Fjord where the India was attacked.—*Reuter.*

List of Officers & Men saved by HM Armed Trawler "Saxon" and
by ships boats of "Index" returned at [Stralsund?] as [Fleetberg?]

W. [Sellachannier?]   R[oyal?] N[avy?]

Commander   G.E. [Ready?] R.N.
Lieut. (not)   John Henry [Biggs?] R.N.R.
Sub Lieut. (temp)   Claude John [Oate?] R.N.R.
    (act)   Harold [Innocotehate?] R.N.R.
Surgeon   [Henal Conultis Lawson?] R.N.
Asst. Paymr.   Charles James [Hyrne?] R.N.
[Engineer?]   Charles William [Ssteen?] R.N.R.
    Frederick William [Pine?] R.N.R.
[Midshipman?]   Ronald Charles [Hast?] R.N.R.
Sub Lieut.   [Ernest Cuthbert Aillitts?] R.N.R.
[Eng Sub Lieut?]   Francis Cuthbert [Poltimer?] R.N.R.
[Midshipman?]   Harold [Hope Jenkins?] R.N.R.

Petty Officer   Arthur [Vaunce?]   [201616?]
    William [J...] [Clork?]   [got a act list?]
    Fred [Hunt?]   Emr. R.F.R.   [Not?]
Lead. Seaman   Albert C. [Craw?]   R.F.R. [4143?]
    Chas. R. [White?]   [197760?]
    Edward S. [Paxton?]   [168340?]
    William G. [Beayon?]   [201889?]
Able Seaman   Samuel E. [Summerfield?]   R.F.R. [4288?]
    Henry [Zerank?]   S.S. or [3204?]
    Fred. E. [Lampson?]   [171702?]
    John T. [Wells?]   R.F.R. [6007?]
    William [Haskell?]   [198676?]

---

26. Able Seaman   John H. [Caines?]   R.F.R. [2286?]
27. "   William [Jones?]   W.F.R. [3302?]
28. "   Henry G. [Hill?]   R.N.V.R. [130. Bristol Divn?]
29. "   Hugh [Davis?]   R.N.R.
30. "   John S. [Alford?]   R.N.V.R. [2680 London?]
31. "   Charles H. [Cox?]   [180401?]
32. "   Sidney G. [Steele?]   R.F.R. [2169?]
33. "   Alfred S. [Burch?]   R.F.R. [454?]
34. "   Herbert [Harrison?]   [194177?]
35. "   William H. [Mortimer?]   R.F.R. [7777?]
36. "   John W.H. [Greison?]   R.N.V.R. [2866 London?]
37. "   Allan G.C. [Artcoll?]   R.F.R. [0009?]
38. "   John T. [Wright?]   [167886?]
39. "   George [Ward?]   [213827?]
40. "   George H. [Comes?]   R.N.V.R. [860 Z. London?]
41. "   Alfred S. [Hanson?]   R.F.R. [5583?]
42. "   John [Willm Barratfield?]   R.N.R. [7069?]
43. "   Robert [Maynard?]   R.N.R. [1840?]
44. "   Bernard [Piddock?]   R.N.R. [6629. A?]
45. "   Reg. [Parsons?]   R.N.R. [2166?]
46. "   Elvey [Taylor?]   R.F.R. [210340?]
47. "   William T. [Keele?]   R.F.R.   * [Hospital at Delos? Henry?]
48. Cook   Ernest [Duggan?]   R.N.V.R. [191. Z - Clyde?]
49. "   Joseph P. [Magill?]   R.N. [...]
50. "   Matthew [Milligan?]   R.N. (temp)
51. Steward   Henry [W. Kiley?]   R.F.R. [101040?]
    James [Frensley Foster?]   R.F.R. [101059?]
52. R.F.A.   Richard A. [Clark?]   R.N.V.R. [Z. 16. Clyde?]
53. "   William [Gillan?]   R.N.V.R. [1760. Clyde?]

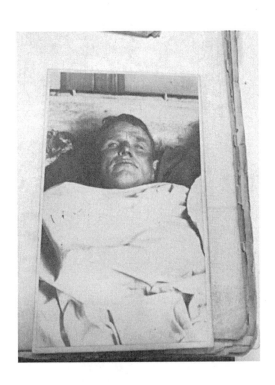

A photo of one of the deceased crew from the files at the National Archives.

Next is a map of the site of the wreck of HMS India. It is approximately six miles from the nearest shore on the island of Helligvaer and locals report that even to this day wreckage from the ship occasionally washes up on the beaches. Local hearsay reports that smoke could be seen from the direction of the sinking ship.

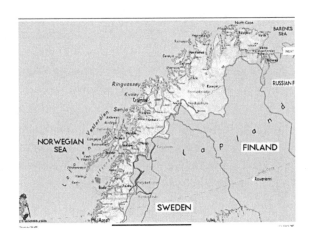

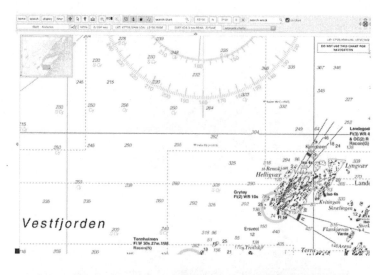

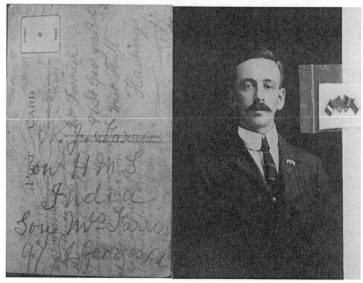

Front and back view of postcard written by Walter Farrier. It is dated 16 November 1914 and reads – "Dear Mother and Dad, sent this to let you know that we did get the Germans and got back quite safe. Expect to be going again this week. Will let you know if I do. Am sending on letter. Surprised to see Tom where he is. Hope Dad will soon be well. Love to all, Walter."—Over the top is scrawled. "WJ Farrier, on board HMS India, return to clerk's office." The dates are confusing as HMS India was not on the water in a war capacity in 1914. Not sure how it all matches up!

8th BATTALION, ROYAL FUSILIERS: DIED 4/8/16.

S/No:- 801188
STOKER W. J. FARRIER.
Went down on H.M.S. India on August 8th last year. (1915)

S/No:-T/2586
PTE. T. FARRIER,
5th Royal Sussex.
Killed in action on May 17th last year (1915)

PTE. P. H. FARRIER,
13th Royal Fusiliers.
Wounded. Now in hospital at Norwich.

No:- 27715
PTE. A. E. FARRIER,
Royal Fusiliers. At the Front.

Four brothers. Sent by Mrs. Farrier, 21, St. George's-road, Hastings.

A clipping from a Hastings Newspaper from 1916 with the four Farrier brothers, three who died and one who was seriously injured.

Memorial from Bodø and gravestone from Narvik.

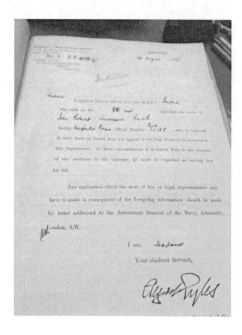

The official letters sent to the next-of-kin of the deceased and of the men who were listed as deceased only to be found to be alive later.

Telegrams "Navy Accounts, London."
In any letter communicating on this subject, please quote

No. P.N.F. 4105/15.

The Accountant General of the Navy,
Admiralty,
London, S.W.

Admiralty.

24 August 1915.

Madam,

    With reference to the letter from this Department dated the 14th. instant, I have to inform you that Thomas Joseph Sanders, Chief Armourer, (Pensioner) Official Number 145068, late of H.M.S. "India", is now reported to have been saved when that vessel was sunk on the 8th. instant. He is at present in Norway, but his precise address is not yet known.

    I have to add that any distress which the receipt of the official intimation may have caused you is deeply regretted, and to request that you will be good enough to return to this Department the notification in question, with its accompanying enclosures, in the attached envelope which need not be stamped.

    I am, Madam,

        Your obedient Servant,

        W. Boxall

        Accountant General
          of the Navy.

Mrs. E. E. Sanders;

    227 Westfield Road,

What to Do with the Sunken Sailors?

Do they stay or do they go? What to do with over two hundred shipwrecked sailors in a neutral country during war time.

The sinking of *HMS India* in neutral waters during war time opened the proverbial tin of diplomatic worms. The Hague convention had been written around eight years earlier to try and deal with occasions and events like this but the interpretation of it could cause issues and contrary interpretations. The telegrams started flying back and forth between Norway and London the day after the sinking and the letters and telegrams continued for almost six weeks while the case was argued back and forth.

The main issue was the prospective internment of the crew and what guidelines were in place to decide who was to be interned and who sent home. The files are now kept in the National Archives in West London and make for compelling reading. It is easy to imagine the men of the Admiralty and the Foreign Office in their offices pacing back and forth trying to work out how to save over a hundred men from indefinite incarceration. To me, I imagine it in black and white..

The cast for the movie features the following characters:

Sir Edward Grey, Viscount Grey of Fallodon—the main force behind British Foreign Policy in the First World War. He served the longest term of any Foreign Secretary, ironic for a man who hated travel and it is said that he was driven almost blind by stress and overwork during the early part of the war. He was released from office at the end of 1916 after serving for eleven years. His photograph shows a man with a closely shaven, sharp face.

Sir Mansfeldt de Cardonnel Findlay—British Diplomat to Norway from 1911-1923. Most colourful description comes from a fellow diplomat turned journalist, RH Bruce Lockheart who states "one of the tallest Englishmen in the world and certainly the tallest man in diplomacy. He was a good organiser and, aided by Charles Brudenell-Bruce, ran his huge Legation (Christiania, in peace time a diplomatic backwater, had, owing to the blockade, the largest staff of any Legation or Embassy during the war) with great efficiency."

The photo portrait of Findlay housed in the National Portrait Gallery shows a man who has a neat moustache, strong eyebrows and hair pomaded slickly to his head.

Sir Walter L.F.G Langley—Assistant Under-Secretary of State. The writer of many of the letters on file, Langley often passes the messages between the Foreign Office and the Admiralty and the Foreign Office and the British Legation in Christiania, Norway. One imagines he would need to have the patience of a saint being the one who is often in the middle of all the messages flying back and forth.

Sir Edmond Slade—Vice-Admiral for the Royal Navy.

Vice-Consul J.N Aagaard—British Vice-Consul stationed in Narvik, the town in Northern Norway close to where *HMS India* sunk.

The action takes place in offices with telegram and telegraph machines firing out messages on a frequent basis and men seated at leather topped desks furiously scratching out letters to their peers in other war offices. The first telegram comes through the day after the sinking. (a note: the archives often only house one side of the correspondence and, at times, the file copies answer unseen telegrams or letters.)

09/08/1915

Telegram: 879

1:35 p.m. from De Chair (the Commander of the 10th Cruiser Squadron).

Informing of torpedoing of HMS India 8 miles off Helligvær and that of the 350 crew, many have perished and the others have been saved by 'HMS Saxon', the Gotaland' and 'India's own boats'.[13]

It is followed two hours later with a reply from the Foreign Office.

Telegram: 880

3:45 p.m. from Foreign Office

Already starting to discuss The Hague treaty and whether the survivors are classed as "shipwrecked seamen and allowed to return to the United Kingdom".

---

[13] All of the telegraphs, telegrams and letters quoted in this chapter can be found at The National Archives in files ADM 1/8429/227 and ADM 116/1440

More details are needed and some appear from the Foreign Office just over an hour later.

Telegram: 881
4:50 p.m. from Foreign Office
An official report forwarded from Narvik reads "India" torpedoed August 8th, 5:45 p.m. Swedish steamer "Gotaland" brought 10 officers, 72 men and 4 dead to Narvik. Captain Kennedy with 7 other officers, 52 men and 7 dead, 3 of whom were officers arrived in Narvik on Armed Trawler "Samson (sic)". Two boats with 48 men and 3 dead arrived in Helligvær."

A few hours later a telegram is received from Norway from the British Consul based in Christiania (now known as Oslo). Mr Findlay is passing on information he is getting from Narvik, close to the sight of the torpedoing. Narvik is almost 1400km from Norway.

Telegram
8:15 p.m. from Mr Findlay
Those who landed in Helligvaer "appears that they must be interned. I should be glad to hear your views." He also outlines that "Norwegian government are informed that "India" was sunk in Vestfjord which is claimed as territorial waters. They have not decided what to do."

The next day and the first recorded telegram arrived from Christiania at 4:30 p.m. and informs of the current status of the crew and that one of the Royal Navy vessels involved in the rescue has departed from Narvik, to re-join the squadron.

10/08/15
Telegram
4:30 p.m. from Mr Findlay
"Captain and other survivors of "India" brought to Narvik by Armed Trawler "Saxon" have been interned and that "Saxon" left at 1:00 a.m. today"

Under an hour later it would appear that the fate of around 100 of the crew has been sealed.
Telegram

5:15 p.m. from Foreign Office

"It would therefore appear that in present case there can be no question of internment of seaman landed from neutral vessels—On the other hand survivors brought to Narvik on Armed Trawler May possibly be held liable to internment unless they left with her before expiration of 24 hours, but this question is still under consideration."

The next day sees the arrival of a brief report from the British Vice-Consul based in Narvik and it tells of the arrival of the dead bodies in Narvik. On the same day, the Foreign Office starts to think about how to get the sailors that were rescued by the neutral ship "*Gotaland*" back to the United Kingdom.

11/08/1915

Letter from Norwegian Vice-Consul Aagaard to Mr Findlay

"Yesterday when the 11 dead were drives through the town to the Chapel the coffins were all covered with flags and flowers."

A second letter to the Admiralty from the Foreign Office is marked Secret and Pressing and deals with how they might get the permitted survivor's home.

A week after the torpedoing of *India* and the Admiralty and Foreign Office are losing hope that they can save the remaining surviving crew from indefinite internment.

12/08/1915

Langley at the Foreign Office discusses the prospective internment with the Admiralty—"With regard to the second and third categories (all men not rescued by the Gotaland) Sir E. Grey finds considerable difficulty in suggesting any convincing ground against the internment of the men included in them."

A question seems to have arisen over why Commander Kennedy did not manage to leave with the men who managed to get back to the United Kingdom when he obviously was very aware that it would be the outcome for many of the men. It takes another week of written discussion and sorting out the rest of the men before Commander Kennedy's report reaches London.

13/08/1915

Telegram 810 from Mr Findlay

11:30 p.m.

Tells of Captain Kennedy refusing to leave HMS Saxon when she landed at Narvik for fear of internment.

Telegram 909 from Mr Findlay

URGENT

"Norwegian Naval Officer in charge of internment telephoned tonight following. Government decided that the survivors on "Saxon" and those landed at Helligvær shall be interned at Trondhjem but that the 81 men saved by neutral ship outside territorial waters are free from 9 p.m. 12 August." He asks how he should get them back to the United Kingdom.

14/08/1915

Telegram 927 from Mr Findlay

"Interned survivors from "HMS India" leave here today, 7 p.m., in Norwegian guardship to Fordlodingen. Will take mail steamer there and travel to internment camp at Lillehammer via Trondhjem. They are on parole."

The Foreign Office obviously tried everything in its power to free as many men as possible. Seeking clarification in a telegram (number 758) on 15/08/1915 of exactly how the men in the *India's* own craft made it to shore. The sticking point being that if the Norwegians assisted the men, then they too might be free to return home.

On the 18/08/1915 a further telegram (number 958) from Mr Findlay alerts the Foreign Office to the issue of the German protest the release of some of the men.

Mr Findlay does not hold back on his opinion stating, "I observed that Germany having broken every rule of law and humanity was hardly in a position to pose as an authority. There could be no question the case in point Norwegian action was entirely justified."

The translated German letter reads as follows.

Imperial German Embassy

Kristiania 18th August 1915

Mr. Minister,

It has come to the knowledge of the Imperial Government, that the Royal Norwegian Government has decided, that, the part of the crew, rescued by the Swedish steamer "Gotaland" of the English auxiliary cruiser "India", which sank recently near the Norwegian coast, not to intern in Norway but to release. The Royal Norwegian Government grounds her decision on the application of the principles of the Hague convention of 18 October 1907 about the war at sea.

With respect to another incident in the past, the Imperial Government has had the honor to express a completely different point of view in such matters to the Royal Norwegian Government. The Imperial Government has still the standpoint that, following the generally acknowledged law of nations, members of the armed forces of a country in the state of war, and acting accordingly, crossing borders into neutral territory, either by land or sea, are to be interned until the end of the war. If the Norwegian Government deviates from the generally acknowledged law of nations basing her decision on the X Hague treaty, it is the point of view of the Imperial Government that this is in contradiction of Article 18 of the aforementioned treaty, which stipulates that its rules are applicable only between the signatory nations and only when all belligerent nations are signatories of the treaty. However Great Britain has never ratified the treaty; resulting in the fact that the ratification by Germany and Norway is completely not significant in the present war, in the very least with regard to Great Britain.

The release of English crewmembers must surprise the Imperial Government, especially since Norway has good reason to enforce its neutrality in the most resolute way against England. Repeatedly were German passengers violently removed and taken prisoner of war, from Norwegian vessels by the English naval forces. So far the Norwegian Government was never successful in getting atonement for such violations – to which other neutral powers protested , partly with success. An even more severe violation of Norwegian neutrality was the sinking of the German steamer "Friedrich Arp" by an English naval vessel inside Norwegian territorial waters on July 8 of this year. The complete crew was taken prisoner of war and brought to England. This act of violence is still not revenged and the German seamen are still held prisoner of war.

The internment of the English crew could have been an efficient way for the Norwegian Government to enforce her protests and thereby bring the attention to the severely damaged German rights. Unfortunately the Royal Norwegian Government has decided to ignore such amicable ideas and released the English crew without considering the endangered German interests.

The Imperial Government must protest against this measure which is sensed as being unfair treatment and has charged me to bring this protest to the attention of your excellency.

With this I acquit myself of that duty etc. etc.

A. Oberndorff

Sixteen days after the tragic torpedoing and loss of life of approximately 160 men, a summary of Commander Kennedy's report of the incident arrives at the Admiralty. He outlines not only exactly what happened on the 8 August but also why he decided to stay with his men and not return to the United Kingdom.

21/08/1915

R. 9:50 p.m.

No. 988

Following for Admiralty with reference to Admiralty telegram to me, 14 August:

Following summary of Captain Kennedy's report:

"After completing search of Swedish S.S "Gloria" Northward of a position on the first 67.30 North and between 11.30 East and 13.30 East, at about 10 a.m. another ship was sighted about 11 a.m. making for Taen Island inside the 3-mile limit. "India" closed to identify and found her to be Swedish ship "Atland". This took "India" several miles N. Of her patrol line again and at about 12 noon urgent wireless message was received from H.M.S "Virginian" ordering them to send "Gloria" to Kirkwall.

Course altered to steer for centre of Vestfjord and speed increased to 16 1/2 knots. At 2 p.m., when North of Husobaran Islands course shaped Southward for centre of patrol line, speed 14 knots zigzagging, about 3 p.m. steamer observed in shore just Northward of Tael Island. Course altered to intercept her and about 4 p.m. "India" came up with her just north of Helligvaer Light and just inside the 3-mile limit.

"India" steamed past and signalled her. She replied that she was the S.S "Hillhouse" from South Shields to Archangel in ballast and hoisted the Red Cross ensign. No name visible and the ship seemed to be very suspicious, but Kennedy considered that he could not interfere. (In view of subsequent events Kennedy thinks she was a motor ship and decoy of the submarine.).

She was a large ship capable of carrying about 6,000 tons of cargo, painted black and with two black masts and her inboard upper works were dirty yellow coloured: the master wearing a white coat and white peaked cap. Smoke being sighted north-north-west, course altered. New ship proved to be the "Saxon". Course then altered back to centre of patrol line and shortly after steamer reported south-East making towards the Taen Islands. Course again altered to

*intercept her. Few minutes after received signed F.T.P to C.Q which was not
answered "India" was torpedoed about 5:41 p.m."*

Report by next bag on 23 August.

24/08/1915.

6:40 p.m.

No. 1005A (R)

Your telegram No. 807

*Following is further extract from Captain Kennedy's report which bears on
the subject of your enquiry.*

*"My reason for deciding to go to Narvik in the "Saxon" was to avoid
submarine following me if I went South and made for Virginian etc.*

*We in the "Saxon" were told that we had to remain on board until it was
decided whether we had to be interned etc. At about 11 p.m., Captain Einang of
the Norwegian Navy asked me to speak to him on shore when we were already
in Norwegian Government vessel "Michael Sars".*

*He then informed me that if I decided I could take the "Saxon" out to sea
with all she had saved; I then most reluctantly decided that as there was no
accommodation, no food and that everyone was worn out, we had better go to
camp, etc."*

On the 23/08/1915 a three-page letter from Vice-Consul Aagaard to Sir E
Grey outlines the arrival of the survivors into Narvik—"I at once sent a
messenger ashore to get articles of clothing sent on board soonest possible as
many of the men were almost naked."

He then goes on to describe the funeral given to the dead who had arrived
with the rescued men— "The ladies of the town kindly offered to arrange the
decorations at the chapel and they literally covered the coffins with flowers. The
wreaths were, however, too numerous to be counted—and many little children
brought heaps of flowers." The rest of the letter concerns the transport of the
survivors to Trondhjem for internment or to Bergen to return home to the United
Kingdom.

There is then a three-week period with little to no communication until mid-
September when the issue of internment raises its head again and the letters from
the Foreign Office start up again. By this time, the survivors picked up by the
Gotaland had made their way or are on their way back to the United Kingdom

and the remaining survivors have been shipped the more than 1000 kilometres down to the internment camp near Lillehammer, Jørstadmoen, the place where most of them would spend the next three years of their lives. But still there is pressure from the Admiralty to free at least some of the men.

13/09/1915

"Sir E Grey is very doubtful of the soundness of the argument that the men who escaped in the "India's" own boats and were towed part of the way to shore by Norwegian motorboats are in the same position as ship-wrecked sailors picked up by neutral merchant ship. He has, however, instructed His Majesty's Minister to apply for their release on this ground."

Another letter from Langley at the Foreign Office to the Under Secretary of the Admiralty (maybe Graham Greene) discusses the three methods of rescue and the possibility that those in the *India's* boats may be eligible for release. He also makes a reference to Commander Kennedy who "was prevented (leaving) by material circumstances only from taking advantage of this permission."

Commander Kennedy had decided that the *Saxon* had neither the food stores, room, clothes, or blankets to take the survivors back to the United Kingdom and so with great regret he agreed to stay and therefore commit them all to internment.

It is a letter from Langley at the Foreign Office which finally lays all the toing and froing to rest, he writes that a "telegram from Mr Findlay from which it appears that the *"India's"* boats were not towed but were merely piloted to shore by a Norwegian boat."

Because they made it to shore by themselves and without the physical assistance of a neutral boat there was no grounds for release for these men either. The 108 men rescued by the *Saxon* and the lifeboats from the *India* were to be interned for the rest of the war. On the 15 September 1915 no one had any idea that that would be another three years and almost two months until most of these men were truly set free.

What were the papers saying?

From the 18 August the British papers started sharing the stories of survivors who had been reported drowned or missing to their families, only for the families to receive personal mail or official notification that their loved one was very much alive.

The Scotsman reported on the 18 August:

"On Monday, the parents of Petty Officer Charles Clinton RNVR who reside at 14 Percy Street, Ibrox, Glasgow received official intimation from the Admiralty that, as their son's name did not appear in the list of rescued from H.M.S India it was feared that he had been lost. Yesterday, however, they received a postcard from him at Bodø, in which Petty Officer Clinton says, "We have been safely landed in Norway". Clinton and his companions after escaping from the doomed ship, appear to have landed on the island of Hellevar (sic), from which they were taken by a Norwegian gunboat."

The Scottish Maritime Museum website also writes about Charles Clinton.

"One of the most interesting wartime stories concerns Charles Clinton, aged 24. The scrapbook has a black-edged death announcement from his parents dated 16 August 1915, detailing his death at sea during the sinking of the HMS India. On the following page, however, is typed letter from the supposedly deceased Charles, dated the following September and sent from Norway. In this he explains how he survived the attack that sank his ship and caused his misreported death.

Further correspondence details his slow progress back from Norway to Scotland. Four months later a postcard from Jørstadmoen, Norway, dated January 1916, gives thanks for "the box of cigarettes—news of a big fire in Bergen. The post office has been destroyed and I'm afraid our mails also." Perhaps this is why there is such a long gap between letters.[14]

Bergen was where much of the mail from the UK was processed before being sent on to Jørstadmoen and a fire would have been devastating for those men, like Arnold, who waited so desperately for mail to arrive.

One of the stories was also reported in a paper at the time. The People's Journal reported on Blacksmith's mate William Gardiner and his story on 21 August 1915.

"The gloom with which this intelligence cast over the missing man's household was lifted in a rather dramatic fashion on Tuesday when a postcard came to hand from him telling of his safety. The postcard bears the Norwegian post-Mark and its contents are quite in keeping with the characteristics of the true British Tar.

Addressed to his brother, it runs—"Dear Pal, this is where I have been dining today. I suppose you have heard about the ship? I have lost everything.

---

[14] Scottishmaritimemuseum.org

We had three hours rowing in a boat – the goods! Hope to see you soon. I am quite well. From W.G, somewhere in Norway."

Gardiner was a blacksmith to trade and joined the Royal Navy Division in October last. He joined H.M.S India only recently and was on his fourth trip when the vessel went down."

On the same day, the Dundee Evening Telegraph reported the following:

"The parents of Andrew Johnston, a native of Linlithgow, who was on board H.M.S India when she sank and who was supposed to have perished, have received a postcard from their son stating that he has been saved. He writes that he has been landed at Hellingvoer (sic), Norway and that he was leaving for another destination which he did not know. He adds—"We are being treated like lords." In another postcard to a friend, he says the ships head went down in a very brief period and he got clear.

The next week sees more reports surface across the country of men reported dead or missing but found alive. On the 21 August good news was reported in Kent in two different papers. The East Kent Gazette reported on Able Seaman Herbert Harrison from Milton Regis

"His wife and relatives mourned him as lost, as his name appeared in the list of "missing" men. But just before going to Press we were informed that Mrs Harrison received a letter yesterday (Friday) from her husband, posted from Norway, informing her that he was saved and is well. The sudden revulsion from grief to joy can be better imagined than described. Herbert Harrison is to be heartily congratulated on his rescue from a watery grave."

The Thanet Advertiser reported on three Ramsgate men including Cook's Mate Henry John Allen, who was engaged to be married. They state that the "glad tidings of his safety were received yesterday (Friday) morning by the 11 o'clock in letters, from the missing seaman himself" and were reassured that he was "safe, in good health and as happy as could be under the circumstances. He could not tell them anything about it, he added, but they would hear in good time."

The other two men had not made personal contact yet and "Anxiety is still felt for the safety of the two young men, as a few of the survivors have since been reported to have succumbed. It appears in messages received from Christiania that many of the survivors were very exhausted."

The Portsmouth Evening News reported on the 23 August that Leading Seaman Walter James Beynon "has been saved and the good tidings has been received with great satisfaction in the town." On the same day the Daily Record, Lanarkshire reported that Mrs Laggan of Alexandria had received a letter stating her husband was "alive and well. It was written in Norway and the letter stated that he had been landed there along with other members of the crew".

The next day the Surrey Mirror reported the good news received by Mrs Buck in Kew as "she has since received a picture postcard and letter posted in Bodø (Norway), saying that he is 'OK' and still has the two lucky farthings she gave him". Mrs Gillon in Govan, as reported by the Dumfries and Galloway Standard, received a letter from her son, William.

The good news continued into September when the Middlesex Chronicle reported on a "Feltham Sailor's Adventures" writing about Charlie Simmonds, Second Cooks Mate whose parents had even received a sympathy message from the King and Queen before they got a telegram announcing his safety and letters from their son. He wrote:

"We have nothing to do with the exception of a little work in the morning, but they have given us some thick clothes. I see by the papers I have been missing till last week. We had a fine time coming through Norway. Later he wrote: "I can't tell you much because we are only allowed to write postcards not letters. My mate was picked up by a Swedish steamer and that lot went home. Some were picked up by one of our armed trawlers. After we struck I ran to my boat and she was lowering full of men. I jumped in and the stern was under water. Then we cut the boat ropes and away she went. The ships boilers exploded and her head went up in the air. It was just like looking at the church. Then she made the last dive and it was all over in about 8 minutes. I could hardly realize it. I landed in a pair of white trousers and a shirt and cap, and we did not sleep much that night. Next morning three dead bodies were washed up; also my serge suit and some of my letters, so I was all right. They are treating us very good right up to the present."

Where Was Arnold?

Having been rescued by the *Saxon* with around sixty other men, Arnold was taken to Narvik, arriving at 10 a.m. on the morning of the 9 August. After a day spent in Narvik 58 men boarded the *Michael Sars*, a Norwegian ship and were taken to the Norwegian Army camp Elvegårdsmoen, about 30 kilometres away, where they met up with the men who had rowed to Helligvaer and had been taken to Bodø. They remained there until the 14 August when they were put on the *Michael Sars* to Lødingen and then transferred to the Norwegian ship *Polarlys* which took them to Trondhjem, where they were shepherded onto a train to Fåberg and then to Jørstadmoen, the permanent camp, arriving on the 17 August. Arnold must have been exhausted and potentially more than a little traumatised and worried at what the future would hold for him.

What were the family doing?

Back at home, Arnold's wellbeing also seemed to have been on the mind of his family. The files at the National Archives contain a letter from R Feaver:

"9 The Avenue
Gravesend
16 August 1915
To the Secretary
Admiralty
London SW
Sir,

 My younger son Richard Arnold Clarke was serving on board H.M.S "India" as Engine room?—Clyde. Z16—and I am deeply thankful to view he is reported among those saved, in the list printed in the London papers of Friday 13 August announcing the loss of that vessel.

 I shall be very grateful if I may receive instructions advising me in what way I can put into communications with my son either by cable or letters to assure him we know of his safety and would like to hear from him.

 I desire also to enquire whether we may be allowed to send him either money or a supply of personal goods as I presume all his personal belongings will have been lost.
With respect, yours faithfully
R Feaver Clarke

 P.S: My elder son is 2nd Lieut. in the 96th Royal Field Artillery—Milford. Both sons are members of the Institute of Civil Engineers."

I am unaware of any reply from the Admiralty but hopefully, R Feaver's mind was set at ease relatively quickly.

It had been a stressful couple of years for R Feaver with Edith having provided drama of her own. Edith had spent much of 1913 and 1914 studying at the Dalcroze Institute in Hellerau, Dresden. She had been sent by Madame Bergman-Österberg from the Bergman-Österberg Physical Training College and was thoroughly enjoying the experience. Winnie had also spent time there in 1913.

Unfortunately for Edith, she was still in Dresden when the war broke out and for a month the family did not know where she was. I had thought that this might be family folklore that had been exaggerated over time but in her papers, she has claim forms for personal goods that she had to leave behind and in one of the highly decorative birthday cards made by Queenie (the one made for her 50th birthday), it is written

Caught there by the world catastrophe,
For a month we heard nothing of E.R.C
But she made her way out of Germany.
The Hun could not daunt her, our bold E.R.C.

The First Few Months—
"Well, News is Scarce."

The British internees arrived at Jørstadmoen in the summer of 1915. It had been a long journey from the northern part of Norway down the coast and then inland to Jørstadmoen. The men were under the watchful eye of armed guards the whole time who had "sharp ammunition and polished bayonets. A military band led the march from Fåberg to Jørstadmoen."[15] The crew of *HMS* India must have wondered what their lives were going to be like from this point forward.

Jørstadmoen is a village in the municipality of Lillehammer and internees were taken to a military training camp that had been in place there since the nineteenth-century. The "Gudbrandsdalens" battalion of the 5th "Osloplandenes" Infantry Regiment of the 2nd Brigade trained there and those soldiers became the guards for the internment camp under the command of Colonel Holtan.

Initially there were one hundred men guarding but once the barbed wire fences were constructed in September 1915 the number of guards was reduced to around sixty men. Photos of the early days show tents set up as well as the barracks which were arranged in a U shape. Officers were initially given tents of their own, whilst the men were in the barracks in rooms of around seven men. Records show that Arnold was in Room V with Thomas Sanders (Chief Armourer), William Gillon (ERA), William Hammond (Donkeyman), Richard Dunn (Storekeeper), Robert Lawrence (Baker) and Lorenzo Chircop (Captain's Valet).

From here on in, most of the story will be told by Arnold himself. He was a prolific letter writer and so were his sisters, primarily Queenie but also Winnie

---

[15] Rønning, O (Husemoen, O & Hosar, K *Fra drgon og musketeer til electronic og data: ekserser plassen Jørstadmoen.* Lillehammer Thorsrud Lokalhistorisk fori. 1998.

and Edith. His letters tell the story of his time in Norway and by connections also the time of the other men who were interned. The letters were kept by Queenie and then Edith until her death.

As mentioned in my opening ramble, I came across the letters whilst researching the lives of his sisters, lives that were documented in letters, travel journals, photographs, and keepsakes. It was finding that many of Arnold's letters were being sold around the world that piqued my interest and it was also the story of his and the other men's, internment which seems to have largely ignored by the history books.

So, from here, this is Arnold's story with me just filling in the gaps and providing the stories of the camp and the other men who lived there for a long time.

The first letter is a postcard and is dated from 23 days after the sinking of the India and 14 days after the crew arrived in Jørstadmoen. Arnold writes his name in the top left-hand corner followed by the number 43; this was his prisoner number for the time that he was interned. He only uses it on the official release post cards and then discards it at the start of 1916. Arnold writes to Queenie with instructions on how to contact him and updates on the goings on in camp, he mentions the erection of the barbed wire fencing. There is no doubt that this is a kind of prison.

1 September 1915

I haven't got Winnie's new address, at least I have mislaid it, but I have remembered the essential ones from where I hope to get letters and here's a tip, on the top of the envelope put 'Prisoner of War in Norway' and it comes with free postage—Up to the present I have only received one letter from Will but there must be a whole budget waiting me (and others) somewhere; I feel sure plenty of things are happening too.

The weather is very good here and beginning to get packing in the dawn hours. We had a good time last Sunday. The Scotch layman took divine service in the morning and there was a grand football match in the afternoon v Gövick. They were a rattling good team and walked all over round the 'Indians' to the tune of 8-2 and it did the chaps a world of good by taking them down a peg or so.

All the wealth and beauty of Lillehammer and district came and visited the scene and as you can guess, the time passed quickly. The elegant wire erection has near made ends meet and saves a lot of bother but 'stone walls do not a prison make, nor iron bars a cage' as I think the poets sing. As this card represents 25% of my allowed weekly correspondence, please give my love to everybody and kind regards to Miss Mac. Ever yours, A.

Very quickly routines are established and a sense of boredom and homesickness are felt, even at this early stage. There is obviously an intention to keep the men busy and "in line" (somewhat literally) as Arnold speaks of going out on daily marches and there is a photograph of men marching through a township. However, the opportunity to see the local town, in what would become a regular outing, sounds like a good escape from the tedium of the inside of the camp.

3 October 1915

As we are now allowed 1 letter and 4 pc it brings the % down a bit but today is Sunday and I am busy sending off the 4 pc and then will have to exist another 7 days. Luckily or rather due to all kind friends 'Clarke ERA' has not had to go one day without getting one thing or another from the mail, otherwise I should be in sick bay, I think.

We continue to march out when fine and bore each other indoors when raining—chiefly the latter of late. Although you talk of beginning term it is curious to think that when this arrives it will be verging onto half term holiday. I have received the parcel from Miss Standfield and hope the letter acknowledging it gets back without being chucked overboard or torpedoed. I have had one letter from RGS of 24 Aug. She mentioned she was working at a hospital (military) and I rather envy the officers—

My unchanging repertoire is now played daily on the— (while the others take their afternoon siesta), but there is always hope of improvement if the piano does not break down. Well, news is scarce, the only variable being how much we walk a day which averages 10 miles altogether well but wishes to all. Ever yours A.

20 October 1915—postcard

This shows one of our routes when out marching. Have marked the position of the camp. 13 P. O's were allowed to go to Lillehammer yesterday. The other 13 today. We were taken over a collection of very old houses. I then had a ripping feed followed by an hours shopping, not the least interesting bit was a goods train shunting! More of this visit in a general letter. Hoping things progress favourably ever.

Yrs, A

From the very beginning, Arnold received regular post from his sisters and packages from his father with magazines, books, and papers. He also received baked goods from Nurse Bates, the family housekeeper. He established a habit of being careful what he said to whom. In his 7 November postcard he comments on a poem he received from Edith and confesses to not having the inspiration to write himself and that the only poem he has would not be suitable to share. He takes a more careful approach and remains positive when writing to Nurse Bates.

7 November 1915—postcard

The Muse has run dry here. I have got hold of a small poem which expresses one feelings here very well but it wouldn't wash here. We get a bit of skating now and again. It is a fine sport indeed, so is sliding. There's excitement in both and certainly the first is rather graceful at times. I often wonder what England is like now and how true the papers are. Lots of the fellows here have had letters censored to rags and I feel certain plenty of letters never get through. Although it doesn't put you off.

18 November/12 Dec to Nurse Bates

Frost, snow and sun are ever with us still but it does not take so much to keep warm as you would expect.

These five letters are the only remaining letters written by Arnold in his first few months in internment but interestingly what has been found is a few letters that were written to him. There are not many surviving letters written to Arnold, for reasons that will become apparent but one would be that he would have had limited ability to store things.

The letters from home, however, give us an idea of what is happening in the family. Two of the postcards are from Winnie who has just started lecturing at Cambridge University and her cards are full of excited commentary about her new life and one is from Queenie poking fun at Winnie's showing off!

27 September 1915

Revelling in the use of my very own desk! You see a glimpse of our large dining hall but it gives you very little idea of the height and size. A wee dot shows you my place at the High. Hope the boxing gloves have got through safely name have proved useful. Very glad to hear some of the correspondence has at last arrived—I have not had the pleasure of tackling the renowned bookshops here yet but hope to do so very shortly. WSC.

4 October 1915

Don't you think this looks rather imposing? That is not a chapel but a hall up which the staff have to walk solemnly to each—there. Had to do it alone the other day as I was late! I might appreciate your climate better than this—we too have had heavy frosts—also most lovely sunshine. No news re more visits of 3? To Gravesend. Had a fire alarm drill at 10:20pm for practice.

14 October 1915

Winnie is swanking her architecture at you. I would be beaten, so I send you this very fine specimen of English Architecture with which you are familiar. Kindly eliminate the awful poodle and substitute Caro who is far better looking. Have at last seen the photo you sent. I like your sick (?) sweet smile! Q (I think that Caro might have been the family cat).

The final card is a special one written from one brother serving his country in war to his brother who is interned in a prison camp. The card itself is quite worn and I have not seen an original copy, so it is hard to read. It has been sent from a Field Post Office and at the top Wilfrid has written On Active Service (although a censor stamp has been placed over the top).

5 November 1915
My dear A,

I don't quite remember if I sent you one of these before or not. I met one of these chaps this afternoon. He is also in one of the columns. One has to keep a most eager outlook; for one does not know who one might meet, I wish I could get into—with some of the relations. Bill.

What about the rest of the crew?

Some online searching enabled me to find a few examples of letters sent by other members of the crew. As mentioned in the last chapter, there were several mix-ups with the reporting of survivors and quite a few families received notification that their loved one had drowned in the North Sea only to receive an apologetic notification from officials that they had been wrong and the man in question was alive and interned in Norway.

These stories made happy reading for local newspapers to pass on in a time that was dominated by so much tragedy and loss. There was also a quota of families who received the tragic news that their loved one was lost only to then receive a letter from the reported dead man! A couple of examples of these can be found in postal museums.

The Bath Postal Museum has a copy of a letter from Cyril Woollford, an Ordinary Signalman, who says he expects that he has been reported as missing. Cyril is one of the younger members of the crew being only twenty when the *India* went down. The card is dated 28 August 1915.

Dear Gladys,

Just a card hoping to find you quite well as it leaves me the same. I dare say you have seen in the Newspapers that I am missing but "home" is the only place I'm missing from. I have not heard from you, so I expect that you thought me among the fishes, but I am not luckily, but all my belongings are. I am only allowed to write these beastly postcards owing to them having to be censored. Your letters to me are also censored which is rather annoying but never mind as long as the censor's donor find any (spying) in them (don't laugh).

The weather here is lovely and I hope you are getting the same. You must let me know if my ma is upsetting herself about me as she will not tell me herself. No doubt she was when she saw I wasn't in the saved in the papers. I am not allowed out yet so cannot get any little curios from this place which no doubt you would like but may be able to get some later. I hope you received my postcard quite safely which I sent last week.

The place where I am now I shall be until the end of the war, which I hope will soon come to a close. Don't forget to let me have a photograph of yourself when convenient. Well Gladys dear I think that I must come to a close as there is not much more room to write here, closing with kindest love to all. Hoping to hear from you soon.

I remain your sincere friend,
Cyril
P.S. Excuse writing etc in a bit of a hurry.
Remember me to your sister.

Cyril writes of having seen what was in the newspapers. Commander Kennedy was instrumental in making sure that he and the officers and interned crew, would have access to British newspapers, magazines, and periodicals. He subscribed to The Times, Morning Post, Daily Mail, Daily Mirror and the Illustrated London News as well as to National Geographic and Land and Water. Mail was regularly arriving, often in under a week from Britain, so the papers would have kept the men relatively up to date with local news.

Cyril writes to Gladys again in mid-September (13 to be exact) talking more about early life in the camp. It has been censored in a few places but gives another view of Jørstadmoen. It is quite a lengthy letter but here are some excerpts:

We are getting on very well here and I think that we shall be alright when the place is properly finished, as they are practically rebuilding the place in order to make us more comfortable for the winter. I had some photographs taken yesterday (Sunday) and will send you one if they are good—We are shortly being dressed in the Norwegian Sailors dress which I think will look very nice. They will be lovely and warm for the winter and no doubt we shall require something warm—

I suppose that it is getting very dark at night there being very little light. It is light here until about 8 p.m. still but of course this place is a great deal farther north than "Brighton". I am afraid, by the look of the papers that I shall have to remain here some considerable time, as it appears that the "war" will last through the winter. I tell you it is horrible to be here, away from all your friends, etc and I am longing to get back to dear old Brighton.

What were the family doing?

1915 was an interesting year for Arnold's sisters. Dorothy had left her secretarial post at the King Edward Sanitorium and was studying farming techniques through Reading University and was at a placement in Dorset. Edith had been offered a position as a School Inspector with the Board of Education and was released from her teaching responsibilities at the Bergman-Österberg Physical Education College to take on this quite prestigious role.

Queenie had made the move to the New Forest to start teaching at Branksome College, a small school run by her friend Irene Macnamara. Winnie had begun lecturing in Physical Education at Homerton College at Cambridge University. Homerton was a women's only College, like Newnham where Queenie had studied. It is quite an achievement for one family to have two daughters represented at such an esteemed educational establishment as Cambridge and before women were even allowed to vote or hold official degrees.

Wilfrid spent the majority of 1915 training in England with his battalion. He was in training camps in Salisbury and Berkhamsted and as Winnie's August 1915 28th entry in her holiday diary for Branksome College states—*Edith (who had come home to celebrate a last evening together with Wilfrid) left first at 8 o'clock. At Waterloo we found Wilfrid's train to Milford cancelled, so he was able to see us safely off.*

So, we can assume that Wilfrid spent time at the Milford camp as well. His letter shows that by 5 November, Wilfrid was on the continent, on the front in Ypres and Arras where he stayed all through-out the winter and into the next year.

The only recorded contact of the sisters and father encountering the war is found in Winnie's travel diaries of 1915. Two holidays were taken at Branksome College where Queenie was to begin teaching in the Autumn term, father, Queenie, and Winnie spent time near the seaside on these holidays.

Winnie writes of troops leaving from Waterloo, of discussing the war debt, of submarines in the Solent and of the Indian Hospital at Barton-on-Sea. The Indian Hospital was a hotel that had been taken over by the army for the treatment and rehabilitation of injured Indian soldiers. It created interest in the then quite provincial New Forest.

16 Apr—From another platform at Waterloo, a number of men were going off and crowds had assembled to send them away and give them a hearty cheer.

20 Apr—After tea, Mr Carter got out his stamps for me and later his maps and we discussed the war.

26 Apr—I was anxious to see the Indian Hospital. Whilst we were standing looking, the sentry said, "You May come in Miss", in spite of a large notice prohibiting entrance. We gladly accepted, the man telling us it was alright if we kept to the high road carefully/. It was a thrilling sight to see all these Indians about the place—such fine faces many of them have and have intelligent eyes.

29 Apr—Great excitement during tea as we heard the buzzing of an aeroplane and soon found the machine right over our heads. It was difficult at first to find it because of the sun. It kept roaming round the neighbourhood for some time.

Later on Mac had a staff meeting in the middle of which the house was startled by very rapid, insistent firing, which seemed to come from the Island. Later on we heard it again, it was really alarming. We heard later eight submarines had been seen and two of these caught. It did not appear in the newspapers.

28 Aug—An aeroplane flew over us about 6 o'clock, traveling very quickly in the direction of the Island.

29 Aug—Beginning a discussion soon after tea on the war loan.

6 Sept—In the evening, we all four went to supper at Mrs Tewson's. Conversation mostly centred on the Indians as Mr Tewson's work is at the hospital.

Royal Naval Barracks, Chatham.

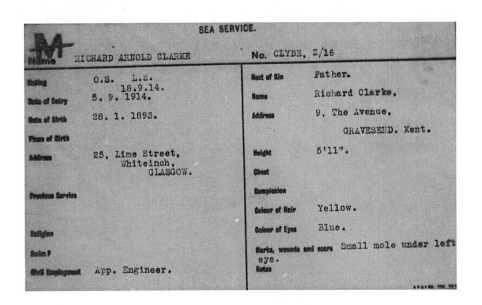

SEA SERVICE.

Name	RICHARD ARNOLD CLARKE
No.	CLYDE, Z/16

Rating	O.S. L.S.	**Next of Kin**	Father.
	18.9.14.	**Name**	Richard Clarke,
Date of Entry	5. 9. 1914.	**Address**	9, The Avenue,
Date of Birth	28. 1. 1893.		GRAVESEND. Kent.
Place of Birth		**Height**	5'11".
Address	25, Lime Street, Whiteinch, GLASGOW.	**Chest**	
Previous Service		**Complexion**	
		Colour of Hair	Yellow.
Religion		**Colour of Eyes**	Blue.
Swim?		**Marks, wounds and scars**	Small mole under left eye.
Civil Employment	App. Engineer.	**Notes**	

The official documents from the Admiralty and War Office for Richard Arnold Clarke.

R.N.V.R. Division CLYDE. No. Z.16

Name in full *Richard Arnold Clarke.*

R.I.C. N° 4413

Date of Birth 28ᵗʰ Jan 1893
Place of Birth
Occupation App. Engineer.
Whether formerly R.M. or R.N.

Front of post card send to Queenie on 26 December 1914—"It was pouring hard and we just walked into the shop and had them taken."

Wearing the uniform provided by the Norwegians—many of the India crew are said to have been very put out at having to wear a Norwegian uniform.

Survivors of H.M.S. INDIA'S Camp,
Elvigaurdi, Norway.

Our Camp at Nordvik Norway 1915

These photos (here and on the previous page) are from Charles Nelson's album and show the very first camp near Narvik. The thought comes to mind that they were lucky it was summer. Not only were they able to survive in the North Sea, but they also did not have to camp in the snow! The second photo is of some of the survivors and I wonder if it might be just the officers. I think I can identify Lieutenant Alltree in the front row and Midshipman Jenkins in the second. The sepia photo on page 127 is from the collection of Seaman Robert Charles Maynard and is also of the interim camp.

There is no identifying writing for this card, but it is reasonable to assume it is Norway and Arnold writes on 3/10/1915. "We continue to march out when fine and bore each other indoors when raining—chiefly the latter of late."
We also know that the men were marched to camp from the train on the day of their arrival in Jørstadmoen.

This postcard is said, by several sources, to have been taken at Jørstadmoen but there is a chance it was taken at the temporary camp in the north of Norway. The uniforms are interesting and are probably not British uniforms, but replacement uniforms supplied by the Norwegians. Arnold is standing in the middle at the back.

Above is a photograph from the Charles Nelson collection of a view across Jørstadmoen, Fåberg and Gudbrandsdalslågen.

Below is one of the postcards of the Jørstadmoen camp. It shows one of the dormitories and probably dates around 1916.

The three following photos are of the crew of HMS India—the first photo would appear to be taken at Jørstadmoen. The building looks like one of the cabins, but it does not look like the full crew that would have arrived on the 17 August. The photos below are said to be of all the rescued men but not officers. It was taken near Narvik before the men were transported to Jørstadmoen. The man peering through the life ring is William Tilley and note the guards on the hill in the distance—keeping an eye on the men. One of the guards is obviously armed and patrolling the area.

A modern photo of the only remaining dormitory at Jørstadmoen and an older photo demonstrates what it was like during WW1.

A postcard found in the family archives from the time that Arnold was kept at Jørstadmoen.

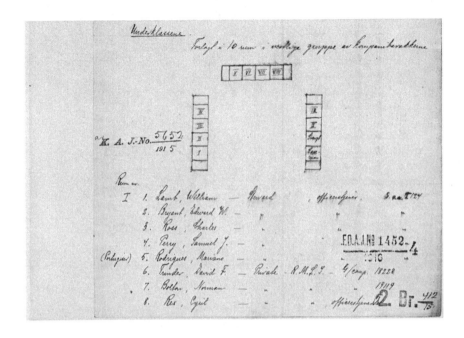

The original lists and map of the rooms and the men allocated to them. Arnold was in room 5.

A photo of some of the internees in front of one of the huts at Jørstadmoen from the collection of Seaman Robert Charles Maynard.

THEY HAVE ONE REGRET, AND ONE ALONE.

...officers of the India, who are now interned in Norway.

A happy group of the India's men on a Norwegian hillside.
The one regret of the men of the H.M.S India is that they are out of the fighting. They
have nothing to complain of in Norway's treatment of them.

From the Daily Sketch, 10 September 1915 (which neatly dates the photos!) must have been cut out by R Feaver or one of the girls. The Daily Sketch was a conservative newspaper and I question that the only regret is that they are not actively fighting.

Three of the early postcards—all of these were sold in the 1984 sale and belong to collectors. I have only ever seen these copies of them.

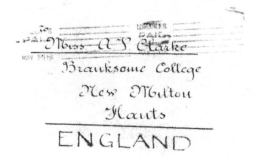

Post cards sent to Arnold from Wilfred and vice versa. Two brothers involved in the same war but having totally different experiences.

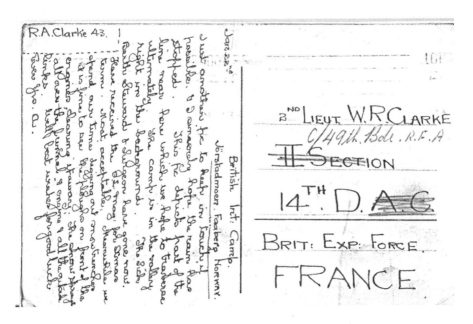

Wilfrid Randall Clarke looking ever so dashing in his uniform—what horrors he must have seen in Ypres and on the front.

These are copies of photos of the crew at Jørstadmoen. On the next page is from Charles Nelson's photo collection and shows the officers skiing with some of the Norwegians.

Internerte englændere i leiren ved Lillehammer.

A newspaper clipping from Norway found in the collection of Fireman William Tilley.

From William Tilley's collection, the photograph to the right looks like the muster that the interned men were required to do every morning and I think at other times of the day as well.

First Half of 1916 –
"Hopes, Ambitions and Ideals have Gone."

The family archives contained very few letters written and sent in 1916. It is hard to know why. Now might be the time to extend on the comments I have made regarding Arnold's letters being sold on the open market. My father-in-law, Arnold Richard (I know, it gets very confusing with all these Richards—R Feaver, R Arnold, and A Richard!), had found a letter online whilst doing research on *HMS India*.

He was surprised and intrigued and contacted the internet sales room, unfortunately they were unable to give him any information as the sale had passed and they were not at liberty to reveal details of who purchased the letter. When I started researching in early 2020, I remembered this find and started my own searching. I started with eBay and immediately found two letters with envelopes for sale for £125 and £325 respectively! Pardon? That amount of money for a letter. I could not comprehend why they were this valuable and I had no idea how they had made it into the market. The Aunts had been so careful to keep everything and my father-in-law would never have let those letters go if he had known of their existence. I kept searching and kept finding more letters and postcards that had been sold in philately sales—all for considerable amounts of money. I managed to purchase one letter without an envelope for only £10 and that seller kindly included a copy of another letter as well. Why was this letter so much cheaper than the ones with envelopes?

It then occurred to me that it was not the letters that were incredibly valuable but the envelopes. I started looking more carefully at philately websites and with philately clubs and got answers. The Scandinavian Philately Society, whose contact person lives a mere 15 minutes from me, was able to fill in some gaps. A gentleman by the name of Roger Partridge was a past member of the club and an avid collector of WW1 mail from Scandinavia amongst other things.

A research document of his explained the mail from Jørstadmoen was highly sort after as it was and is, so rare. The censor markings and mail markings make it valuable and Arnold was such a prolific writer and his sisters, so good at keeping his mail, that the envelopes from his letters are well known and highly prized by collectors. They feature in books and have been used for lectures and presentations to philately societies.

My only question then was, how exactly did these letters make it into the market from the collection that had been looked after so well by Edith, Queenie, and Winnie? A partial answer came through another article written by Roger Partridge. The letters had been placed in a sale in the Hampshire in 1984. Edith was the last of the R Feaver's children to die and she passed away in 1984 and she lived in the New Forest.

The contents of the house she lived in and had lived in with her sisters for many years, were packed up and most of them shipped to Australia but somehow, this collection of Arnold's letters was sold and no-one knows by whom. It has become one of those family mysteries. I have now seen these letters being sold all over the world. Mr Partridge seemed to have had the biggest collection, but he unfortunately passed away in the past few years and consequently, I am sadly unable to talk to him.

I have now found thirty-two letters from varying sources online or with other collectors and one from Wilfrid to Queenie and I am sure there are more out there and I continue my hunt. The family, incidentally, had forty-three letters. Many more would have been written over the course of three years but I will never know their fate – lost, censored, in private collections, thrown away.

So, back to the known letters. As I said, the family collection for 1916 was very sparse but I managed to supplement it with many from the collectors, both from Roger's work and from letters found online and through other collectors. The first piece of mail is a postcard dated 11 January; Arnold writes to Queenie.

Thanks very much indeed for your letters of 27 Dec and 6 Jan. You'll observe it hasn't taken long. There has been a nasty gap in mails—but it isn't your fault because everyone is suffering similarly—beside for leading our 'leisured life', we are prone to think everyone does likewise.

He then goes on making mention of what seems to have been a few of his favourite activities whilst in internment—art and skiing.

I must say sketching and painting seems to be much more attractive than stodgy maths and perhaps however much I worked it wouldn't get me any the better job. I don't know and it's not much use encouraging here. Have had skiing regularly this week but don't seem to make decided impressions in the snow!

Skiing becomes a frequently mentioned activity in winter letters and cards and there are postcards with Arnold and others on their skis. It is confirmed in a later letter that guards were present during these leisure time activities, particularly in the early days. There was little chance of escaping the reality of being incarcerated.

A card written to Wilfrid later in January (22) 1916, alludes to both Arnold's desire to keep in regular contact with his brother as he serves on the front and that communication must be getting through in one way or another as Arnold is aware of the weather in France –

Just another pc to keep in touch if possible and I sincerely hope the rain has stopped.

After explaining the view on the postcard Arnold makes mention of two of the men who must have gone home.

The sick berth steward and surgeon have gone now. Records show that the Tempy. Surgeon, Frank W Lawson was repatriated on 15 January 1916. The only steward not listed in a later head count is Mariano Rodrigues so it's reasonable to assume that he was repatriated at this time. These men were the first of quite a few to leave the camp and not return in 1916. It must have been hard to see them go and know that they were heading home.

This final part of the card outlines some of the work the interned men have been made to do and Arnold ends wishing his brother the best of luck, being aware of the danger he was in.

Meanwhile, we spend our time digging out snow trenches. It is fine to see the ploughs on front of the engines clearing it away. The snow strays all over the funnel and engine and all the outer links. Well, best wishes for good luck. Ever Yrs, A.

The 2 February 1916 letter to Queenie has a feel of loneliness and isolation that becomes quite common as the time progresses. There is a feeling of a need for regular contact from home. Arnold comments on how regularly he writes and wants to know if they are making it home. The mystery in this letter is the mention of Surbiton. I have no knowledge of who lived in Surbiton—maybe a sweetheart?

It was my turn to go marketing to Lillehammer today and it occurred to me to try this and send this as a valentine though there is no cause for it. The best part of the whole day was on the engine while it shunted. I haven't been very well this week either. I haven't had a letter from WSC since 1 Jan. I haven't heard from Surbiton either since 12 Dec. I regret, therefore I haven't written either. How long do my letters take getting thro' home? I write home every Sunday and Wednesday. Are many letters going adrift? I sent some paintings home yesterday. Trusting to hear from you again. A

In a desire to know more about the camp, Winnie has obvious sent a letter full of questions and in the postcard of 21 February Arnold replies covering each question and giving an idea of what his day-to-day life is like.

2. The day 8 a.m.-11 a.m. passes quickly. Meals, Carpentry, painting, skiing 2-4 p.m., Bridge each night 7:30-10 p.m. 3. Will write you a pc each Monday, as in Scotland.

He then goes on to speak about a visit to the dentist—a sign that the Norwegian captors are prepared to offer a certain level of medical care to their internees. He also describes the scene of two men waltzing at the end of the room. This is another "movie moment" for me, a moment that is so easy to picture. Two interned soldiers waltzing with each other to a gramophone as there is no one else to dance with but the whole time imagining the girls they have left behind.

Have just come back from Lillehammer today where a lady dentist has been giving my mouth beams from the drill. However, a stopped tooth is better than none at all. We climbed Jörstad Hill on Saturday on skis. It was magnificent, perfect weather and glorious view. The swift descent was not the least exciting. I hope to send you a parcel ultimately. Meanwhile, the other end of the room there is a gramophone dreamy waltz and two of our number waltzing.

Best wishes, A

On 11 March, Arnold writes a postcard to Winnie with big news in it. He talks of his influenza and of a big concert but then *I think also the presentation of some plate to the Cmdr. and his wife as a wedding present.* Commander Kennedy has got married and the crew got together and gifted him a large silver platter with all the crewmen's names engraved into it.

Commander Kennedy obviously fell on his feet quickly after arriving in Lillehammer to be married only six months after first setting foot in the area—it certainly did not take him long to settle in. Further research finds that his wife was the daughter of a Norwegian Naval Commander so there is a possibility, he knew her or knew of her prior to arriving in Jørstadmoen.

A rambling letter to Queenie on 18 April is the first indication of how the censors are affecting the mail. All the envelopes have censor markings. Both Norwegian and English and a few letters show signs of being tampered with cut out sections. We will never know how many letters were stopped but Arnold develops a habit of acknowledging the letters he receives from his sisters and Father supposedly so they would know what was getting to him and what was not.

The letter is full of information about the camp and camp life including letters from philanthropists, the formation of a band and then, in typical Arnold style, a mathematical equation. He would know that he had an attentive audience in his Cambridge mathematics Tripos educated sister. (The certificates he refers to, I think, would be ones he was designing for Queenie to give her students. His penmanship was quite beautiful and I have the feeling that his clever big sister realised that giving Arnold a job to do would make him feel connected and useful.)

My dear Queenie,

While the censor stops all our letters, there is no option but to write more this end; I posted 3 certificates to you as specimens but I hope to send the other shortly. If they are satisfactory, repeat orders are welcome.

From time to time, being objects of pity, derision or honour—as you like, receive letters from philanthropists, etc, etc. I enclose you a small booklet. It brings to mind 'The Jacobites Epitath'—

'Each night my home beheld in fevered slap,

Each morning started from my dream to weep.

Heard on Jorstad, Lomond's muttering breeze

And pined by Goya for my lovelier Thames.'

The military have given us the use of some old bugles and 2 side drums. It is nice to have a decent bugle of one's own. There is the makings of a good small band here, several having had previous experience. The buglers are of blatant Teutonic origin.

Recently I applied mechanics to skiing. There is one slope we—of, which, by several experts, is agreed to be 45 degrees. For a short distance, you do a straight course to clear trees. Your straight course lasts 5 secs—not more.

Now

$$Accelerate = \frac{final\ velocity\ -\ initial\ velocity}{time}$$

$$g\ sin\ x = \frac{u\text{-}o}{5\ secs}$$

32 x 1/2 x 5 = u = 112.8 fl per second

Allowing a little from friction and wind resistance, the result is still over 60 miles an hour. Alas, that the snow has melted.

The concert last Sunday was a great success.

It is very hard to write letters when none have arrived for so long. One lives only in anticipating the number when they do come. However, I conclude in wishing you a successful summer term.

Yrs, A

By 24 May, the mood of Arnold's letters changes dramatically. He lets Queenie know about the certificates he has completed and then begins to talk about the escape of two of the British prisoners and the effect this has had on the camp. For the very first time we hear of how desperate Arnold is feeling, it is a heart-breaking letter and unfortunately, the first of many in this vein.

He only ever talks this way when writing to Queenie. She becomes his confidant and although we never get to see her replies to his letters, she must have worked hard to try and reassure him and keep him going. It would have been terribly hard for her to receive these letters knowing how depressed Arnold was becoming and not being able to really do anything much about it.

Dear Queenie,

Dispatched to you on 19 May—4 certificates. Another 4 on 22 May.

It was my turn for cook today, otherwise the last four would have gone off today. The first were rotten, the last are not much better, I'm sorry.

I expect you will have heard 2 men escaped. The screw has been on us the whole time but it's awful now. Bayonets and loaded revolvers—I wish I had been a casualty last August instead of a survivor. My 1st ship and only 4 months. 9 solid months without a change of scenery and companions and lord knows how many more to follow. Hopes, ambitions and ideals have all gone. I had better stop before I go too far.

Yours, A

Arnold is careful to protect certain loved ones from his darkest feelings and in a postcard to Nurse on 8 June he speaks of trivial things.

Thank you very much indeed for the large cake which arrived quite safely yesterday. I can assure you that not a crumb was wasted; meanwhile, I hope you are going on well. This postcard shows most of Christiania, The Royal Palace in the background—not unlike Buckingham Palace.

What was happening in the camp?

Early in 1916, the interned Officers from *HMS India* were moved out of the camp into alternate accommodation in Suttestad, a nearby village. Eleven officers were moved to Sole Pensjonet which was owned by Mrs Aslaug Haak. This was a temporary arrangement and later they were moved into more permanent accommodation.

Also, early in 1916, as mentioned earlier in one of Arnold's letters, Commander Kennedy got married. He married the daughter of a Norwegian Naval Commander, Alice Fedora Esther Lundh, on 28 February and as Arnold mentioned, the crew commemorated the occasion with a silver platter.

The engagement announcement and marriage ceremony were unusually close together with the engagement announced in the *Norges Handel og Sjofartstedente* paper on the 11 February and the marriage taking place only seventeen days later. A local newspaper announced the nuptials—"celebrated on the 28th by Miss Fedora Lundh, daughter of Commander Harold Lundh and Mrs

131

Thorpe and Commander W.G.A Kennedy R.N, currently interned in Norway. The wedding ceremony will be held in the English Church at 12."

A Norwegian article[16] describes the Commander as "Commander Kennedy himself, a large, thick-skinned man who really roamed Storgata, lived first at Hotell Victoria and then in the Villa Formo at Gamleveien 119. The class differences were large in the British Navy and this was reflected during the internment as well.

The officers were allowed to have their servants—a total of six men. The officers also developed for themselves an active social life in and around Lillehammer. Roger Partridge writes, "Among their closest friends was one Anders Skar who ran a textile factory and dye-works"[17]. He goes on to explain that in the early 1990s several sacks of Commander Kennedy's personal papers were found in Skar's former residence after 75 years of being kept in an attic.

These recently found papers included an ample wad of bills which show the lavish life Kennedy was able to lead whilst in internment, similar to the life that he had lived prior to the war. A life that included the buying of furs, cognac, a musquash coat, a three-month supply of flowers for the house as well as Havana cigars.

Kennedy was also recognised as being a skilled salmon fisherman, probably a skill he had nurtured in the Lakes District. He was reported to have caught the largest salmon ever caught in Norway to date. Kennedy and Fedora also had the services of a chauffeur—"Petter Henriksen, who drove him wherever he wanted in the carriage." As Partridge notes—"It would seem that Commander Kennedy's period of internment was not too onerous."

One could assume that Commander Kennedy would have access to family money during his internment which would have assisted in supporting the lifestyle he led.

---

[16] (1995) *Briter bak piggtråd*. Pryser, T and Olstad, I. Fåberg og Lillehammer, ye Lokalskrift av Fåberg Historielag. Vol 15, 1995.

[17] Roger Partridge had drafted a document focusing on the philately side of mail from Jørstadmoen. He never ended up publishing it as it started to drift into family history and lost its single-minded focus on philately. Alan Totten, an acquaintance of Roger's contacted me and kindly posted me the complete section of Rogers work that covered the internment of the India crew in Norway. Alan was confident that Roger would be pleased to see his research finally being used.

The crew of *HMS* India were not living the same kind of lifestyle but were anxious to maintain their connection with home. Through reaching out to philately societies I came across five postcards which tell of a lovely relationship between a father and son. Herbert Ripley was a Colour Sergeant from Gillingham; Kent, who had served with the Navy for a few years. He had been married to Elizabeth since 1901 and had three children—Alice born 1902, Herbert born 1903 and Sydney born 1907.

He was one of the crew rescued by the Saxon and, being not an officer, was interned in the camp. Herbert's postcards to his son Bert show a father who is desperately trying to still stay involved in his children's lives even though he is imprisoned hundreds of miles away. They all tell a lovely story of a moment in the life Bert and as they tell this story in a chronological order, I am going to transcribe them in their full (please note that his use of punctuation is limited and these are transcribed accurately!).

19 January 1916
Dear Bert,

Just a Q. P.C for you and no more jangling because one of you is getting more letters than the other. I suppose, Alice has written more often than you have. This is a proper Norwegian house as it is here now plenty of snow still lying about and it would cover you quite up. No room for any more at this time. Your loving Dad xxxx.

6 February 1916
My dear boy,

Your letter reached me last night the one I ought to have got before this. Now, I mean what I say that you can have 10/- if you get a scholarship at the Teck so now you have got something to work for. No more grumbling about the P.C or else I will not send you anymore. Alice has written to me more than you have I suppose that is why she has most. No more with love from your loving dad, H.G Ripley xxx.

22 March 1916
My dear Bert,

I have not got a postcard of a fjord, but if I see one anywhere I will think of you. That's right keep at the top of the class and do not forget the 10/-. I will try

and make you something out of fret (?) wood. Do not try and varnish the paper knife or you will spoil it better leave it till I come home but keep it nice and clean if you have that one to more (?).
Your loving Dad xxxxx.

30 April 1916
   My dear Bert,
Just another one for your collection. How did you get on with the Tec exam anywhere near the top. I am sending you a pattern for a watch stand for your watch and you ought to make a frame for your photo how do you like it. Do you like your box or did you not want it? No more tonight.
Your loving Dad xxxxxx.

21 May 1916
Dear Bert,
   I was indeed very pleased to hear you had one a scholarship and am very proud of it, but you must still stick to your books and keep on learning it will help you in later years. I hope you are right about me coming home in June. I hope to be able to tell you that I am in a few days' time.
Your loving Dad xxxxxxx.

I found myself cheering on Bert and feeling quite proud that he had gained his scholarship. I was also touched by all the kisses Herbert finished each letter with—more on each consecutive card. Herbert seems like such a loving dad! Bert was right, though, Herbert was "invalided home" on the 1 June. I guess that he may have sustained injuries in the shipwreck, but it is hard to know and I've been unable to find out any more information on him.

Mail was an incredibly important means of communication during the First World War. On a personal level, I do not think it is overstating it to say that Queenie's regular correspondence (other members of the family too, but primarily Queenie) with Arnold kept him sane and maybe even kept him alive.

He was not the only man at war to which mail had this level of significance and Royal Mail had to deal with a whole other level of mail delivery during this time. Demand was so high that a specially built mail office known as the Home Depot was constructed in Regents Park. By the end of the war an astounding one million parcels and twelve million letters were passing through this purpose made depot every week.

Mail to men on the front line and to men being kept from those they loved was a literal lifeline and BBC news reported that in 1914 a soldier on the Western Front wrote of his loneliness to a London newspaper and mentioned that he would appreciate mail[18]. Within weeks the lonely soldier had received over three thousand letters and thousands of parcels.

Mail was also a lifeline for those at home as it was often only mail that reassured family at home that their loved one was still alive. The speed at which the mail was delivered is another surprising and impressive feat in a time of war. Roger Partridge noted that one card sent by Commander Kennedy in October 1916 took only four days to get from Lillehammer to London! Remarkably quick delivery even in today's standards.

One of the biggest events in the first half of 1916 was mentioned briefly in Arnold's letter of the 24 May. Two of the British internees escaped from the camp at Jørstadmoen. J.W.B Grigson, Able Seaman and shipwright Charles Clinton managed to escape and make their way back to the United Kingdom. Charles Clinton has been difficult to trace after his escape but after the war had ended, he was recorded as being back at work in the Drawing Office at Denny's Shipyard in Dumbarton.

John William Boldero Grigson was easier to research and his life continued to be interesting after his escape. Grigson had signed up with the RNVR in 1913 and in 1914 was transferred to the Royal Navy division. He joined the *India* on the 13 April 1915 and was one of the few who managed to get a place in one of the *India's* life boats when she was torpedoed.

After escaping on the 19 May it was not long before Grigson was commissioned into the Royal Navy Air Squadron on 20 August. Grigson became a highly decorated Air Commodore who flew in both World Wars but in all the writing I have seen on him not one piece mentions that he escaped from a prison camp. Some assume that he got sent home on the *Gotaland* but the escape is never discussed.

The Grigson/Clinton escape had a knock-on effect for those remaining in the camp. The conditions had become slowly more liberal prior to the escape with an easing on the numbers of armed guards and extra freedoms being allowed to

---

[18]2014. *World War One: How did 12 million letters a week reach soldiers?* BBC News Magazine. 31 January 2014. www.bbc.com/news/magazine-25934407

some of the prisoners but this stopped once Grigson and Clinton managed to gain their freedom and make their way home. Arnold mentions "bayonets and loaded revolvers" were prevalent and the mood in the camp changed.

Considering that the 'gentlemen's agreement' between Norway and Britain stated that men on leave would return to the camp, it seems odd that Grigson was able to move into the RNAS and continue serving after his escape.

Grigson, Clinton, and Arnold were not the only ones unhappy at Jørstadmoen. In late June, contact was made from the camp to the Daily Mail:

"Sir,

Seeing in the 'Daily Mail' the way you have taken up the cause of the British interned, who are suffering so much in Germany I would like to mention that there are ninety odd men interned here. We have been here since 19 August last and have had a very bad time of it. We are not getting our dues. The British Consul at Christiania apparently does not take any interest in our welfare as he hasn't paid a visit to the camp during the nine months we have been here.

We don't pretend that we are as badly off as the people in Germany, but for a neutral country we are treated very badly. We are surrounded by a strong wire fence ten feet high with several rows of barbed wire on top. We have not been allowed outside of this since two men escaped some time ago—we have been cooped up all the winter on account of the snow. The fine weather is just starting here now, but the Norwegian authorities don't think fit to let us out for a little liberty.

There is much discontent among the men who have done nothing more criminal than save their lives. The food we get is not what it should be, being of poor quality and insufficient in quantity, we even have to buy sugar and salt and if it wasn't for the parcels of food we get from home and relatives we should very often go hungry.

The medical treatment to men taken ill is administered in such a way as to border on incompetency. If you could put a few lines in the Daily Mail setting forth our position and let the British public know how we are suffering and that we are having anything but a picnic party here in Norway, it might lead to an alteration being made and our imprisonment happier. Hope you can do something to air our grievances as we are enduring the Horrors of Internment with a vengeance.

Yours faithfully,

Indianus."[19]

There is also feedback from an unnamed source that has been kept in the files at the National Archives. Just listed as from P/W, Fåberg, 3.6.16 the internee writes:

"What the Norwegians say is a pack of lies; they have not treated us fair as they might. We have been underfed and no liberty hardly at all; and when those two escaped they made it a bit worse—Only lately they have fed us better since we made a noise and let us go out a little, then only with a soldier in small groups. Why I could show you a paper where they treat one of our chaps in prison better than they do us."

Indianus would appear to be a 'nom de plume' as there is no one of that name in the records and the complainant from the archives is also anonymous but these letters set off a chain of replies and official mail again as the Foreign Office attempted to smooth over the discontent.

On the 11 June, Commander Kennedy sent off the following letter covering the food allowances for the interned men. This was sent to his Norwegian counterpart and was one of several letters sent over the course of the internment dealing with the victuals and allowances for the men. Their tastes were quite different to those of the Norwegian soldiers and changes were requested to suit the tastes of the British sailors.

Internment Camp

Jørstadmoen

Fåberg

11 June 1916

Sir,

Respecting the scale of provisions for the interned British Seamen at Jørstadmoen, I suggest the following alterations for the next quarter.

Meat—The same amount weekly but issued in different quantities as per attached scale. The salt meat I find is invariably wasted, so suggest it be no longer supplied, but fresh meat issued instead. This is included in the fresh meat scale.

Vegetables—The supply may be altered to 300 grams daily of potatoes and 200g of other fresh vegetables. When fresh vegetable cannot be supplied, I suggest a suitable corresponding amount of dried vegetables which you may fix, be issued instead.

---

[19]Documents quoted in this chapter can be found at The National Archives FO 383/212

Jam or marmalade—This supply is satisfactory, but I suggest jam and marmalade may be issued on alternate weeks, jam not yet having been supplied.

Sugar—I suggest the allowance be increased from 1 1/2 oz. to 3 oz. per day.

Salt—I suggest that the supply of salt be increased to 70 grams per man per week.

Pepper—I suggest pepper be supplied ground to the camp or a machine supplied for the purpose.

The suggested alterations are written in red ink on the former scale attached.

I have to the honour to be Sir, your obedient servant, W.G.A Kennedy, Commander R.N

What were the family doing?

1916 saw relative stability for the women in the Clarke family. Edith had returned to Dartford to teach at Bergman-Österberg Physical Training College. Queenie was teaching at Branksome College and Winnie was lecturing at Homerton College, Cambridge. Father and Nurse were living at 9 The Avenue, Gravesend.

Wilfred spent the beginning of the year on the front in Ypres and Arras before being one of the lucky ones who was able to return to London and take up a role in the Inspection Department (Carriages) in Woolwich, where he was most likely to be involved in the design of weapons which would fit with his qualifications as an engineer. It must have been such a relief to have him home safely.

Second Half of 1916 – "Not Letters but a Bare Chronicle of Existence."

8 July 1916 marked eleven months since the torpedoing of *HMS India* and just under eleven months since the surviving crew from the ship had begun their internment at Jørstadmoen. Most had thought they would be home by this stage and no one had any idea just how long this war would drag on.

Most of the men, at this time, did not have any gainful employment and their days appear to be spent reading, smoking, woodworking, going on marches or walks, getting weekend time in local towns and being that it was summer, sometimes going for a swim. Arnold has his difficulties but continues to only share the worst of it with Queenie. The first letter from this half of 1916 is a card written to Nurse on 4 July who has, once again, been baking for the baby of the family.

Many thanks for the box of little cakes which F. forwarded on recently. They arrived in grand condition and soon disappeared. We had a terrible thunderstorm here last night—the first we have had since we have been here. I wish it meant we were coming home.
Yrs, A.

The letter written to Queenie later in the month (26 July) is quite upbeat for Arnold and gives another look at what day to day life was like. Arnold was a great amateur artist (my husband tells of sitting with him as a young boy and watching him draw with both hands at the same time.) I suspect that he drew, painted, or sketched on a very regular basis, especially in the early days when there was not much else to do and his sisters and father kindly kept him well stocked with pens, ink and paper.

Sadly, few of those drawings exist anymore but the family does own four quite beautiful pieces of artwork done on circles of tree trunks from birch trees. I think these were made as gifts or tokens to send home to his family. They are treasured parts of the family archive now. He also writes in this letter about the food he has been cooking when it is his turn. It sounds better than the official reports or the complaints by the anonymous disgruntled internees, but he points out that the knowledge of the waiter and baker are invaluable and that "Kroners help"!

My dear Q,

Your letter of 16 July last night and your letter of 20 July tonight prompt me to a small return. With regards to pen and ink sketches, I can only say that I have had many hours on consummate pleasure out of WSC's Indian ink and ERC's mapping pens. Many sketches go into the w.p.b and many are for other people. I am getting to like etching and the height of an etcher's ambition is a black and white drawing in 'Punch'. The crucial point of his drawings is facial expression. I think I have given that part of it up.

You would hardly credit today's diet for a P of W, yet (I was cook and had to wash up—I know!).

Breakfast—Plate of Plasmon Gats, Bacon and Eggs (fried), bread and butter and marmalade Dinner—Roast beef, potatoes, greens and horseradish. Stewed rhubarb, tinned cherries and cream.

Tea—radishes.

Supper—Fried eggs or poached.

This shows you what private enterprise does, aided by the professional knowledge of a (late) ships headwaiter and a (late) ships baker. Of course, Kroners are necessary.

It occurs to me that the London papers or other news—will ascertain that with regard to the British force interned in Norway that the Commander is married, a lieutenant and one of the men in the camp are engaged all to Norwegian girls. Please do not entertain any worry on my account. I cannot talk Norwegian and have only spoken to them over shop counters.

We get fine bathing for exercise in the River Laagen. A high dive of 10ft off the rocks into about 20ft of clear fresh water.

I have said too much already in this letter so will pipe down now.

Ever yours, A

By August, Arnold has found himself in a bit of a slump. It is the year anniversary of arriving in Jørstadmoen and he does not think that he will ever leave. Queenie has obviously been attempting to keep his spirits up and has been instructing him to make the most of his time—*I am going to follow your previous advice and get all possible enjoyment—skiing, skating and tobogganing.*

After all, it was hard work that got me Ramsgate, Glasgow and this in succession. I have given up hope of passing the Ass. inst. C.E or of seeing any of you again.

In a country where it is so cold that milk is sold in cubic meters in Winter and so hot in Summer that milk is always sour, it is amazing to find the number of wild berries which grow in profusion.

We found a number of wild raspberry bushes this morning (previously located) and an hour's picking gives us raspberry tart for supper tonight—

For a good many days past, we have been down to the river for swimming. It is not tremendously exciting, but it is excellent exercise—Today is the 1st year anniversary of arriving at Jørstadmoen."

The next letter from Arnold gives an indication of the slight change in circumstances that is about to befall some of the India crew. He speaks of them *"going narrying up in the mountains now."* The opportunity for change seems to be perfect for Arnold as his mental health seems to be deteriorating as time passes.

He writes, *Logically I cannot expect letters if I write none and certainly what emanates from here are not letters but a bare chronicle of existence.* And *They might at least exchange us for the Germans or they don't need us. I don't care much what happens.*

A letter written just two weeks later (2 September) confirms the arrangements for a group of the men to leave the camp and move to the mountains to work on the Dovrebanen, a train line that would eventually run from Oslo to Trondhjem across the Dovrefjell Mountain Range. The line now runs for 548Km and was finished in 1921.

Arnold is very much in the doldrums at this point and ends the letter saying that he appears to attract bad luck and would not be surprised if the train he has to travel on to get to the worksite crashes.

Dear Q,

Many thanks for your letter of 24 Aug from home also for F's forwarding of O.L magazine. In reply to enquirers for pen trays, etc. I regret to be unable to comply at present. We are off this aft: up into the mountains. Bags packed etc. We do not expect to be there for very long into the winter.

If this should miss you at home, I trust you have had a successful term. I do not know about the new address but the above one will find us as our letters will go to Jørstadmoen to be censored.

There are about 30 who did not volunteer for work and are staying behind. I have sent home all my photos, torn up every letter and had a general clean out. Will write and let you know what the job is like. What is to be, will be, I suppose.

I could say a lot if letters were more certain and there was no censoring.

I am sorry this letter is not very cheery, but you can't help feeling a bit bad at times. The train might be wrecked. I always was unlucky.
Yrs A

All remaining letters from 1916 are sent from Hjerkinn and are c/o Vaktchefen, which I think means the Guard or Commander, at Jørstadmoen. Some also mention being sent from Jernbanestasion which simply means train station. Hjerkinn is a village in the municipality of Dovre about 180Km from Jørstadmoen. It sits at the base of the Dovrefjell mountains and is one of the driest places in Norway.

There is an army base in Hjerkinn and it appears that is where Arnold and the other internees from *HMS India* stayed during their time working on that part of the railway. They were accompanied by one Norwegian officer from the camp as well as about twelve soldiers.

On 28 October, Arnold writes:

Dear Q,

I have rec. your letter of 16 Oct. I always enjoy your letters with their weekly bemoanings of the horrors of cold and damp. No wonder you gaze with longing to Italy.

I have passed a most enjoyable week in hospital. Go out Monday 30 October then 2 days to rest my arm and back to Jørstadmoen on 3 November.

By the time this letter reaches you, the submarine question which is convulsing Norway will probably have been settled. I—(censored)

The food in this place is A1. The domestic, for three days, in reply to her "small die mere moat?" had "mere, tak" for answers, so now she brings a lusty helping. Tea is always drunk without milk and the coffee is topping.
Best Wishes, Yrs A

In the letter above, Arnold seems to think that he will be back in Jørstadmoen on 3 November. As all the rest of the letters of the year come from Hjerkinn this did not happen. It is also vague as to what the hospital visit was for, he only mentions injury to his arm, but it is never mentioned again so it must not have been too serious an injury.

Even though he is away from camp he is aware, however, of the total number of men still interned in Norway and in a letter of 25 November he informs Queenie that *last year there were 96 here; now 75. Disposal of 21 as follows— escaped 2. Returned home (unfit)13. Hospital 1. Prison 2. Working out at jobs 3.* I am not sure if those numbers include the officers living outside of the camp or not. I suspect they do not.

Queenie remains steadfast in her attempts to keep in close contact with Arnold and to make him feel a part of the family and useful to them. She is obviously struggling with one of the heaters in the school or at her home and has been writing of her frustrations to her little brother.

He responds on 25 November with detailed advice on how she might go about overcoming her issues—*Were I a resident engineer upon your estate, I should first get a long bamboo pole, tie a bundle of rags on one end (a brush, if money was no object), scramble on the roof and work the brush up and down the flue pipe,—then clear away all soot, (this dome monthly).*

Next I would spend some hours in your coal shed crushing your 'household nobs' into walnut size for use in this stove (and not larger than walnut size). In getting the stove under warm light an ordinary fire with sticks in the bottom (here they use pine logs soaked in paraffin) and gradually fill up through the top with the small coal; during this operation the lower flap should be up to admit all air possible.

The instructions are accompanied by sketches—*"diagrams of comparison"* and he finishes off and reminds her that if *the ashes are removed at 10 p.m. at night the stove should still be burning well in the morning.* His advice seems to have paid off as he comments in his 18 December letter that he *was very pleased to get your letter of 10 Dec and to hear stove was less refractory.*

One letter in the family collection, dated 16 November 1916, is a rare letter written to Arnold's eldest sister Dorothy. I am confident that more letters were written to Dorothy, but this is one of the very few to survive. It is written not only to mark the occasion of her birthday but also to congratulate her move towards her desired profession of being a farmer. He writes:

Was pleased to get your letter of 7 November and to hear you have formed something fairly definite.

The occasion moved me to an 'effusion' and a sketch, both of which I enclose for your perusal and at the same time I wish you many happy returns of the day.

No doubt, in a few weeks you will have acquired some idea of any personal affects you may require in your new career and I suggest the family subscribe and give it to you—some book maybe—'Hints on milking obstreperous cattle' or possibly you will require a 'ploughman's outfit'—but such a subject is beyond the scope of my mere pen.

Sartorial matters agrarian is, I believe, the latest science among the women of England."

This letter and the accompanying 'effusion' are rare glimpses of Arnold wry wit and his super dry sense of humour and I enjoy this side of him so very much. I think it is a look at his true rounded character and not just the young man who is overcome with his isolation and loneliness. The 'effusion' is a poem and it is so charming that I want to share it!

How to knock the bottom out of the Money Market or the metamorphosis of an ink-slinger.
In ancient lay, the poets sang,
'The pen is mightier than the sword'.
Mightier than this, the milk churns clang,
'Back to the land, to the grassy sward'.

For lo! Our eldest D has done,
With shorthand, type and office stool,
Her haven now,—the chicken run,
And in the dairy, fresh and cool.

And hens that could not lay an egg,
Shall see her smile and then lay twenty,
The game old cock, with shaking leg,
Shall rise again and crow in plenty.

With mornings dawn her brood shall rise,
Resolved to shew the world their powers.
{The cocks' shrill clarion to the skies
Wakes us at hopeless early hours.}

With three-legged stool and milking pail,
D to the meadow winds her way.
The cow, with joy, doth way her tail
And gives two ton of milk a day.

'Eggs'—'fresh eggs'—'new laid eggs' and all
Milk without water we shall see.
Down comes the price with a fall
Back to the land has gone our D.

Below this effusion is one of Arnold's beautifully drawn ink sketches of a girl with her sheep holding a crook. This letter and accompanying poem have become favourites of mine due to the warmth and gentleness in them.

The end of the year sees Arnold back on his ski's, *We were out skiing again to-day; after all the experience of last year, it is a great come down to the pride, to take a hill flying rush and, instead of nonchalantly reaching the bottom at great speed, to forfeit assume a recumbent position halfway down* and seems to be in an unusually, if not a bit guardedly, optimistic mood *Somehow we feel we are on the eve of great events. Look where you will, no 'deadlock' appears much anywhere.*

It is extremely fortunate that at this time Arnold did not know that he still had almost two years left before any great event took place and he was able to go home.

What was happening in the camp?

June of 1916 had brought with it signs of unrest from some members of the interned crew. The escape of Grigson and Clinton had stirred things up in the camp and select internees were voicing their unhappiness about the conditions they had found themselves in. The files at the National Archives reveal more information on exactly how the escape took place.

The British Legation in Norway report that Commander Kennedy had requested that Grigson be allowed to assist him with work "outside the camp" and this was allowed after Kennedy had provided a personal guarantee that Grigson would adhere to the rules of his internment and not try to escape. Grigson was provided with a special mark to wear on his arm to make his easily recognisable.

The report goes on to say, "The Norwegian Authorities concerned now believe that the Mark has been used first by Grigson and then by Clinton, the fact that the whole guard was changed on the very time the escape took place, pending to facilitate their passing out of the camp unnoticed. Most likely Grigson has sent the work to Clinton by letter, immediately after he himself had got out and in fact the mark was found, after the escape had been discovered in a letter addressed to two of the interned by the name of Atwood and Woolford."

There were also reports that Clinton may have stolen a bicycle which may have assisted them in their escape. The Lillehammer Spectator reported on 14 June 1916, that letters had been received by a local business which contained money for the repair of two 'borrowed' bicycles. The letters had Scottish stamps on them.

With the escape of Grigson and Clinton and the subsequent tightening of the restrictions on freedoms added to the grumblings on conditions and the growing awareness that this incarceration was not going to end anytime soon, back in England the message was getting through that the crew was unhappy. The unnamed internee whose words have been kept on file at the National Archives[20] continues to voice his frustrations with two missives in July and then two in September.

---

[20] All correspondence quoted in this chapter is from the file The National Archives numbered FO 383/212

From P/W, Jørstadmoen. 27.7.16

The number here is steadily diminishing. Three men were sent home a month ago; another three go home tonight. Gregson (sic) escaped last May.

27.7.16

We are allowed out about two hours a day. I went out the other day. They sent two soldiers with three of us armed with revolvers. The food we get here don't build body at all. I don't know how we should get on if we had any hard work to do.

3.9.16

Fifty of the boys left the Camp yesterday for this railway job at Dombås, leaving 30 in the camp. We were left without a cook, so the Norwegian officer asked for a volunteer and I took it on. It did not care much about turning out a 6a.m. this morning for a start to make porridge for 30 hungry mucks—they seemed satisfied with the dinner (sloppy ash) made by a sloppy cook—

I had an idea that when those 50 went away we were to be given leave; instead of that all leave was today because somebody was supposed to have tried to get out last night; they found a bag of food or something. Nobody in the camp knows anything about it; but no one is allowed out without further orders, excepting of course those youngsters the lady killers, who have walked in and out as they like ever since they came here.

They still walk out because they would not escape. (Line deleted here). If I could only sound my aitches when I talk. You know, where they are not required, "go hon"! I should be allowed to walk and stop till 11 p.m. Also I read all about those chaps having leave from Holland. We could have had the same long ago but for our own officers. I said officers, ten a penny, pick 'en where you like!

The Norwegian Authorities were quite willing to give us leave provided our Captain would stand security that no one would escape. He wouldn't do it like the Captain in Holland did, therefore we are to be kept caged up, while those in Holland enjoy liberty. You don't want me to tell you again my opinion of our officers, you know it already. We have only to thank them for being here at all. It will all come out some day.

6.9.16

They may keep my mouth shut while I am here, but I shall certainly write an article informing the public of Great Britain how I fared in neutral country. I do consider we are treated like dogs; although I see it published in our papers we are well cared for. And again, we are caged up like wild animals at the Zoo and fed equally as well.

Whoever this man is, he certainly does not hold back. I had often wondered what the opinions of the crew were towards the officers and the fact that the officers were allowed to live out of the camp. It certainly highlighted the divide between the men and officers and allowed those living out of camp a totally dissimilar experience of interment than those behind the barbed wire fences being watched by armed men. Several officers married and started families and stories and photos exist of parties with local women and drinking and feasting. This was not happening in the camp where the men were left to primarily create their own entertainment.

This divide is reinforced when looking at Commander Kennedy's official response to the complaints made to the Daily Mail.

14 July 1916
Sir,

With reference to your letter N.L.I/45316, of the 27 June calling for remarks from me on a letter addressed to the Editor of the Daily Mail by a member of the crew of H.M.S "India", now interned here, I have the honour to submit herewith a statement showing the treatment which the interned men receive and which in my opinion is very satisfactory.

I would at the same time submit for your favourable consideration that the Norwegian Authorities may be officially informed "that any man who escaped from Norway after signing a paper promising not to escape would be sent back again". If this could be done I am sure a much greater amount of liberty would be granted and this would greatly assist in relieving the tediousness of the internment and make the men much more happy and contented.

The men are interned in a very large enclosure several acres in extent, which is surrounded by a high wire fence with barbed wire on the top and armed sentries stationed all around. They are very comfortably housed in huts, especially built to make them warm in the cold weather each room has a large stove in it and plenty of fuel both coke and wood is supplied. Each man has a straw mattress and pillow and four blankets. There are about ten men in each sleeping room and in addition, there are four mess rooms fitted with all necessary articles for refreshment.

The cooking is done by the ship's cook of the "India", the food is drawn daily from the quarter master in bulk and is issued very much the same as on-board ship. There is also a large concert hall and a workshop for carpentry (which is not used by the men).

I have also arranged a canteen in the Camp which is run by a committee and is supervised by my second in command, Act. Lieutenant J.H Biggs, R.N.R. In the Hall there is a library of over 600 books, all gifts. There is also in the camp a football and cricket ground and the men have also the use of several musical instruments.

With regard to the victualling the scale originally supplied was the same as the Norwegian soldiers got. As this was not satisfactory I had it altered soon after our arrival. Again, in December, I submitted a letter, copy enclosed, with a new scale, which was at once adopted by the Norwegian authorities. Again in June, last I submitted a fresh letter and scale and this has also been adopted. These letters and scales will, I think, answer the remark in the letter about having to go without food, etc.

With regard to the leave question—until Petty Officer Clinton and Act. Ldg. Seaman Grigson escaped on the 19th May the men were allowed in small parties with only one soldier armed with a revolver in charge of each party and everyone had to be back in camp by 5 o/c p.m. After these two men escaped, all leave and privileges were stopped for a time, but I am glad to say that these small privileges are again being granted. A party is also allowed to go to Lillehammer every Saturday for shopping purposes.

With regard to the statement that the Consul at Kristiania takes no interest in the men because he has not been here to see them, there is no necessity for the Consul to be troubled to come here. I myself am constantly at the camp and I always have two officers on duty living at the Camp and any man can see me or the Officers when they like.

If it were not for a few men who will get drunk every time they are allowed in Lillehammer, the authorities would I am sure be more lenient as regards leave.

I enclose herewith the two letters referred to with regard to the victualling.

I have the honour to be, Sir, Your Obedient Servant, W.G. A Kennedy, Commander, R.N.

Internment Camp

Jørstadmoen

14 July 1916

Report re Medical arrangements

There is a properly equipped sick bay attached to the camp and also a hospital, which is only used very occasionally, all serious sick cases being sent to the Civil hospital in Lillehammer. Soon after Surgeon F.W Lawson, R.N was allowed to go home, there has since been a resident Norwegian Army doctor attached to the camp who is nearly always a resident practitioner in the district.

(Signed) W.G.A Kennedy, Commander R.N late in command of H.M.S "India".

The response to Kennedy's letters is to focus on trying to gain the interned men more freedom by attempting to gain an agreement between the English and Norwegians, whereby men who escape will be returned to camp having signed a document stating that they will not try and run away again. This may answer why Grigson and Clinton were not returned as there was no such agreement in place when they escaped.

At around the same time the newspapers in Britain were reporting on the conditions in Norway and how they were being discussed in the House of Commons. The Nottingham Evening Post, the Sunderland Daily Echo and the Dublin Daily Chronicle give reports on what was happening:

"British Jack Tars Fairly Treated

In the House of Commons today Mr Barnoe asked the Under Secretary for Foreign Affairs if he had any official information to the effect that British Naval prisoners at Forstadmoen (sic) Fåberg, Norway are subject to harsh treatment, inferior food, and deprivation of liberty.

Lord Robert Cecil said the Admiralty had received an official report, dated 14 July, according to which the men in question appeared to be well treated and fed and enjoying a reasonable amount of liberty. Several privileges were temporarily stopped owing to the escape of two prisoners."

The men concerned with sorting out the agreement on the British side were J. Murray are the Admiralty and Sir Maurice de Bunsen at the Foreign Office.

De Bunsen was a highly respected and experienced diplomat who served as Ambassador to Spain and was Ambassador to Austria when the war broke out.

9 August 1916

Sir, (under Secretary of State, Foreign Office)

I am commanded by My Lords Commissioners of the Admiralty to forward herewith, for the information of the Secretary of State for Foreign Affairs, a copy of a report which has been received from Commander W.G.A Kennedy, R.N late H.M.S "India", on the Internment Camp at Jørstadmoen, Norway.

2. With regard to the suggestion contained in the first paragraph of this report that the Norwegian Government should be officially informed that any man who escapes from Norway after giving a signed promise not to escape will be sent back to Norway; it appears to Their Lordships that it would be desirable to pursue the same course towards these men as has been adopted in regard to the men interned in Holland and to give the suggested assurance in the hope that the result may be to secure for the men interned in Norway privileges similar to those granted by the Dutch Authorities.

I am accordingly to request that if Viscount Grey sees no objection a communication in the terms indicated above may be addressed to the Norwegian Government.

I am, Sir, Your Obedient Servant, J Murray.

14 August 1916

Charge d'Affaires, Kristiania

Sir,

The Lords Commissioners of the Admiralty have suggested to this department that the Norwegian Government may be willing to adopt, in respect of the British Naval Ps/W interned in Norway, a procedure similar to that pursued in like circumstances by the Netherland Government, namely, that in the receipt of an official assurance on the part of H.M.G to the effect that any of the prisoners in question who may escape from Norway, after having given a signed undertaking not to do so, shall be sent back for re-internment in that country, somewhat more extended privileges than at present should be accorded to these men.

I have to request to you to make a communication in the above sense to the Norwegian minister for F.A. and to inform H.E that, should the Norwegian Government be disposed to take their proposal into their favourable consideration, the requisite assurance will be conveyed to them by H.M.G without delay.

(for the Secretary of State) Maurice de Bunsen

Telegraph

Decypher. Sir M. Findlay (Christiania) 2 September

D. 1:15 a.m.

R. 11:30a.m. 3 September 1916

No. 3022 (R)

Norwegian Government have agreed to accord greater freedom to interned crew of His Majesty's ship "India" on terms indicated in your despatch—consular and have already allowed 12 men under one Officer to take employment on railway works.

Can you telegraph requisite assurance.

Arnold was one of the men allowed to take employment on the railway works and this was the start of a continued employment on the construction of the Dovrebanen that would occur on and off until the time he left Norway.

This was not the end of the matter, however and men continued to speak up about their treatment and further action was taken to try and appease the disgruntled men..

An odd little letter is in the files at the National Archives is be addressed to a member of Parliament. It seems that one of the internees wrote to his local MP (Major H.K Newton, M.P) who has then written to Lord Robert Cecil, 1st Viscount Cecil of Chelwood who the Parliamentary Under-Secretary of State for Foreign Affairs was.

There is no further action on this letter in the files, so I don't know whether Lord Cecil found it was the mistake he wished for or not, but he had reported to the House of Commons back in July, so he has knowledge of what was going on or at least what had been reported to him.

18 September 1916

My dear Newton, (Major H.K Newton, M.P)

I will enquire into the case of your constituent who is interned in Norway. I cannot help hoping there is some mistake, for, speaking generally, the Norwegians are well disposed towards us.

Yours sincerely,

Robert Cecil

In the September files, we find out who made the original complaint. Albert Charles Ware was an Able Seaman who was born in Somerset and trained at Chatham. He was one of the older members of the crew being born in 1876 and he was one of the survivors to be rescued by the Saxon. It would seem likely that he was the unnamed man from the archive file and also from the letter to the paper. Although the letter from the paper is written by someone with a good grasp of written English, and the unnamed man confesses that "If I could only sound my aitches when I talk" then he might be treated better so they might not be the same man. Ware is firstly referred to by the Foreign Office in a letter to a Major Newton regarding the letter of complaint sent by Leading Seaman Ware.

The Foreign Office reassure Major Newton that they are looking into the complaint and will let the major know of the result. The letter below also refers to the complaint about men in prison being treated better and that fits in with the series of complaints made by the formerly unknown man.

10 October 1916

Sir, (Under Secretary of State, Foreign Office)

With reference to your letter of the 25th ultimo, No 187083/1203/P, relative to a complaint by Leading Seaman Albert C. Ware, late of H.M.S "India", regarding the food rations supplied to the prisoners interned in Norway, I am commanded by My Lords Commissioners of the Admiralty to refer to Admiralty letter of the 9 August last, N.L.I/47617 in which a copy of a report date the 14 July from Commander W.G.A Kennedy R.N. on this subject was enclosed and to transmit herewith, for the information of the Secretary of State for Foreign Affairs, copies of two letters referred to in this report which have been addressed by Commander Kennedy to the Norwegian Authorities in regard to the victualling of the men interned at Jørstadmoen.

In their Lordships opinion it does not appear that the complaints about the bad quality and insufficiency of the rations are justified.

2. I am to add that Their Lordships have no knowledge of preferential treatment having been accorded by the Norwegian Government to a prisoner of undesirable character and to suggest that Ware's complaint may possibly relate to the temporary stoppage of leave and other privileges which appear to have occurred in consequence of the escape of two men.

I am, Sir, Your obedient Servant, W Graham Greene

Albert Ware did not leave to work on the railway in 1916, like some of the other men, so did not even get a change of scenery in that year. I wonder whether, in retrospect, they later regretted not taking the opportunity to do something different. Of course, there is always a chance that they were not offered the opportunity for varying reasons like health, behaviour, or lack of skills.

It is fortunate that Arnold was able to leave the camp. He was given not only a change of scenery and chance to spend time outside the high, barbed wire fence but it also something to do. A job. A chance to feel purposeful. This was so important for his well-being and survival. Especially knowing, as we do now, that he had a lot more time to spend in this country so far away from home.

The complaints made by Ware began a lengthy, war long tussle between the interned men and the Officers, the Legation in Christiania, the Foreign Office, Admiralty and Prisoner of War Office. There is evidence in the files at the National Archives of unrest and dissatisfaction that carries on throughout the duration of the war. At times, the men behind desks ask for more information from the Officers and in late November 1916 Lieutenant John Biggs is asked to author a report.

The report is lengthy and it covers everything from the food supplies to recreation. On the food Biggs writes "The underfeeding, so called, often was the result of quarrels between the men and the cooks. There were originally four cooks in the Camp, but one was sent home with appendicitis. The others suffered from a grievance as they said they worked for all the rest who did nothing and got no extra pay for it.

The consequence was the food was often wasted, I am sure. "I am unsure as to the exact identity of the cooks, but I have a feeling that they were both men from the ship (Arnold mentions his having to cook in a later letter) as well as people from surrounding villages. I do know that one of the internees, William Tilley, married one of the cooks."

Lieutenant Biggs is quite scathing of the complainants and writes, "The man who wrote this was evidently too lazy to work himself and is undoubtedly one of the 'sea lawyers' who are a nuisance always and have damped every effort to do anything at all for the crowd in general."

I was unfamiliar with the term 'sea lawyers' but the Oxford Dictionary soon got me up-to-speed and left me in no doubt as to Biggs opinions on Ware and his type— "sea lawyer: an eloquently and obstinately argumentative person." He reveals that further escapes were attempted "two did try to escape and one owned up later on and got punishment in cells" but stresses that life in the camps isn't all that bad (in his opinion)— "This is the result undoubtedly of being confined for so long and restricted without work to keep their minds occupied. Men who behaved themselves could get out nearly every day.

Many are too lazy to go out. Swimming parties went out every day during summer weather. Skiing parties went out every day last winter and skating parties went too till the snow was too much to clear away and there is arranged two days a week for shopping parties to Lillehammer."

Most of the correspondence on file from the second half of 1916 centres on men requesting leave to visit unwell relatives back home in the United Kingdom. The first request is made but Leading Seaman Edward Penton in September and this is closely followed by requests from Albert Ware, Leading Seaman Charles White, Storekeeper Richard Dunn, and Petty Officer Fred Hines.

All men had requested leave due to unwell relatives, usually mothers or wives and all were granted their requests. By the end of November Midshipman Harold Jenkins and Assistant Engineer Francis Patmore have also joined the request list without having unwell relatives. Leave is approved for all the men and in December they are joined by Able Seamen William Keats, J.T Wright and Samuel Summerfield as well as Cooper C.W Green.

These ten men make the maximum amount absent from camp as allowed by the Norwegian Authorities and they insisted that all men away from camp must not be involved in any war work whilst on leave. The Norwegians also stress that "Interned men whose conduct has been less than satisfactory will not be granted leave."

It is then that the extensions to the periods of leave begin to flood in. Patmore, Penton, and Ware are amongst those who request and have extensions granted and the demand becomes great enough that the British authorities decide to become stricter on allowing extensions. Findlay, from the Legation in Christiania, writes:

"I am of the opinion that continuous applications for extensions of leave from H.M.S "India's" men will eventually lead to leave being refused for numbers of the men who are anxious to get home.

It is unsatisfactory from my point of view to be continually asking for favours from the Norwegian Government."

Lieutenant Biggs concurs and warns that "extensions of leave granted without proper control, will only make it possible for 'schemers' to gain an advantage over better men and delay leave for the others." Looking at how long Arnold waited for leave, I fear that Biggs may have been right and it was lucky for all those restrictions were placed on leave so that many of the interned men got a chance to see their loved ones at least once over the time they were imprisoned.

On the following pages – A collection of Arnold's letters, poems and etchings including instructions on fixing stoves and heaters, a missed visit, a poem for Dorothy, a drawing of another 10th Cruiser Squadron vessel and what I think is a drawing of Queenie entitled "Supercilious Wrath".

Supercilious wrath!

How to knock the bottom out of the Money Market

or

The metamorphosis of an into-stinger.

In ancient lay, the poets sang.
'The pen is mightier than the sword';
mightier than this, the milk churns clang,
'Back to the land, to the grassy sward'.

For lo!   our eldest D . has done
with shorthand, type and office stool,
Her haven now,— the chicken run,
And in the dairy, fresh and cool.

And hens that could not lay an egg,
Shall see her smile, and then lay twenty,
The game old cock, with shaking leg,
Shall rise again and crow in plenty.

With mornings down her hood shall rise
Resolved to shew the world their powers
(The cocks' shrill clarion to the skies
Wakes us at hopeless early hours)

With three legged stool and milking pail.
D. to the meadow wends her way.
The cow, with joy, doth wag her tail
And gives two ton of milk a day.

'Eggs' – 'fresh eggs' – 'new-laid eggs' and all
Milk without water we shall see
Down comes the price with a fall
Back to the land has gone our D.

"Kept Sheep in Arcadia"

R.A.Clarke.   British Internment Camp
c/o Vaktchefen. Jørstadmoen
Faaberg Jernebanestation
NORWAY.

August 2ⁿᵈ

~~Dear Edith,~~

On Monday July 31ˢᵗ, I had a letter from Miss Simpson saying she would be in Norway on Aug 1ˢᵗ & would endeavour to see me.

There are only two trains per diem which arrive at Faaberg St. with connections from Kristiania on the South. One ~~is at~~ arrives 12·55 midday and the other ~~passes~~ arrives 4·30 pm in the afternoon.

There are only 2 trains daily ~~for~~ from Faaberg to Kristiania. 11 am & 5·30 pm ~~etc~~.

Yesterday. (Tues. Aug 1ˢᵗ) I had special leave from 12 pm. till 4 pm. I met the 1ˢᵗ train but regret Miss S. did not arrive. I had almost reached Camp again when the military postman overtook me with a telegram from Miss S. from Lillestrøm Station saying she had missed the connections.

There would not have been time to get here & back in time to leave Kristiania
(The absence of Faaberg Bridge & the ferry add at least uncertainty ½ hr to the programme & we are 2½ miles from Faaberg).

Invoking outside aid (as I am no Norske scholar) I wired back a reply in Norwegian & english to the above effect.

I can only trust it reached her safely.

It is exceedingly kind of her to make the attempt, and even an hours conversation with a countryman

R.A.Clarke. British Internment Camp.
4. Vahtchefen   Jørstadmoen.
Faaberg Jernbanestation
NORWAY.   Aug 26ᵗʰ 1916.

Dear 2.

Your letter from home Aug 16 arrived last night & was most welcome. : Logically I cannot expect letters if I write none, & certainly what emanates from here are not letters but a bare chronicle of existence.

For a good time past the days have been passed in reading sketching & smoking with an occasional swim as a diversion. This latter is now off owing to adverse conditions & climate.

You might ask I. to send me out another small bottle of Indian ink like the one WSG sent me. There is no hurry. Another 4 or 5 weeks will do, as we have another year to do here.

It is pretty certain we are going navvying up in the mountains now. 'Your King & Country need U.' They might at least exchange us for the Germans, they don't need us. I don't care much what happens.

Our weather has broken up now. We shall soon be having 12-20 degrees day in, day out. Please thank E for. her parcel of books & also I. for the apples & nuts which arr⁴ quite safely. I only mention it in care my other letter goes adrift. I enclose a small sketch of one of the 'Muckle Flugga Hussars' to which much maligned unit the 'Indies' me belonged. I remain Yrs A.

H.M. Armed Liner 'ALCANTARA' and S.M.S. GREIF.

These four cuttings from a birch tree have hung in my father-in-law's study for as long as I have known him. They were painted in 1916 at Jørstadmoen by Arnold. One of them is clearly a gift to Edith and another has the Latin quote "Honi soit qui mal y pense" meaning "Shame be to him who thinks evil of it."

This quote was used in many different Navy and Military settings and as a part of the heraldry of the Order of the Garter. The other two cuttings are mementos of Norway—one displaying Arnold's love of the magazine Punch and its witty satire and the other his connections to the sea and the Navy.

Some of the postcards sent from Colour Sergeant Herbert Charles Ripley to his son, Bert. They tell the story of Bert's attempts to gain a scholarship to a local tech school and the story of a father trying to keep in touch and parent from afar.

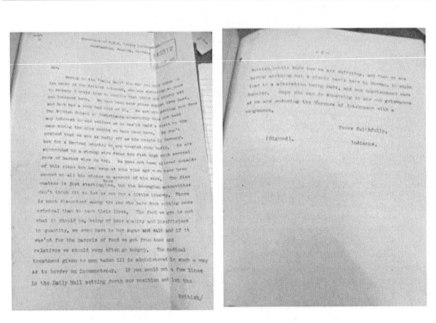

A copy of the letter of complaint sent to the Daily Mail and some of the official responses trying to deal with these issues raised.

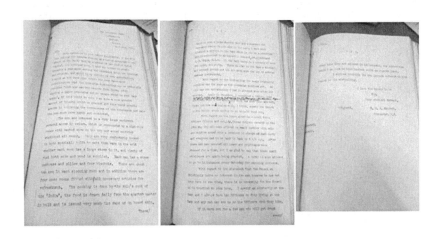

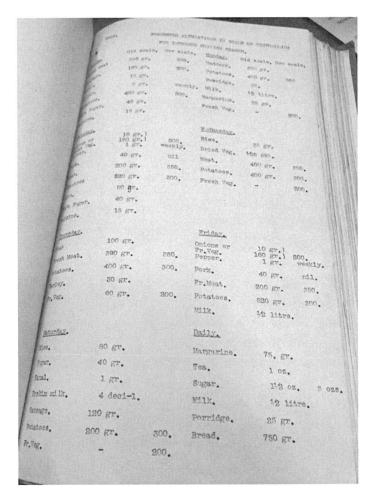

The daily allowances for the internees as negotiated by Commander Kennedy.

Weekly supply of:-

Salt.		
Barley.	21 gr.per man.	70 grns per man
Jam or Marmalade.	30 " " "	
Cheese.	200 " " "	
Pepper.	120 " " "	
	—	7 grns per man.

Dealing with the fallout from the public complaints made about the camp by an internee.

MURRAY

174525

MILITARY

Decypher. Sir M. Findlay. (Christiania) September 2
D. 1.15.a.m.
R.11.30.a.m. September 3rd,1916.
No. 3022. (R).

. . . .

Norwegian Government have agreed to accord greater freedom to interned crew of His Majesty's ship "India" on terms indicated in your despatch 9 Consular and have already allowed 12 men under ficer to take employment on railway works.

Can you telegraph requisite assurance.

. . . .

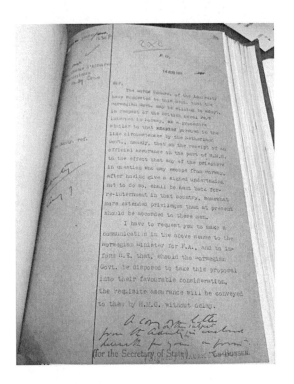

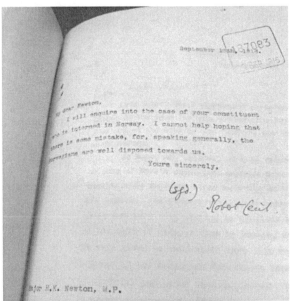

From the official files at the National Archives the letter written to Newton MP and the anonymous complaints from one of the internees at Jørstadmoen.

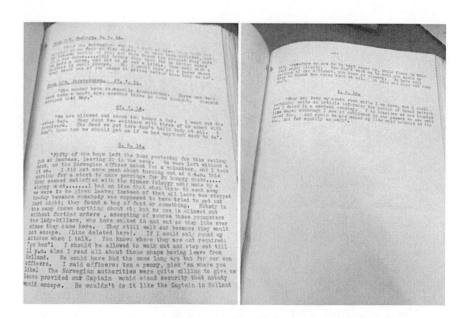

Skiing in the winter of maybe 1916, it is hard to tell the exact date. Arnold is on the very left. The lower photograph is from the collection of Seaman Robert Charles Maynard—I am unable to identify the individual skiers in this one.

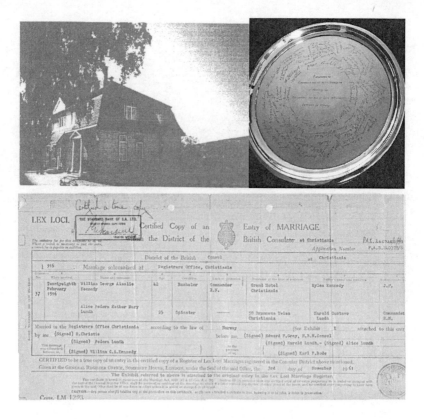

Photos of Commander Kennedy and his new wife Fedora on their wedding day. Also shown are a photograph of their wedding certificate showing that they were married at the Consulate in Kristiania. The menu from their reception is signed by some of the guests, I can make out the signatures of Lieutenants Biggs and Alltree however none of the other seem familiar.

There is also a photograph of a silver plate that was gifted and signed by the crew of HMS India. In addition, a photograph of Villa Formo where the married couple lived.

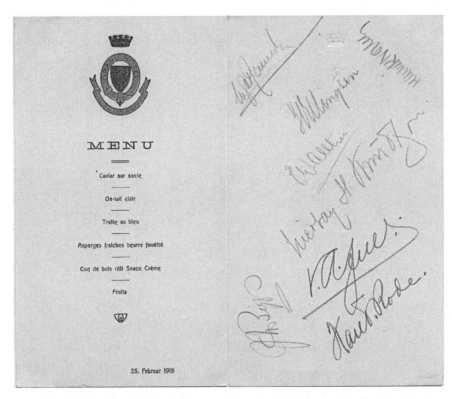

MENU
——
'Caviar sur socle
——
Ox-tail clair
——
Truite au bleu
——
Asperges fraiches beurre fouétté
——
Coq de bois rôti Sauce Crème
——
Fruits

25. Februar 1916

Photographs from the album of Senior Engineer Charles Nelson. He loved skiing and also seemed to enjoy a healthy social life!

Self on Ski 1916 near Lillehammer - Norway

Frank Wold Lillehammer 1916

Hjerkinn

Photographs and postcards from Hjerkinn where Arnold and others were sent to work on the Dovrebanen railway. The postcard interests me as it is written to R. Feaver but it does not look like Arnold's writing. The humour is recognisable with him commenting that the train (which is not seen at the station) is temporarily delayed.

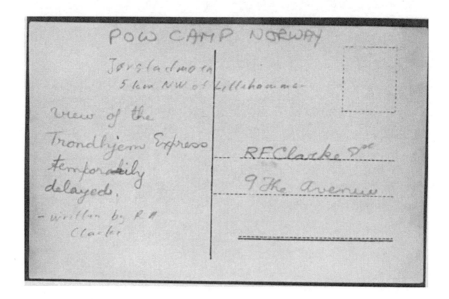

POW CAMP NORWAY

Jørstadmoen
5 km NW of Lillehammer

view of the
Trondhjem Express
temporarily
delayed.
- written by R H
Clarke

R.F.Clarke 9º
9 The Avenue

Washing day at camp, a photograph from the collection of Seaman Robert Charles Maynard.

First Half of 1917 –
"The News Is Forced."

At the start of 1917, the internees have been "guests" of the Norwegian Government for 511 days. In that time the Battle of Gallipoli had been fought and the Gallipoli evacuation had been completed, the Battle of Verdun had begun, the British Conscription bill had been passed, the Battle of the Somme had begun and the first use of tanks was seen in the same battle and one of the biggest sea battles, the Battle of Jutland, had been fought not far away in the North Sea with 6000 British sailors losing their lives. But still the war raged on and still in a quiet valley in Norway around 80 British sailors waited for the news that might let them return home.

That valley is situated 190Km from Oslo (what was known then as Christiania) at the top of the Mjøsa lake, the largest and deepest lake in not only Norway but also Europe. Through the valley runs the Gudbrandsdalslågen, a river that feeds into the Mjøsa and the valley itself is named after that river Gudbrandsdalen (in English, the Gudbrand Valley).

It is a large valley that sits in the middle of a collection of smaller valleys. There are three main sections of the valley—the Norddalen (Northern section) around Dovre, the Midtdalen (middle section) and Sørdalen where the Fåberg/Jørstadmoen camp was based. The Norwegian playwright Henrik Ibsen was inspired by his travels through the area to write Peer Gynt. The titular character may have been based on a local man. The area was primarily used for farming at the time of WW1.

Arnold starts 1917 back in the camp at Fåberg. It was winter which means his primary source of entertainment would have been skiing, reading, drawing, and smoking! The first letter does not appear until mid-February and begins a recurrent theme of the troubles of keeping in regular contact due to irregular mail. On 19 February he writes to Queenie:

My dear Q,

For over a fortnight, we have had no letters or news of any description, there it was most cheering to receive last night your letter of 4th Feb, F's letter of 7 Feb and DC's of 6 Feb; in the interim I had not given up writing, for should you get mine of 10 Feb it will probably call forth a stirring reproof.

I sympathise with you in your burst pipes and wintry conditions, but time soon slides on and you will soon be basking in April's sunshine.

It would appear that Father is anxious to get Arnold home on leave but there appears to be a process that must be gone through and I wonder that a healthy, young, single man might not be as high up on the list of those applying and being granted leave as a man who has a wife and children at home. However, there seem to be improvements being made at the camp.

Which reminds me that in my last letter I explained the situation in regards leave. Would you tactfully explain the situation to F?—The war apparently bids fair to carry on indefinitely.

There were rumours that we were to have a new bathhouse and also electric light. This we dismissed as idle talk, but the first is practically an accomplished fact and the second should be finished shortly.

I am sorry my letters are not in the super cheerful strain.

Best wishes Yours A

Late February also sees Arnold in contact with Wilfrid who is still working in the Inspection Department in Woolwich, but it is still Queenie who gets the most mail (or who kept the most mail?) and who gets the real insight into everyday life at the Fåberg camp. Both of the following letters/cards were written on the 28 February.

Wilfrid

Please excuse a P.C this week. Have not heard from you for over a month but that is not to be surprised at under existing conditions. Hope everything is going well.

Yrs, A

My dear Q,

When letters etc only come about twice a month you can guess their value. I was very glad to get yours of 12 Feb today with a pathetic lament of the householder's unequal fight with cold. All pipes in this country are at least 9ft below the surface. During the latter part of our stay 'up country', pickaxes were discarded and we used to blow up the frozen earth.

It is pretty evident you have not received some of my latter letters otherwise the reply would have—and trenchant; never mind—it's all one to me.

Latterly they have stacked enormous quantities of tree trunks and wood fuel inside the camp—sufficient for nearly another two winters and it is still coming in. Over half the camp has had the electric light in and the new bath house is practically finished. Being a mathematician you will deduce from this:

   a.   we shall be leaving shortly.
   b.   We shall not be leaving here for a couple of years.

The days pass quick enough. I have learnt in a small way, the art of string netting. Up to the present I have merely turned out a few nets for boiling the mess's potatoes, but I hope to make hammocks after a bit of practice.
Please, excuse more.
Best wishes
Yours A"

By March mail is still only coming through to Arnold in dribs and drabs but Arnold decides to entertain Queenie in his 7 March letter with descriptions of some of the visitors that have been brought into the camp and what he imagines would happen should an important visitor call by.

He also mentions, for the first time this year, about opportunities for work on the railways again and that there were 'bad reports' regarding the first team of workers. I've yet to uncover any official reports linking to this claim so am unsure as to what the 'bad reports' actually were. I suspect it may involve drunkenness and an unwillingness to work efficiently, but I can say without a doubt, that Arnold would not have been included in any such report.

My Dear Q,
Many thanks indeed for your letter of 18 Feb. It is only the 3rd mail in six weeks; they buck ones spirit up immensely,—do letters.
Your reference to Bishop Bury is interesting; were not he and Miss Hobhouse, the subject of pertinent questions in Parliament recently?

When we were here first, we had visitors occasionally. The first was an educated young Norwegian, who spoke English fluently; he belonged to some International Prayer Union; in his address, he informed us we were the "GUESTS(!)" of the Norwegian Government. We are,—but it takes yards of barbed wire (pigtraad), regular counting and a company of soldiers to entertain us.

The second visitor was a lady, who ran down the morals of every country and town, she could pronounce in English (This diatribe included Norway). She then played (and she could not play the piano as well as I) 'The Dead March'. This was only 16/15 Sept. We since found out she is a religious maniac, well known in these parts.

The third was a 'press correspondent.' Although no evidence is forthcoming, I have a shrewd notion he was spurious and of Teutonic tendencies.

Thus you see that,—should a Bishop or anyone be sighted in the offing—the chances are that the person would only see the lime lighting clique. (I give way here.)

However, take it, he gets further. It would probably arrive on one of those happy days when we: Breakfast (8:30) Fresh Herrings (fried) coffee.

Dinner (12) Roast Beef, Roast potatoes, cabbage, green (and Brown) peas, stewed prunes and custard oranges, coffee and cigarettes.

Tea (4) Beautiful white bread, butter, marmalade.

Supper (7 p.m.) Egg and onion omelette, cheese, cocoa.

The above is no Fantasia, but, on occasions,-concrete face. Eminently satisfactory, you say. I agree. Sometime later, when the Bishop is still faring sumptuously (elsewhere) and things altered a bit, you just walk in and have a look at the grub and then walk out again, fully convinced that once 'trespasses had been forgiven,' but that the petition preceding it, had been temporarily overlooked.

Twice this week the names have been asked for of those willing to work on (a) a local—scheme; (b) next June, on the old railway job, up country, at Hjerkinn; I fancy the first is cancelled; with regard to the second, it would seem that, though a bad report was returned of us, they valued the work of some of us. But in any case, I rather fight shy of going up there again. Beside I'm hoping for something to turn up by next May—incidentally, I've had the same hope for the last nineteen months.

So, you see that we are all still jogging on in much the same old way. I haven't heard from W.R.C since 20 Jan and the letter from W.S.C last night was the first since 28 Jan. Whenever a mail turns up here, I always rely (and get) one from you. I won't say anymore. Of course, I don't worry if I don't get any letters—I've been away too long for that, but I shan't be sorry when it is all over. Best wishes and all good luck

Yrs A

P.S. This is the longest letter I have written in N.

He is similarly chatty later in the month, especially with the news to share of the fire in the barracks Arnold had been staying in. John Thiesen, in his book Prisoners of War and Internees in Norway in World War 1 1914–1919, makes mention of a fire that happened in one of the Barracks in the afternoon of the 26 March 1917.

Arnold can shed more light on the situation as well informing on the continued desire to move men up to work on the railways again. He also reflects on the unsurprising importance of the letters from home and how often he returned to them for comfort and reassurance. It must have been disheartening to lose yet again what seems to have been most of his personal belongings, especially when he must have had so little that he could call his own. He points out that his letters from home were read and reread countless times and the photos helped him pass many a night.

31 March 1917 (from Partridge collection sent in by Alan Totten)

Dear Q,

As it is some time since I wrote to you, here is another of the series, in time about to welcome you back to Branksome and labour for another summer. Certainly time passes quick enough.

It becomes a habit to write and say there has been no mail for x days and there's nothing doing. However, the former is true when x = 8; in regard to the latter, our house was burnt to the ground last Monday night and there is to be a church service tomorrow.

The fire broke the monotony a bit. We are having a housewarming at present. An interned housewarming means you have pulled all the salvage out of various sacks and boxes and separated the socks out of the frying pans and cleared trousers from a mixture of tooth powder, soda and sugar—but man is only born to trouble as the sparks fly upwards—and no life was lost.

I enclose a photo (of him skiing) which may cause you to smile. This is an awful country for weather. The thaw had progressed favourably and half the snow had gone. Then, suddenly, it started to snow hard and we were subjected to a day of it and the thaw starts over again.

I hope your summer term proves successful. I am sorry that all your letters were destroyed last Monday.

They are hustling about a bit to try and get some of us up to Hjerkinn on the railway job. I suppose this in order to relieve congestion in the rooms.

Just before going to that uncertainty last year I sent home all my photos and things. I used to pass many an evening looking at them;—There is no decoration or comfort about the present quarters. Possibly, however, I shall paint them and then there will be another fire or earthquake—perhaps even the war will end, but the day of miracles is over.

Ever yours A

P.S. many thanks indeed for your letter of the 11th just arrived.

The mail seems to be arriving more frequently to Fåberg by April and it cheers Arnold immensely to have regular contact with his beloved family. He is quick to reassure them that he is physically fit even if he struggles mentally. The 6 April letter answers a question that had been on my mind. In many of the photos the internees are going about their business or leisure without guards being present.

The granddaughter of Charles Nelson pointed out to me that in one of the photos taken of the whole crew the armed guards can be seen watching closely from the top of hill behind all the British Internees. In this letter, Arnold informs Queenie that "of course, the soldiers stood behind the camera," so even though leisure activities were allowed they were still usually done under the supervision of armed soldiers.

My dear Q,

About every Friday now we get a few letters. Yours of 15 Mar, RFC's of 18 Mar turned up trumps today. Many thanks indeed for yours. It makes life worth living to get them.

I should lie to read an essay by you on the artful artisan and the harassed householder; hitherto the trouble of houses have been spared to me, so I do not feel that kindred feeling.

You need not worry about us. We shan't starve until this country goes to war, which is not at all likely. Variety is the soul of life (and food) and we raise the wind frequently.

Casting the mind back over past years, one wonders whether Good Friday's over times in Glasgow were not worlds better than this. It is snowing like blazers now and a week ago we thought the snow was all gone.

I have forgotten if I have previously foisted on you one of the enclosed photographs. Since the fire I have gone a drift a bit on letters because my letter sack and contents perished. However, it shows you I am alright and nothing to be proud of. Of course the soldiers stood behind the camera; don't turn away with the idea we roam at our own sweet will.

It is a work of energy to do any carpentry or write a letter nowadays. Even in a letter the news is forced, so please excuse this and it is hard to settle in the new quarters.

The book "Bindle", which WSC sent, has cheered all hands. It is going all round and making a laugh.
Best wishes for a successful summer term.
Yours A[21]

One of the hardest things for Arnold when faced with the task of writing letters home on a regular basis was to find things to talk about. His days had a repetitive pattern to them, as you would imagine and he struggled to find different topics to write about it, but he desperately wanted and needed to stay connected.

9 April, he promises, "I am going to try and drop talking about war and weather, but it will be a hard job." He then goes on to talk about men returning from leave to find the barracks burned down and speaks half-heartedly about a Bridge game.

---

[21] The Bindle book Winnie sent Arnold was written by Herbert John Jenkins and published in early 1916. The humourous books centered on the character Mr Joseph Bindle and were very popular through war times.

The latest spasm is the fact that the 9 who were on leave in England return tonight. They won't half do a moan, when on returning from a comfortable home in Blighty, they have to sort out their salvage from the dump. I have never been (nor ever wish to) a rummage or 'great' sale at reduced prices, but I cannot make a shrewd guess at its going on.

F tells me that you will be at Branksome all Easter on the gardening stunt. I wish I could be there to help you, even tho here one can sit with the legs up on a rest and smoke all day. There was a bridge tournament recently. It goes without saying my partner and I went down.

We were only there to make up the number. It was only a case of dealing the cards. Our opponents just took up the tricks and the points. Perhaps, I am lucky, but don't know it.

As I shall shortly expect a caustic letter of reproof from you, I had better retain a portion of brains to reply there to meanwhile, Ever Yrs, A

One of the most interesting letters in the whole collection is one that I discovered in the papers of author John Thiesen. I have found no other letters that relate to the one he writes of, so I am having to fill the gaps.

23 April 1917
My dear Q,

Perhaps you will be surprised at yet another letter, but there is something I fancy I can explain easier to you than anyone else.

It was intimated to me on Sat 21 Apr that Commander Kennedy had received a letter from the Secretary to the Admiralty concerning me. I was up at Lillehammer today and saw the letter which was to the effect that I should seek employment outside.

It seems to be rather out of proportion to trouble the Secretary of the Admiralty with the employment of interned ERA's when there is the submarine menace to occupy them.

Who wrote to the admiralty about me?

The reply will probably be to the effect that the person in question has not mingled at all with the Norwegians and has taken no trouble to learn the language; that probably during the ensuing summer months he will he working on the railway job up at Hjerkinn; any other job would involve protracted negotiations with trade unions etc (this caused the delay last year); moreover the cost of living is extraordinarily high; more so, now that America has come into the war.

Then I may as well tell you that for a long time, nine men have been all ready and only wait the word to go on leave. In the batch which follows them is my chance.

You long do you think the war is going to last?

Ever Yrs, A

It seems to me that a member of the family, Queenie or Father I would think, have written to the Admiralty expressing their concern with Arnold's mental health and well-being. They have obviously done this without him knowing. I have only seen one letter to the Admiralty from the family and that was the one written by R Feaver in the weeks after the sinking.

It would not surprise me, seeing how quickly R Feaver sought to get information on Arnold's well-being in the early days that he would do so again if he had concerns; however, Arnold seemed to try and hide his innermost thoughts from everyone but Queenie so maybe it was her. Saying this, I cannot really discount any member of the family as I feel that they all would have been trying to make Arnold's life as bearable as possible.

This is one of the things that I hope continued research will find an answer to. Arnold is quick to show that he knows the exact reason he is not high on the list for employment outside of the camp—he has no desire to make a home in Norway. All he wants is to go home. He does not want to learn the language or get to know the locals. He wants to be with his family in Gravesend or New Milton or even back out at sea doing his part for the war effort and not in Norway behind barbed wire fences being watched constantly by armed guards. His next letter (12 May) once again finds him struggling with things to write about and the promise to not talk about the war is broken.

Every night this week we've been for a good long walk doing between 8-12 miles after supper. Of course, correct thing would also be to do physical exercises before breakfast but I gave that up after the first nine months here.

There seems to be plenty in the papers nowadays about meetings, conferences and interviews, but in the majority of cases it seems they are 'words, idle words', for things go on much the same, all save prices which rise steadily.

It is hard to write a letter week after week, when one hasn't got one to reply to and still less news to put in it so best wishes and good luck.
Yours A

What was happening in the camp?

Arnold was not the only one struggling with the monotony of living in the camp. While conducting my research I contacted the Scandinavian Philately Society and their President put me in contact with Patricia Adams who was incredibly helpful.

Patricia was familiar with the work of Roger Partridge who was the man who I think had purchased most of the collection from the sale in Hampshire in 1984. Patricia had copies of a lot of Roger's writings as well as a small collection of her own including the postcards from Herbert Ripley to his son Bert from early 1916. She also has two postcards from early 1917.

They are written by Able Seaman Frederick Ernest Sampson to Mr & Mrs J Carter, Police Station, Stoke Holy Cross, Norwich, Norfolk. Research finds that Frederick was born in Suffolk in 1877 and enlisted in 1893. After the war he joined the Police Force as in the 1939 register we find him listed as a First Police Reserve and he is married to Gertrude. He died in Norfolk in 1953.

The two surviving postcards written by Frederick Sampson are both from early 1917 and both written to Mr and Mrs Carter. I have been unable to find out anything about the Carter's but the letters are signed with a degree of formality and so, it seems unlikely they were close family members. Frederick, like Arnold, thanks the Carters for letters and gifts but struggles to find positive things to say about his life in the camp.

26 January
Many thanks for apples, they are splendid but had a good knocking about, only part of the box arrived here, pleased to hear you are all as usual, as this leaves one fairly fed up, been here too long, very cold here now, but let's hope the end is nearer than we think, haven't any interesting news as usual so trusting this will find you all in best of health, with best wishes from yours sincerely, F.E Sampson.

18ᵗʰ March

Many thanks for your letter of 3ʳᵈ, came rather quick, glad you got the frames allright (sic), I thought they would suit you especially being made from the old box, they've really been further than you have, if I could get away I'd give you a hand with the garden but no luck yet for a while by the looks of things but hope you will have a good crop of everything, no exciting news from me as usual. Best wishes from F.E Sampson.

The boredom of camp life meant that for some internees the opportunity to escape it all by drinking in local bars or creating a bit of trouble proved too tempting. An article from a local history book, *Faberg og Lillehammer—Ek lokalskrift utgitt av Fåberg Historielag,* sheds light on the trouble a small number of the English internees could get up to both inside and outside of the camp and early 1917 features a couple of notable incidents.

In January, the station master complained that a small group of the English interns from Jørstadmoen were arrested for disorder and intoxication. Private Albert Hopkins and fireman W Price were sentenced to three days in prison after their big day out. This was followed in March by an incident in the camp. It is described in the article:

"March 17, there was a great spectacle in camp. Some Englishmen who have been in town were full when they returned. The worst were Haars (I think this is supposed to be Fireman S Hawes) and Jack Philip (Private). Jack Philip has returned from Akershus (a prison) a few days before where he had spent 30 days.

When they came into the camp, one of the guards was supposed to take him and have him on the square, but this was probably not to the Englishman's taste. He flew at the guard and struck him on the head, the guard shot at him with the revolver but did not hit. The Englishmen inside the fence kept storming this, including Felice Spiteri (Fireman) and Edward McKeever (Stoker).

There have also been tales that have drifted down through descendants of internees that report of another attempted escape from camp in the first half of 1917. One of Commander Kennedy's descendants relates that "on 30 June 1917, two runaways were put in front of the martial court in Kristiania. One got 45 days of arrest, the other got 35 days."

I cannot say for sure who these men were, although records show that Trimmer Frederick Haddow spent time in Kongsberg and Kongsvinger prisons and Fireman Charles Temple was at Dombås. Maybe they had attempted another escape?

Life may have been more settled for those who had managed to obtain precious leave and visit home. Indeed, it must have been so interesting that getting a few back to Norway proved to be a bit of a challenge. The National Archive Prisoner of War files for 1917 contain a telegraph from Mr Findlay at the Legation in Christiania enquiring after Keats, Summerfield, Wright, Hammond, and Buck, all of whom had leave that had expired over four weeks ago. Six days later, he is reassured by W Graham Greene that "the ratings are en route to Norway."

Things were not as challenging for the Officers. Many of them seemed to just be living close to normal lives albeit in a different location. Charles Nelson, Chief Engineer/Chief of Staff, writes to his bank on Cornhill in London on 23 January to *Please keep those in your care until such a time as I may return to England and place any I may send from time to time to my current account.* I am not sure that the interned crew were spending much time thinking about their bank accounts.

The one thing that is rare when researching the internee mail from Jørstadmoen are letters written to or from sweethearts. I suppose that these private missives were either protected or destroyed and so didn't make it into the sales or collector's market. However, a lovely letter from early 1917 was amongst the items Roger Partridge had in his vast collection. It is written from a Miss F Baker to Rob, who I and Roger have been able to confirm as Seaman Robert Charles Maynard. The letter reads:

Miss F Baker
27 St. Jude Street
Bethnal Green
19.1.17
My dearest Rob,

I now take the greatest pleasure in writing this letter to you but I am sorry to tell you that at present I feel really ill and it's a wonder I am here but never mind God is good and I am still safe at present. Say dear, I received two letters from you today and I am answering yours of the 12th, you say dear that the bunk is doing a roaring trade well I think that's the best place when its cold out and you dear will take care of yourself.

Say dear you tell me that you were sorry to put me to so much trouble that's all right Dear I only hope to God that you will be with me soon and all I can say I hope you will repay me "well" you know. Dear Rob, I daresay you will be surprised to hear what I have to tell you but Tom has been taken in the London Hospital on the last—as got to go under an operation so you can guess Dear something is wrong.

I don't believe you would know him if you were to see him really he looks terrible but we must hope that he gets over it all right. He was supposed to go back the night he wrote that letter to you what I have sent but of cause he was to (sic) ill to go back. Now dear, I do hope that you get what you want you say you will get me some more cards when the weather permits you right you are but take care of yourself; now Dear, you must forgive me but I cannot write more tonight so must now close with best love and wishes.

Your loving sweetheart, Florrie xxxxxxxxxxxxxxxxxxxx
Best respects from all at home.
Good night and God Bless You

I think that the things I find most endearing about this letter are the fact that she signs off as his sweetheart and the at least 20 kisses that are included at the end of the letter. I could not leave it not knowing what happened next and a quick search on my favourite genealogy site happily revealed that Rob and Florrie married in the third quarter of 1917 in Bethnal Green, so I can only assume that he was lucky enough to get leave and used his leave time wisely to marry the girl he loved.

My later contact with his family confirmed that he was married in September of 1917. Records show that he was back in the camp in Norway by February 1918 as he was one of the performers in the Variety concert.

Things are even rosier for the Commander as he welcomes the birth of his son on the 29 April. The birth notice reads "On Sunday 29 April at Fair View, Lillehammer, to Fédora the wife of Commander W.G.A Kennedy, R.N., late HMS "India", prisoner of war interned in Norway—a son." [22] It becomes increasingly obvious that the Commanders experiences of internment are completely different from the ones being had by his crew.

---

[22] This clip was in a collection of scans sent to me by Sindre Torp, a Norwegian gentleman, who had been involved (in collaboration with the Barltrop's) in attempting to develop a website about the sinking of *HMS India* and the internment of her crew.

What were the family doing?

Stability is still the norm for the rest of the Clarke family with Dorothy working on the farm in Dorset, Edith teaching at Dartford, Queenie teaching at Branksome and Winnie still lecturing at Homerton. Father is living at 9 The Avenue in Gravesend. Wilfred spends the start of the year at Woolwich in the Carriages Department, but the second part of the year sees a change for him as well as a couple of changes of scenery for Arnold.

Two photographs of the hut fire from the collection of Seaman Robert Charles Maynard. An amazing shot of the fire as it burned and then the charred remains. It remains unclear as to whether the fire was deliberately lit or not.

Second Half of 1917 – "I Regret My Letters Often Get Left Unwritten Nowadays."

The summer of 1917 was a cool and wet one in England but was fine enough in Norway for swimming and walking. Whilst having these pleasant enough activities available to him they were still not enough to distract Arnold from the ever-present reality that he was nearing the two-year anniversary of having been torpedoed and imprisoned in Norway. His letters of July and August hold little in the way of optimism and much in the way of defeatism, loneliness, frustration, and sadness.

19 July 1917
Dear Q,

Many thanks for your letter of 3 Jul. I am impressed by your subtle invitation to New Milton and to bring a screwdriver and hammer with me.

However, work and I have fallen out. It was once explained to me that "in the sweat of one—etc, etc", bread and clothing were earned. That, like a lot of other things, is a fallacy. I get board, lodging and clothing, free gratis and for nothing.

I cannot imagine what England must be like with all its restrictions and the new Women's Franchise. Let's see, you just top it, don't you? They certainly can't make much more of a hash of things. I have certainly given up hope. I suppose a bomb or so round a few prelates or politicians back gardens might shift things a bit. Meanwhile—things go on (or back).

Last Sunday, one man started to go mad. A day later he turned into a raving homicidal maniac and was taken to Gjovik Asylum in a motorcar. It shows what can be done.

A statue of justice as adapted for Norway should show the sword's edges, jagged and round; the scales weighted and the bandage cocked up over one eye.

The days pass quickly enough. Swimming, tennis, reading and walking. At one time I was rather fearful of the time when friends and relatives would take me to task for all the sins of omission and commission during this period, but I don't care a rap now for the odds are not much that way inclined.

I do not know where you have elected to pass the summer holidays, so am sending this letter home.

I enclose a few issues of used Norwegian stamps, which I request you turn over to E.R.C. The 2/40 ore specimens have (I am told) only been in circulation since 1 July 1917.

Best wishes to all,

Yours A

The lack of incoming mail also wears on Arnold as the only thing that seems to keep him going a lot of the time is the regular letters from his father, brother and sisters. He sends a brief postcard to his father who is on holidays in Wales saying, *Please excuse P.C. I have put off writing night after night in the hopes of a letter coming through, but none seem to come. Your last letter was very near a month ago. I hope all goes well.*

Nothing much else to say. Yrs, A

Only two days later, on 9 August, a letter to Queenie reveals exactly how low Arnold's feelings have sunk when he relates that he thinks he might have been better off being one of the casualties of the torpedo attack.

My dear Q,

Many thanks indeed for your pc of 22 July arrived tonight. I regret my letters often get left unwritten nowadays—owing to being absolutely despondent nowadays.

There is all this talk of the secure preparations for 1918 and 1919. It would appear that I am never to see you again. Still it's no use worrying.

The time passes quickly enough, but it knocks the stuffing out of you, considering that in 8 weeks the thermometer will be permanently under zero for another dreary desolate 8 months. Honestly, the supreme casualty list seems to be about the best off.

Best wishes to all

Yours A

Six days later and he is in slightly higher spirits and composes a letter reporting on a list of his day-to-day activities. He still cannot help but refer to the war and questions, *I wonder how many are enjoying it?*

My dear Q,

It is over a week since anything arrived, so one must stop putting off writing. Your two cards were the last arrivals (15 and 22 July). By the time this letter gets home, you will have finished your holiday, (which I hope was successful) and will be packing for another Michaelmas term. Almost I find myself wishing you a Merry Christmas.

About now, many millions souls will be tightening up the belt and setting the jaw a little firmer while the oldest game in the world goes on for another winter (?). I wonder how many are enjoying it.

The swallows are getting ready to fly now and in a fortnight we shall have a frost and an end to bathing. Yet somehow time passes fairly quickly. Monday is, de rigeur laundry day; last Monday our stove jibbed. In five minutes it's 29 component parts were laying out on the grass. Then followed a feline-like expedition to the tiles and a go at the flue.

Having disposed of 2 pails full of dirt, ash and soot, I assembled it and it goes fine now. It was like old times, being hot and dirty. I know I shall get yours to do IF ever I reach your place.

Last Thursday, there was a dance in a small way in the camp, but I wasn't there. Next Sunday, the keener spirits are getting up another. A ticket is enclosed, but as distance intervenes, you need not worry to come.

The immediate water supply of this barrack consists of two pails behind the doors. Their existence is known to many. We are quite used to cats and dogs assuaging their thirst from them but recently as I was sitting reading, two young bulls from a neighbouring herd of cattle walked in and drank the lot.

I will not wander into political news, but there is—money in circulation, all the breweries are on strike throughout the country and we are having homegrown cauliflowers, turnips, new potato and cherry tart tomorrow for dinner.

Meanwhile, I remain, with best wishes to all,

Ever yours, A

The last letter of the summer of 1917 vacillates between chatty news and uncharacteristically damning views on those in positions of superiority. Arnold has yet to have leave and leave has been granted to many men at the camp by this stage. He must have been thinking that his turn would come soon but it does not look like he was given any indication of when.

He writes of an inspection by General Buller but has little faith that it will change things for the men behind the barbed wire. In fact, he has little faith that anything will result in change for the men imprisoned at Fåberg.

24 August 1917
My dear Q,

Many thanks indeed for your letter of 29 July, with its description of the prize givings. I am glad it was a success. You will be well into the Michaelmas term by the time this letter arrives. (By the way, I always thought you didn't hanker for a cap and gown—being above the pomp and vanities.)

It is the hardest job imaginable to write a letter nowadays. The reversion from summer to winter depresses one beyond measure.

I got hold of a stray photograph recently so am enclosing it. It shows the refreshment bar for the 1st dance. There was a dance last Saturday night. It rained in torrents. I only stayed 10 minutes and then packed up—fed up. My dancing days are over.

General Buller from the British Legation was here last Wednesday to investigate things in general. It was a chance to hear someone who spoke English. It's a rotten shame about the leave, but I suppose if the legation people are quite comfortable with their relatives and friends near them, a fat cigar and 3 good square meals a day, it doesn't matter a nap about anything else, least of all us, whose kindred interests presumably they represent.

We have got a cavalry unit on the—now. After getting so used to the old bugle calls it came as a shock to hear a smart trumpeter on the job. It recalls old times.

The last few days we have been doing well out of our little allotment. Out of 55 turnip plants planted 47 came up successful. The peas are good, but not enough. No flowers for me if I ever get a garden.

It's all very well people saying, "it can't be much longer" and all that. We have heard that yarn before—months ago. A bomb or so round some of the

Bishops and politicians' quarters would prove an aid to digestion. A big article appeared in neutral papers recently.

A personal statement by the Kaiser was to the effect that before he and his family starved, a fleet of aeroplanes is going to blow up Windsor Castle. (though I failed to see how that produces bread and butter). A further statement on tonight's paper by K Bell on W Front says that God "is going to do all sorts of terrible things to the 'hovedfienden' (that's the English). However, not the slightest tremor of this reaches here.
So yours, A

The next letter is dated 23 December. One of the reasons that there was a large amount of time between letters is that Arnold was finally granted leave. It is only through obscure references that I was able to work out that he got the chance to return home in November (I think) of 1917. Wilfred's obituary mentions how lucky it was that the two brothers got to spend time with each other when Arnold returned from Norway on leave.

Men who got the opportunity to travel home went in groups of 7-10 and could spend approximately 3 weeks at home with their families before returning to Norway. The British Government had an agreement with the Norwegian Government that all internees would be returned to the camp to see out their internment and not re-join the war.

Two days before Christmas Arnold writes to Queenie to apologise for missing her birthday and acknowledge the first mail that he has received since arriving back in Norway. He also comments on the arrival of new internees from the wrecking of the British trawler the "Lord Alverstone."

23 December 1917
My dear Q,

Tonight there arrived the first mail since we landed here. Your letter of 10th Dec arrived; you always turn up trumps. RFC's 'Observer', 'Graphics' and 'Punch' for week ending, 8 Dec also arrived. I am very grateful for them.

I entirely overlooked your birthday so tender my sincerest apologies. I also congrats on your part in Metric system debate. From the Engineering pt, it is ideal, but I rather fancy we were sort of pioneers in standardisation and measurements so it is really only the enormous cost that stands in the way.

There was a change here when the men of the out of convoy scrap came here to be interned. They are the only survivors (except for some in Germany) off the convoying trawlers and—poor beggars—they have had a hard time of it.

It is bitterly cold here now. 25 degrees Celsius. I have bought a grand pair of skis and had some good runs on them.

When I started to come back, I had good resolutions. One is kept pretty busy though in the numerous little domestic duties, mainly of having wood and drawing water, but at other times I cannot settle down to any occupation, just smoking and thinking.

I don't know what sort of show Christmas will be here, but I don't care a nap now. Give my love to N and tell her I have kept the pudding for Christmas. I have turned out a curry supper since I came back. It was a success.
There's to be a dance for Boxing Night, I believe.
With best wishes,
Yours, A

What was happening in the camp?

July started with an official count of all the men in camp. The number on the 17 July was 78 names. From what I can tell this did not include all the officers who were still living outside of the camp but still considered to be interned. Soon after this, a smaller group of men returned to Hjerkinn to continue working on the railway, Arnold did not appear to be among them. His leave application might have had something to do with this, but this is conjecture on my part as I do not really know why he did not go.

Late August brought with it a visit from Sir Hon. Henry Yarde-Buller. Yarde-Buller had worked as Military attaché prior to and during WW1 and from 28 December 1916 he was Military Attaché (General Staff Officer), Christiania and Stockholm. Created a C.B in 1917 and a K.B.E in 1919, he was sent to the camp by the Legation at Christiania to see how the men were faring and try and deal with the ever-present rumbling dissatisfactions of some of the men.

Arnold refers to his visit in his letter of 24 August, but whilst he was happy to hear another English voice, he didn't hold out much hope for any significant change in circumstances for the interned men—*but I suppose if the legation people are quite comfortable with their relatives and friends near them, a fat cigar and 3 good square meals a day, it doesn't matter a nap about anything else, least of all us, whose kindred interests presumably they represent.* He might have been right.

Yarde-Buller took a few weeks to get his report together but when he did it was a lengthy one. On the 18 September, the official report was passed onto Mr Findlay at the legation in Christiania and then shared with the Foreign Office. Yarde-Buller reports that Commander Kennedy was indisposed "but kindly placed an automobile at my disposal and detailed Lieutenant Alltree, one of the officers on duty for the month, to accompany me."[23]

He describes the camp as being "10 kilometres from Lillehammer" with plenty of space around the buildings, a recreation room provided "due to Commander Kennedy's initiative" and ample grounds which include a football field. There are reported to be about 40 men in the camp with a further approximately 30 away at Hjerkinn and few employed at the Legation in Kristiania.

The first issue Yarde-Buller investigates is that of the victuals provided for the interned men as there had been complaints about the lack of fresh fruit and vegetables, the hardness of the meat and constant problems with the milk. He states, "I saw the milk which was, as stated above, quite undrinkable." He then met with men from the different barracks to hear complaints—"I said a few words and then asked them to speak out, frankly."

He comments that most of the complaints were ones that he already knew about and then, a bit dismissively in my opinion, he states, "I particularly remarked two men as being the type of habitual grumblers and this was subsequently corroborated by Lieutenants Alltree and Nelson." He then goes on to list the complaints as:

a) Insufficient change of blankets.
b) Lack of clothing (they were supplied with Norwegian Navy uniforms when they arrived and some had supplemented with clothes sent from home or bought in nearby shops).
c) Poor quality of food.
d) The question of limited leave.

Yarde-Buller starts by saying that he has requested that the milk supplier be put on notice and then sums things up by stating that "I do not consider that the

---

[23] The Yarde-Buller report transcripts are from The National Archives file FO 383/449

men have any cause for complaint beyond the hardship of a long internment in a neutral country owing to war exigencies."

He outlines that they can walk for two hours in the morning and in the afternoon and the "privileged" men get a further two hours. All of this is without an armed guard or "escort." He also points out that they are allowed occasional visits to Lillehammer and that special applications for leave are seldom refused.

He reflects that all men have been offered work on the railway and "those who for whatever reason have elected to stay in camp appear to have got into a mental condition, due no doubt to the length of their confinement, which exaggerates irksomeness of their position. He then makes recommendations:

- He recommends that the interior discipline of the camp is handed over from the Norwegian guards to the British officers.
- Complaints should be immediately made to the attending British Officer "this would have the effect of preventing the men from harbouring grievances which often grow into imaginary hardships".
- A British officer should always be present at the daily rations issue.
- The internees should be measured and supplied with new British Naval Uniform and boots.
- A supply of naval tobacco, leaf and tin should be supplied periodically.

When I first read this report my initial feeling was that Yarde-Buller was quite dismissive of the feelings of the interned men but with further thought I wonder that there really was not much else he was able to do above and beyond what he did. These men were being held as prisoners and they could have been in far worse situations than what they were in. It was not the thing to send counsellors in for the men to talk to and so whilst Yarde-Buller recognised that the men were struggling with their mental health at that time and in that place, there was nothing more he could really do than to try and provide distractions and make them comfortable. He could not do the one thing that so many of them wanted and that was to allow them to return home, permanently.

Attached to the report written by General Yarde-Buller were the official regulations for the camp and they make clearer the rules around leaving the camp for exercise or visits to Lillehammer. Men could go for walks in groups of no more than four without an armed guard accompanying them, but no more than twenty men were allowed out of the camp at the one time. These rules, however, only applied to those who did not meet the criteria below:

"All men who have not signed a declaration that they will not attempt to escape men who have not been photographed and men who for some other reason—such as bad behaviour in or outside camp—cannot have the same freedom but may be permitted to go for walks with a guard from 10-12 p.m. and 2-4 p.m."

The regulations also state that "All requests for permission to Lillehammer or extra must be given to Petty Officer Hines, otherwise they will not be considered."

The poor mental health of some of the men was highlighted most by the tragic case of John Thomas Wells. Arnold wrote in his letter of 19 July, *Last Sunday one man started to go mad. A day later he turned into a raving homicidal maniac and was taken to Gjovik Asylum in a motorcar. It shows what can be done.*

I am confident that the man he was referring to was 38-year-old, Able Seaman John Thomas Wells. From the time Wells is taken from the camp we find nothing about him until the sad letter dated 8 November that has been kept in the file at the National Archives.[24] The letter reads:

"Sir,

I have the honour to confirm herewith my telegram of the 20 October 1917 reporting the death of John Thomas Wells, Able Seaman RFR o.n 187363, which sad event took place suddenly at Prestestæter Asylum near Gjovik on 20 October.

Owing to the very awkward communications between Gjovik and Jørstadmoen, he was buried privately at Gjovik on 26 October. Four of his shipmates accompanied by a sergeant of the guard were allowed to attend the funeral.

I enclose a copy of the death certificate and also a list of private effects of the late A B Wells, as to the disposal I await your lordships command.

The address of his wife is:

Mrs Fanny Wells

5 Sherwood Street

Bromley-by-Bow

London."

---

[24] Letter can be found at The National Archives file FO 383/327

The most heart-breaking sentence, for me, in this official letter is "which sad event took place suddenly at Prestestæter Asylum." It seems clear that John Thomas Wells took his own life in this Norwegian Asylum on his own, away from all he knew and loved. One can only imagine how shocking this must have been for many of the men at Jørstadmoen. They would have been witness to a man going mad, a madness that led to his eventual suicide.

Back in the camp, life was also proving extremely challenging for another member of the H.M.S *India* crew. The Scandinavian Prisoner of War files for 1917, held in the National Archives, contain several letters concerning the plight of Private Albert North Hopkins, a career sailor who had joined the Navy in 1901 but had taken leave prior to the war and become a commercial traveller selling soap. He re-joined the Navy at the start of the war. In a typed letter dated 13 November 1917 and written to Waldorf Astor Esq, Private Hopkins outlines his troubles:

"Sir,

My weight is now about 6 stone 3lbs. Am in bed, with the doctor attending me.

If I die, please do your best for my wife and child, at 31 Queen Street, Plymouth, Devon. Service 4 years in Marines, then invalided. 9 ½ years on Royal Fleet Reserve, then invalided. When war broke out in the Wiltshire's a few months and then the marines.

Yours respectfully,

(sd) A.N Hopkins"

In December, obviously not having received a satisfactory reply yet from Astor, Hopkins attempts to find support from the Lady's Emergency Committee of the Navy League. On the 13 December he writes:

"Dear Miss Matheson,

Just a line to let you know, I am in bed and do not think I have long to live. I am about 6 stone 3lbs now.

Why I am kept here I don't know.

Yours respectfully,

Pte A.N Hopkins

Age nearly 42"

Three days later Commander Kennedy gets involved and writes to the Admiralty that he "has the honour to report that Private A.N Hopkins is in an indifferent state of health. He is very thin and anaemic and today has been sent to hospital suffering from giddiness. The camp doctor has, at my request, had Hopkins under special observation for some months and endeavoured, at my request, to have him surveyed by a Norwegian medical board with a view of invaliding him".

Kennedy writes that he has been informed that the only grounds for invaliding are cancer, lunacy or pulmonary complaints and so requests that the Admiralty could seek a "prolonged leave of absence" for Hopkins. It is 13 February when Mr Findlay from the Legation confirms that "Private Hopkins also J.T Wright repatriated considered unfit for Military service."

The final event for the camp in 1917 was the arrival of approximately twelve new British men. The trawler *Lord Alverstone* had only recently been built and was requisitioned by the Admiralty and turned into a mine sweeper. It was acting as a convoy escort to a Scandinavian fleet with other British vessels when SMS Emden and destroyers of the German Third Half Flotilla attacked them.

The *Lord Alverstone* was sunk but all twelve of its crew were rescued and taken to Jørstadmoen where they joined the seventy or so *India* crew who had now been there almost two and a half years. I wonder if the new faces were a welcome change.

What were the family up doing?

Things had continued to remain static for most of the Clarke clan but by saying this, it does not mean that they did not notice the war around them every day. R Feaver had brought his family up in the Kent seaside town of Gravesend and he continued to live there with Nurse Bates with his daughters and Wilfrid making frequent visits.

Gravesend is situated on the Thames Estuary and so, found itself the witness and the victim of air raids during the war. The air raids were conducted by Zeppelins and Gotha planes who used the River Medway and the River Thames as navigation aides to help them find their way to London. There are reports of Zeppelins dropping incendiary bombs on Gravesend in 1915, 1916 and 1917 with damage to property but fortunately, no serious casualties were reported.

The sight of the Zeppelins looming above must have been a terrifying sight for the townspeople of Gravesend and in 1916 they were able to see the Zeppelins come down in flames in Essex, across the estuary, on three separate occasions. Gravesends proximity Chatham, which was a major port and Navy training town and therefore a target for the Germans, would have also explained the frequency of air attacks.

In September 1917, the barracks of HMS Pembroke were hit and destroyed. These may have been the very barracks that Arnold had stayed in when training in 1914/15. R Feaver and Edith (in Dartford) would have been very aware of this war being fought right on their doorsteps as well as on the continent.

Queenie would also have been very aware of the war with the New Forest being somewhat of a hub for training and being a staging post for troops preparing to leave for the continent. So much was going on in the New Forest it would have been hard not to be aware! There were airfields being built in Beaulieu and Calshot and a grenade school and trench mortar school that later merged to become the Southern Command Bombing School would have been making a regular racket.

A War Dog Training School was set up in the Forest with trenches being dug for training purposes. I wrote earlier about the Indian Hospital but there was also a hospital for injured New Zealand troops and a cemetery holds the remains of almost one hundred New Zealand soldiers.

The war also influenced the Forest itself. New Forest Ponies were taken to be trained to be war horses and most never returned. Much of the Forest itself was felled as Timber was needed for the war effort. Troops were brought in from as far away as Canada to assist in the preparation of timber and then later coal and from the Southampton docks ship loads of men were being transported across the channel to encounter the hell that was trench warfare in France and Belgium.

Wilfrid was the one to experience the greatest amount of change in 1917. He had arrived back from the front in the first half of 1916 and was sent to Woolwich to assist in the design and engineering of weaponry, but his mind had obviously been on greater things and on 21 August 1917 a letter [25] was written to his superiors at Woolwich:

"The service of this Officer is applied for by the Royal Flying Corps for instruction in aviation. He has served 6 months in France and has been passed fit for the above duties. Can he be spared please and if so, may he be ordered to report forthwith to the Commandant School of Military Aeronautics, Reading, taking camp kit with him.

Captain for Major G.S"

---

[25] Found in Wilfrid's file at The National Archives WO 339/14533

There are handwritten notes following this letter that was found in Wilfrid's file in the National Archives and by late September he had commenced his training where he was "enthusiastically devoted to this work and made good progress, passing his examinations successfully."[26]

Before heading to Grantham for further training, Wilfrid managed to get a few days at home where serendipitously he managed to cross paths with Arnold who had "obtained leave for a month on parole in England—and arriving had three days with his brother."[27] What a reunion that must have been for the two brothers who had not seen each other for maybe as long as three years. What joy it must have been for R Feaver to have his two sons together even if for only three days. How bittersweet knowing what was to unfold over the next few months.

On the 23 December Wilfrid wrote to Queenie in what is the only surviving letter from his time at the Royal Flying Corps in Grantham. It is written on official paper but is a jolly, light-hearted letter that must have been treasured.

My dear Queenie,

I remember you saying how unfortunate it was to have a birthday just before Christmas because people usually amalgamated the events as far as gifts were concerned. I am afraid you will think I have done this with my letter. But really it is not the case. Just lately I have been going hell-for-leather and although I made one strenuous effort to toddle down to Grantham and invest in something for you, it fizzled out at useless.

But this is no bar to me wishing you many happy returns of the day today and as you will probably get it on Christmas Day, also a very happy Christmas.

I hope you will make things fairly hop at St Brendan's (Aunt Di's House in Wimbledon). Raise the place out of the dusty reveries of a year. Fickle old Goss and make Mary fairly nip about.

What about the old moke? Do give it a lump of sugar from me and also a good dig in its fat old ribs.

Bye the bye before I leave the present subject. What would you like? I remember you saying that there were two things that made Mac's eyes sparkle one was whiskey and the other a cheque.

Which of these would you prefer? If any (and state reason).

---

[26] Wilfrid's obituary

[27] Wilfrid's obituary

I have been absolutely throttled by duties of all descriptions just lately. But I am trying not to lose sight of the fact that I am here to fly. Among other things I am taking a gas course!

But now I really must turn in as I was up betimes this morning training two machines.

And with the cheeriest of wishes to one and all.

Good-by-ee

From Wilfrid."

MATHS. TRIP. CANTAB.

A letter and postcard from 1917.

Last Thursday, there was a dance in a small way in the
Camp, but I wasn't there.   Next Sunday, the keener
spirits are getting up another.

A ticket is enclosed, but as
distance intervenes, you nee[d]
not worry to come.

The immediate water
supply of this barrak con[sists]
of two pails behind the ~~doors~~.   Their existen[ce]
is known to many.   We are quite used to cats &
dogs assuaging their thirst therefrom, but the oth[er]
one hot morning recently as I was sittin[g]
reading, two young bulls from a neighb[ouring]
herd of cattle, walked in & drank the [lot]

I will not wander into political [matters]
but there is iron money in circulation
all the breweries are on strike throughout
the country & we are having home gro[wn]
cauliflowers, turnips & new potatoes & cherry tart
To morrow for dinner

Meanwhile I remain, with best wishes to a[ll]
Ever yrs.
A.

RAC
SUNDAY
INVITATION
DANCE.
INTERNMENT CAMP, JØRSTADMOEN, 8 to 12 p.[m.]

From Seaman Robert Charles Maynard's collection, I love that this photograph shows the men in casual poses. I also love the name given to the postcard— The Mornings Argument.

From the collection of John Roland Anderson. I find it so tricky as I recognise so many of the faces now but still find it so hard to put names to them. I think Anderson is second from the right.

Two letters from 1917

A letter from Arnold which mentions his skiing prowess, or not. Photo ankle deep in snow, unsure of what year.

Blacksmiths at the camp—the one on the right is William Gardiner.

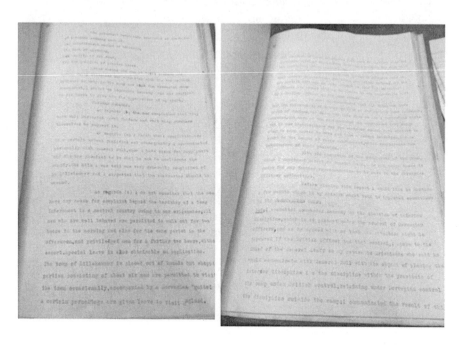

Yarde-Buller's report on conditions at the Jørstadmoen Internee camp as seen in the files at the National Archives.

50 TS.
ROYAL FLYING CORPS.
SPITTLEGATE, GRANTHAM
23-12-17

My dear Queenie

I remember you saying how unfortunate it was to have a birthday just before Christmas because people usually amalgamated the events as far as gifts were concerned. I am afraid you will think I have done this with my letter. But really it is not the case. Just lately I have been going Hell for leather and although I made one strenuous effort to toddle down to Grantham and invest in something for you, it fizzled out as useless.

But this is no bar to me wishing you many happy returns of the day. today and as you will probably get it on Christmas Day, also a very happy Christmas.

I hope you will make things fairly hot at St Brendan's. Rouse the place out of the dusty reverie of a year. Tickle old Coas, and make many fairly nip about.

Wilfrid's letter to Queenie written from the Royal Flying Corps at Grantham.

What about the old moke?
do give it a lump of sugar
from me, and also a good
dig in its fat old ribs.

Bye the bye before I leave
the present subject. What
would you like? I remember
you saying that there were
two things that made mac's
eyes sparkle one was whiskey
and the other a cheque.

Which of these would you
prefer? if any. (and state reasons)

I have been absolutely throttled
by duties of all descriptions
just lately. But I am trying
not to lose sight of the fact that
I am here to fly. Among
other things I am taking a
gas course! →

But now I
really must turn in
as I was up betimes
this morning dethroning
two machines
And with the cheeriest of
wishes to one + all
good-by-ee
from
Wilfrid

A Show in Camp - Fancy Dress 1917

First Half of 1918 –
"London Seems a Long Way Off."

1918 provides us with the largest amount of surviving mail with twenty-seven letters and cards across the year dating from the 1 January until only days before peace was called and the Allies claimed victory over the Triple Alliance. After being granted leave in late 1917 and being able to spend time back in Gravesend with his family, returning to Norway must have been disheartening for Arnold. This was exacerbated by the ever-present fact that he had no idea of how long he would remain in Norway and when he would see his family again. Would it be another 2 or more years?

The first letter is written on the first day of 1918 and provides updates on what is happening in the camp and how they saw the New Year. Arnold seems happy enough to socialise over card games or when skiing with others but seems to shy away from the party scene—he just cannot muster the enthusiasm to party when he feels there is no cause for partying.

My dear Q,

This is the first letter of the New Year and although a circular every Sunday seemed about the utmost output possible, somehow I thought I would write tonight as I don't seem to be able to turn my hand to anything.

I wonder how Christmas and the New Year passed with you. We had a sing song on Christmas night and a dance on Boxing night and of course, saw the New Year in. I didn't take an active part in either. I have had some good fast ski-runs and some good games of bridge in the evenings.

The net result of trying to knock off smoking is that all spare moments are spent smoking and thinking. There has only been your one letter as yet and there have been no other mails of any description and no news either for some time.

This afternoon I spent transferring etcetera's from the 1917 diary into the 1918; but it is no use trying to look forward yet, just plod on. The cafes and many other places like this out here, are closing down after today, owing to the times and I suppose, this is only the beginning.

Has any decision been reached yet, regarding the future life of No 9?

Four of the men are still working up Dourefjeld on the railway. They came down here for a holiday at Christmas. It is not a great catch up there, though, of course, it is absolutely out of touch with civilisation except at such time as they muster rucksack and cards for bread, coffee etc and go to fetch provisions. I don't know whether I shall go up there yet. Perhaps.

The 28 will bring another reminder of the passage of time, worse than New Year, but it soon slips by into the past and nothing happens.

The big Lillehammer ski jumping and long-distance running championship sports come off on the 10 and 11 February this year; they will certainly be worthwhile to go and watch.

It is about time I finished up now, so goodbye.

Ever yours, A

The letter includes a brief note to Nurse to thank her for the Christmas Pudding she has sent over which seems to have been shared around! *I want to thank you very much for the Christmas pudding. It was a huge success. I made some custard for it and also a curry the same evening. No one was ill!*

Skiing is the one thing during a cold Norwegian winter that keeps Arnold's spirits up and all his January letters mention time spent on the local slopes. On 11 January he writes, *We go skiing but there's not overmuch snow about. I usually managed to come in covered with ice and snow, which shows I still have a lot to learn in the art of steering, stopping and starting. In the woods today I passed a place where I was laid out last year, I successfully negotiated it this time.*

About ten days later the snow seems to have really come in allowing for more time to be spent out of the camp and perfecting technique on the skis—*It has snowed pretty nearly all this week; There is about 3 feet laying everywhere, but of course it is much warmer,—only 10 degrees of frost. We are planning some grand ski-ing picnics now the snow has come. I am possibly speculating in a second pair of skis.*

By the start of February, he relishes the freedom he gets when on the slopes—*There hasn't been much time for skiing, but one day I was out on the jumps; for a few times I landed like a crab—on my side, with skis uppermost. Eventually, I managed to do it correctly and though the style, take off, flight and landing were execrable, I managed to clear about 40 feet. Today, there was a dense white mist on the hills, which hid everything. It was rare sport dashing down at full speed with no guide at all. I had more falls than ever I have had for many a day.*

But there is no escaping the camp and the unavoidable actuality that he is still imprisoned and life in the camp in the middle of winter brings stress and agitation to many who are in there with him—*As regards food, there was a bit of a row at New Year. The authorities cut down things a bit, but we wouldn't take salt tack. We get the same as the civil population, but you cannot buy anything in shops without cards and restaurants have nothing but a small drink of sugarless coffee to offer.*

There are, however, still efforts, on the part of many, to make life in camp bearable and even fun. Arnold has written of the dances and sing songs that he did not take part in but on the 3 February (as related in the 5 February letter) Arnold does take part in a concert.

Yesterday, after a lapse of 23 months, another concert was arranged. There is not much use in describing it, so I enclose you a programme and also another for the collection. As the concert was over at 10:30 p.m., permission was given to have an impromptu dance, till midnight. Although I was in working rig, I had some good dances.

We are so lucky that the programme from this night still exists, in fact we still have both copies that were sent from the camp in 1918. It has been put together by someone with wry sense of humour with the front page stating that the "Varieties Theatre, Jørstadmoen" is hosting a "Grand Concert at The Internment Camp."

The inside of the programme lists the acts as put on by thirteen of the men, there is a collection of songs and sketches over two parts that look highly entertaining. Around the outside of the programme is a border with mock advertisements for mock businesses run by the internees. W.H Oakley advertises that "ASSETS. Bought, Lent, Sold or exchanged". H Hill states that "Special Notice. Reduce your Weight. The only sure remedy." All men are reminded "BATHS! Open Wednesdays & Saturdays. Inspection invited. Don't miss one."

Handwritten in one box is "Dovrebanens Anlægget. 1000 Navvies wanted. Knowledge of Norse not required (only blasting) Payment by results. 1 Krone per her perhaps. Men with webbed feet preferred." A box in the lower right-hand corner of the back page reveals what role Arnold played "Scenery by W H Oakley. Lighting and Effects by R A Clarke & C H Woollford." It is pleasing to see Arnold getting involved and even enjoying himself a bit. This light-heartedness would be dealt a severe blow in the next few days.

On the 7 February, Arnold received a cablegram from Edith with the most tragic news he would receive since the death of his mother almost twelve years earlier. Wilfrid had been killed in a flying accident at Grantham. He wrote to Queenie the next day.

My dear Q,

Edith's cablegram arrived last night. I was going to cable back but I couldn't. I don't know how to write. How is Father? I am dreading the next mail out.

Yours ever A

This letter is heart-breaking in its briefness and the sentence, *I don't know how to write,* says so much. It must have been devastating for Arnold to get this news in such a way. No one to tell him personally that his only brother had died. I wonder that Arnold never speaks of any other person from the camp. Never alludes to any man he may have skied with or worked with, smoked with or played Bridge with. I get the feeling that he was reticent to form personal relationships in camp and this would mean that in this time of great sorrow and great need he may be even more isolated and alone. This is conjecture on my part but reading between the lines, loneliness tinges so much of what he writes. It, understandably, takes him while to get past his sadness and under a week later he writes to Queenie again. There seems to have been talk about him getting compassionate leave, but this is shut down by Arnold in this heavily censored letter.

Dear Q,

I don't know why I should write to you tonight. I had E's cablegram a week ago (Thurs 7th); missed writing the usual Sunday letter; last night we had mail and I had yours of 27 Jan.

I expect ERC will manage all the affairs. Similar circumstances have happened to other men in the camp and one must wait till all have been on leave before any go again; there are many to go also, so there could be no chance of getting home for another month before August.

Temporarily I am storekeeper for clothes and provisions. British navy gear and tobacco is on the way out here. Provisions have also been applied for and I suppose despite the economy warnings of food ministers, the British govt will politely accede to all their requests. (Big chunk cut out—censors?)

getting the worst time of it. I am dreading the next mail out.

There seems something fateful but lucky that leave did come off. There are times when I don't care whether I ever see anybody again. To get this jammed straight on top of 5 years in Glasgow doesn't seem exactly justice; but I suppose there is no such thing as justice or honesty. It's all—so, one must go in with the swim. I suppose conscientious objectors and the German prisoners are all on full rations—only others go hungry.

I had better stop now and pick up a Tennyson.

Ever yours, A

P.S. I don't know who the Member for your division is but would be no harm if you feel like it, of ascertaining whether the principle of sending food out here is right. The Hague convention should, like other things, occasionally be brought up to date.

There is a letter that is dated 22 February but does not have a year written on it. I have a feeling it is also from 1918 as it makes mention of 7 February and how slow the time is passing. When you read on to the description of the weather it seems clear how much slower the time would pass when not only are you grieving but the weather is bitterly cold and inhospitable.

My dear Q,

Very nearly a fortnight has gone by since 7 Feb and every night there is no mail. Somehow, the days have gone but a few have seemed interminably long.

Latterly, we've been having a heavy snowfall coupled with wind. Over a foot fell yesterday. One result of these was to break the cables from the power station. All Gausdaal and a part of Gudbrandsdalon were in total darkness for three hours last night and things are not much better tonight. There are no standbys in the shape of paraffin or candles as these are unattainable.

Events in the Baltic provinces and in North Eastern Europe seem highly complicated and the newspapers here contain long articles every night. I suppose there is a silver lining in the clouds London seems a long way off. Yours ever A

P.S. Perhaps, I might mention that this week one of the stokers is to be married to a Norwegian girl in Lillehammer. 3 of the officers besides the Commander have all married Norwegian girls recently and five other men are engaged. It doesn't seem right on England anyhow.

At the start of March Arnold is still really struggling in dealing with his grief and loneliness. He has obviously not been writing home a lot as he just does not know what to say. Conditions in camp do not seem to be getting any easier either.

My dear Q,

Many thanks indeed for your letters of 3 and 10 Feb, both arrived tonight. I hardly know how to answer them. I have been feeling pretty rotten these last three weeks and a long letter would be only be in this strain.

The weather has been pretty bad and all the electric light seems to break down pretty regularly every other night. There is no paraffin."

However even Arnold can see that maybe the war can't last another year— *Surely the whole thing won't hang out another year. This country is badly off for food and the civilian population has its rations cut down again this month. We get our rations all right, but they are to be cut at the end of March—or all else sent out from England. The uselessness of it and they talk of food of shortage and lack of manpower.*

It would be nice to think that as he moved through March Arnold started to feel better, but his letters show that he continues to struggle and it is exacerbated when he is told about the changes to the mail regulations and that he is only allowed to write two letters a week. I can imagine that back at home people would write regularly to those they knew were fighting or imprisoned. They would see it as a good thing to do, which it was, but Arnold found it difficult to reply. He did not have a lot to say. There was not much happening in his life, not a great deal to report on and he knew that if he said too much, he was at risk of being censored and his letters turning up unreadable. There was also, now, the challenge of having to decide who to write your two precious letters a week to.

One solution for this was to write a circular but Arnold often did not want to share his troubled feelings with the whole family.

13 *March 1918*
My dear Q,

A new regulation is coming out here that only 2 letters a man per week are to be written. I have had a fair amount of letters and papers and I don't know how to answer them. The next mail will probably bring more. E's 2 books arrived last night, also Father's parcel of tobacco. This was labelled 'parcel number 1', but it was all knocked about and the address hardly legible as it has been wandering round plenty German prison camps.

I ought to write to Miss D.T-S but somehow, can't begin. There is also a letter from G.J Davis.

I'm feeling pretty queer as well. There was a job recently I thought I might get as a motor mechanic. However, it has fallen through. I'm not going to apply anymore, then I can't be disappointed. I have had enough disappointments. It is just as easy to sit by the fire and smoke all day and there's less trouble.
Yours A.

Arnold refers to "Miss D. T-S" in this letter and it was late in the process of writing this book that I was contacted by Rolf Scharning, a Norwegian gentleman living in London who was a member of the Scandinavian Philately Society. He apologised for taking such a long time in contacting me but wished to share a letter he owned.

The letter was one of the rare ones still in existence that were written to Arnold. It is dated 12 March 1918 and the address of the writer is given as 7 The Avenue, Gravesend. The house next door to R Feaver and Dorothy. The letter is signed Dorothy and a bit of quick research unearthed that a Dorothy Mary Thomas lived at number 7 and she was twenty years of age in 1918.

Interestingly, the list of Wilfrid's effects that were shipped to his father after his premature death includes about eight letters written by Dorothy from number 7 dated from December 1917 to the time of his death in early February 1918. The letter written to Arnold is a bittersweet and tender one and reading between the lines Dorothy and Wilfrid may have been in the initial stages of a love affair.

7 The Avenue
Gravesend
12 March 18
Dear Arnold,

How can I write to you? At such a time as this mere words appear such a mockery and yet to me the genuine condolences of many friends have been one of my greatest comforts. Although I have not written you, believe me, Arnold, I have been much with you in thought and feel that I must write you a few words to express, however poorly, my very tenderest sympathy in the great loss.

It has been one of my constant thoughts of sorrow that you should be so far away and yet Arnold you could do nothing even if you were in England with your people so that although you are all alone with no one to help you, do try to bear up bravely.

To us at home the blow fell as a bolt from the blue. As you know Wilfrid arrived home on Friday at 6:30 in the greatest of spirits—I cannot describe all, it is still far too bitter but suffice it to say that we went to Town on Saturday and the whole of the weekend we together spent the most joyous and happiest time of our lives.

Wilfrid returned at 6:15 on Monday. Arnold, if you could have only seen the boy! I have never seen him so thoroughly and absolutely buoyant enthusiastic and pleased with everything. And yet, Arnold, it is God's wish. It is most terribly hard to understand why He takes our best but I feel sure that he is serving in some other way and has special work to do in that mysterious Hereafter of which we know so little. It may by that he is a ministering Angel to us below to draw, to strengthen and to comfort us.

It seems so natural that he must be doing something for he was so keen to achieve something here. But yet to me I can't realise that he has gone. It is an impossibility. It may be a childish belief but I still feel as though I can still talk to him here quite naturally although I can't see him. Yet there are times when I feel that I cannot suppress my whole self and I have such a restless longing which I cannot satisfy. This I hope will soothe although—God only knows what it means to me.

I had never realised that Wilfrid was my centre about which all plans revolved, but I do sincerely hope this sorrow will so influence my character as to make me a better,—and stronger woman. I have stuck to my work as best I possibly could although it is sometimes a great difficulty but I have been strengthened by the desire not to be less plucky than Wilfrid.

Mr Clarke has borne up most bravely. I had a nice letter from nurse at New Milton as of today and I am glad to say she also seems to be much better. The girls have all been really fine!

Arnold, I am afraid this whole letter reads very sadly. I only hope it will not add to any depression if so don't read it but simply tear it up. I have also neglected to thank you very much indeed for your letter but am sorry to state that the whole of the middle first sheet was mutilated. It ran on— "and now having let off steam." I, therefore, concluded you had already let off too much concerning Parliament. But the whole Censor seems to be perfectly ridiculous, in its discretion as to what should and should not be passed.

With best wishes from all,

Yours very sincerely,

Dorothy

P.S. I have enclosed a small poem which I think is a great help.

It is impossible to know what Arnold made of this emotional letter. Whether it was comfort to him or exacerbated his own pain, we will never know. We also don't know if he found the words to write back to Dorothy but the pain they both suffered must have been one shared by so many who lost loved ones in a long and brutal war.

At times, the new lower limit of two letters a week was too much for Arnold. He was running out of things to say and was in no frame of mind to write idle chit chat. At these times it was always Queenie who he leant on and relied on and once again, he writes to her asking her not to share the letter as was usually done but to keep it for herself.

20 April 1918

My dear Q,

Many thanks indeed for your letters of 7 April, 31 March and 24 March; we have had a big batch of letters and papers this weekend, but it was your letter of 31st which prompts me to answer. This letter is for you and need not be sent round; I shall write the O after this and that will make the two for the week. Sometimes the weeks allowance had proved 2 too many for me.

Since I came back off leave I haven't written a letter to anyone outside of the family, at least only one to Miss Thomas. S Davies, J Starbuck and G Hedge and others all wrote recently, so they will put me down as a churlish curmudgeon for not answering and perhaps, they won't be far wrong. There's plenty of people I would like to write to, but it is not worth it.

We've had our first issue of Navy rations and tobacco tonight. Bully beef is grand and we shall be having some good suet duffs in a day or so; it must be a bit galling to the Norwegians to see us living like lords on stuff from home. Some of the uniforms have arrived also. When everything is perfect, I suppose we shall shift.

Last Sunday, the English clergyman from Krjstanja was coming to give a service, but it was cancelled. We have gone without for 3 years, so they may as well spare us the infliction and reserve their energy for any different from us, who can give Job himself a 3-year handicap and beat him, —hands down.

We had another dance last Sunday night. It wasn't bad.

I believe there is to be a bit of a bust up in this country on 1 May. Things promise to be a bit lively—in fact, they've had a small taste already of it in the big towns, but no more need be said while the Censor is hanging in the offing.

It is possible to get up for an early morning run, now that the snow has all gone. Besides it is not much use getting up early as it makes the day longer and we only get 10 1/2 hours sleep every night. It is extraordinary to see the illustrated papers and see pictures of ordinary life with people working. It looks uncanny, something impossible to be true. However, I shall not make its acquaintance for a long while so needn't worry.

Have reached the limit allowed for letters, so will finish.

Yours A

P.S. I've written a home letter every Sunday for nearly 20 years, but it will go by the board now.

The blows kept coming in the first half of 1918 with the news in early May that Aunt Di had died. I get the feeling that Aunt Di was a bit pious and curmudgeonly, but she was a generous woman who had kept an eye on her nieces and nephews after their mother had died and she had been an important part of their lives.

She was 82 when she died and had lived a very full and benevolent life but her passing was still keenly felt by all members of the Clarke family and especially Arnold, who was once again grieving on his own away from those who could support him. Incidents like this made it almost impossible for him to drag himself out of his depressive state.

9 May 1918 (Aunt Di died 6 May)
My dear Q,

I received the cablegram from Grav this afternoon and again, I am not looking forward to the next mail out. It's hateful to be tied down here and a censor on all letters. It makes letter writing a thing to be avoided at all costs, but it is easiest to write to you. Is the war ever going to stop?

I am afraid I am beginning to give up hope of ever seeing anybody again. It doesn't take much to make one wish one could go through that gate with them. At any rate, it can't be so very much worse than this and one would at least have company.

One new activity has marked the progress of this week. The frost is sufficiently far down in the soil to let the surface be worked. We have matured and turned over our small allotment, but we shall not be planting seeds till the 2nd week in June.

I would be much obliged if you would get a few enclosed packets of seeds in letters. One packet in a letter would pass muster. Lettuce and radishes are the only things that grow. We buy the small plants of cabbage and turnips from the farmers when ready for transplanting. Seeds are not very easy to get and have risen 500% in price since last year.
I am afraid I can't write any more tonight.
Yours A.

The next two letters are in a similar vein. Arnold is at his lowest, I think, of the whole time in internment. He maintains his regular contact with Queenie, but it is not an easy task for him. His garden patch brings brief distraction but not enough to bring any lasting comfort.

He reflects on what life will be like out of internment and cannot imagine it. He also mentions, which he has done in one previous letter, B.S or B Standfield. I have not been able to determine who she is but think her first name might have been Barbara. I wonder that she might have been a love interest for Arnold but have no way of knowing if this was the case or not. She is certainly one of very few people mentioned who are not family members.

16 *May, 1918*

My dear Q,

   It is awfully hard to write a letter nowadays. This is the 2nd attempt. The other went in the fire. However your letter of April 24th arrived tonight and prompts me to answer.

   Glad to hear the weather is favourably. You should see our garden. It's something like a garden (but not much).

   After the winter I dropped taking the temperature as we don't pass the thermometer on our summer break to the camp.

   A few things are happening on the weekend. Tomorrow is 17 May—Norse's Independence Day—free beer, bands all day—dances all night,—then come the Whitsun holidays, also we had a new guard and there is to be a dance next a Sunday. We have had a football match every 2nd day with the Soldiers, as they raised a fairly smart team,—all 'Kristiania bhoys.'

   8 men came back off leave from England tonight. 'It makes Victoria station seems a—of a long way off.' England must be full of wounded.

   There might be something else doing next week but will be writing again later.

   Your letters come as a godsend. I wish BS would drop a line now and again, but I suppose she is a Londoner of Londoners now, too busy to look round, but I expect I would be too churlish to answer if one did come.

   I will always write my two letters per week, but I am afraid they are not interesting and don't contain much.

Best wishes, Yours A

16 *June 1918*

   *As the postman has not yet come, there is time for a few lines for yourself. This month always brings memories. (*Mother had died in June 1906) *Yesterday and today, things all seemed to go wrong. There are no textbooks, no one to ask and no tools. However, I've done something and can only trust the morrow brings nothing worse. As Yarrow states "it is better to do wrong than to do nothing."*

   The changes produced lately seem to bring a lot of things into view—Income tax, rates, insurance, matrimony and etc etc—things I rather fight shy of. I often wonder if the d_ old war will ever stop. It would be a strange thing having liberty to go and work where you like. I don't think I should stop at home tho', but probably go to sea on worse jobs than this. After all, the fascination of the Wanderlust is almost as great or greater than any others, at least I think so, but not as certain.

The weather is rather inclement just as present, up to the present we have made an embankment 80 yards long, about 10 feet high and 20 feet broad at the base, but this sort of work is very, very slow and Norwegians 'never' use machinery. Their railways are built by pick and shovel and all their rock blasting drilled by hand—all transport by horses. It breaks one heart at times on thinking of it.

I think I have said enough for the present.

Hoping to get your reply.
Yours A

By mid-June Arnold has had another change of scenery and is once again working on the Dovrebanen railway, this time in Oppdal. In the June 18th letter he mentions "dispatching" the seeds sent by Miss Macnamara to the mess gardener. (Gardening had been another outlet for some of the interned and the article *'Briter bak piggtråd'* shared with me by Lars Fruergaard-Jensen tells that "The kitchen gardens flourished outside the barracks where the people lived, having first camped in tents for the first time[28].")

He comments a bit later in the letter that he does not think that they will send the British Navy uniform "up here." In a letter with the same date on it, he confirms that they have been "up here" for three weeks now. Oppdal is approximately 230km from Jørstadmoen and is a primarily mountainous region. Arnold mentions how hands on the work was, blasting through rock so that railway track could be laid.

18 June 1918
Dear Q,

Last mail I received Miss R Macnamara's letter and packet of seeds. Please, thank her very much indeed for them. I have dispatched them to the mess gardener. By the same mail also and copies of the 'Nation' from WSC, also tobacco. Many thanks indeed for then, I would like to write to W but I expect she will be leaving Homerton and possibly the term ends soon.

---

[28] Pryser, T & Olstad, I. (1995*). 'Briter bak piggtråd'* p113

The Magazines are very interesting but deep as are the themes it discusses, they don't concern or rather, affect us, but it is good to read them.

The uniform has arrived at the camp, but I doubt if they will send any on up here. To all intents and purposes I am civilian pro-term:

In Miss M's letter she mentioned the play Branksome was doing this summer. It must be rather handy for you, having an unofficial dramatist attached to the staff. I suppose the end of term is always a great time for you (but I don't hold with children's plays unfortunately).

Best wishes to one and all,

Ever yours, A

18 June 1918 (Opdal)

My dear Q,

As there are but few pages left on the pad, here's the usual Sunday letter.

It is nearly 3 weeks since anything came up from the camp, so things are getting a bit stale.

The time is slipping by fast. It has been grand weather today. This time last week the deluge was just beginning. It was 5 days before we had complete details, but the damage down the valley is even worse than at first reported. 3 big wooden bridges on the railway have been completely demolished. Embankments, farms and houses all went under. There was no loss of life but several farms have lost their entire stock.

The foreman of this section was shifted yesterday to take charge of a gang of Germans (interned) at work. He didn't at all seem to relish the job. There have been one or two round this part of the valley, but I haven't met any yet.

No more for the present as I am dog-tired and half asleep.

Ever yours A

The June 26th letter is the best description of his surroundings we get from Arnold in the whole three years he is interned and whilst he can still see no end to his predicament there is a sense that the work that he is doing is keeping him occupied and he provides us with a line which has become a personal favourite of mine. He is writing about the lack of alcohol where he is working and says that if he were able to get hold of some, *"I would show a sponge a few things in the way of liquid-absorption."*

26 June 1918

My dear Q,

Here is the usual mid-weekly letter. As it is nearly a fortnight since the last letters came up from the camp, it is rather hard to write a letter.

Midsummer day has passed. We have had two days off work this week. It rained without stopping for three days. Now and again to liven things, the wind lashed itself into a fury. Above the howling of the gale and the pattering of the rain drops, one heard the roar of a thousand cataracts, howling and echoing in the rocky passages down the mountainsides.

Just opposite this farm is a peak shaped not unlike the pictures one sees of the Matterhorn, snow-capped and cloud encircled.

This place is not densely populated at the best of times and early mornings on days like these is awful. Half my time is spent in the cab alongside the furnace and the other half, beside the log fire here—keeping warm with a pipe and something to read. Luckily, there we the papers and 'Nations' etc, which people have sent out so it has not been so bad.

It has just stopped raining but by the black clouds, round the summits, we are in for another dousing. Oh and from a flat country no snow and water (h & c) from a tap!

Log cabins and grass roofs may look romantic and picturesque, but they do not err on the side of water-tightness under abnormal rainfall.

A second attempt to finish this. The landlady has been telling me that a wooden bridge on the railway from Störem to Trondhjem has been carried away by the floods; another river has risen and washed the road away at Presthus; finally the telegraph wires have carried away. We are entirely cut off from the outside world pro-term, but probably only till the end of the week. Thus it seems it was a bit of a storm.

It is quite easy for the telegraph wires to go. Their poles are not preserved or strengthened like ours. Just chop down a tree, lop off the branches,—drive in an insulator and tie the wire to it and finish.

I was having a conversation with the local 'rationeringem' official. (He likes riding on the engine). He is by way of being a bit of a mountaineer and has been up all the Dovrefjell peaks. 'But the old order changeth, giving place to new.' No more of that game for me now.

Years ago, I remember learning the mountain chains of Europe: Dovrefjell being somewhat familiar sounding, remained in my memory—but I never guessed I should have such a long, close and financial connection with it.

There's times (oft-recurring) when one gets fed up to the very hilt with the war, Norge and everything. Even a good swear (polyglot) doesn't seem to ease the feelings. There's thousands of Micawbers now, but it's 'one' thing, not 'something' they wait for.

The reason why this letter is so long, is the fact that these are the last pages of the writing pad and it will be sometime before I shall get to the distant store, in time to catch it open and purchase another.

There's no doubt, in outlandish places by oneself, one sinks into habits of sloth and laziness. If ever fate should cast me on a British warship again, I shall be under arrest from morning to night. But there is no chance of the war stopping.

The muck-rake and the slough of despond are not so bad after all; as regards the crown of glory (mythical) overhead,—well, a bird (or rake) in the hand is worth two (or a crown) in the bush. It is very lucky indeed that Norge is a 'dry' country. Such people as I have met, always ask me if I can get whiskey from the camp. The crew of the 'Berlin' get their leave and spirits from Germany. If I could get some now, I would show a sponge a few things in the way of liquid-absorption. (cleaning fires is a thirsty job.)

I rather fancy you had best burn this letter. If WSC or ERC sees it, they will drop on me like a ton of coal—but they've never been out of England for more than a few consecutive months.

Ever yours, A

P.S. The censor cannot grumble at this letter because I am working a d-d sight harder than (her/him)—(N.B to censor— please erase to suit). 7 days a week, 5 a.m. every morn.

The hope for Arnold leading into the second half of 1918 is that the railway work provides enough of a distraction to carry him through the rest of the war.

What was happening in the camp?

Unrest was the mood that kicked off 1918. The letters sent by Private Albert Hopkins towards the end of 1917 reignited discussions over conditions in the camp and an unfortunate incident very early in the new year set an unsavoury tone to the start of what would be the last year at Jørstadmoen.

A long letter written by Commander Kennedy to the British Legation on the 7 January outlines the "trouble we had in camp here on the 1 January and subsequent days." He explains that a new rationing list had been sent to camp and he had encouraged the men to "accept it for about 14 days and then I would try and have it amended. On the 1 January the ration for the day was Salt Meat. This the men absolutely refused to touch and said they would go on a hunger strike."

They were talked down and replacement meat was arranged using temporary supplies from Lillehammer "but when they came to draw the meat, they again refused to take any, this time on the ground that there was a great deal too much bone and, on the 5 January, they refused to muster in the morning and the gates were closed and all privileges stopped."

He goes on to explain that he then went and met with the officers and inspected the meat "which was by the way nearly all ribs and very little meat." He then arranged for the old rationing to be restored and considered that things were then back to normal. However, "the men also complained that a guard with fixed bayonets had been marched into camp on the evening of the 4 and patrolled inside the camp. This they resented very much and I think was the reason for refusing to muster in the morning."

Apparently, the Camp Commander had been informed by telephone that someone "had heard on good authority that the men were going to burn the camp down. I assured the Camp Commandant that I did not think that there was any likelihood of any trouble occurring provided the guard was kept out of the camp." With all the skiing and swimming and niceties of the camp, I think that, at times, it is easy to forget that Jørstadmoen was a Prisoner of War camp and that the men inside it were being held against their will by armed guards.

The Norwegian article shared with me by Lars Fruergaard-Jensen confirms that whilst the officers were "allowed to move freely outside the camp within one of the districts commands specified area. The privates, on the other hand, were not allowed to go outside the 'enclosures. 'Faced with any attempt to do so, the records in question will have unrelenting use of their rifle, which should always be loaded and with full magazine.'[29]

---

[29] Pryser, T & Olstad, I. (1995) op. cit. p 115

It is obvious that more freedoms were allowed than stated here but the Norwegian guards still, theoretically, could use force or weapons if they saw fit. It is no wonder that the English internees felt frustrated and confined.

A book concerning the local history of Jørstadmoen, published in 1998, writes about another barracks fire that occurred in early April 1918. It tells of the fire catching in one of the stoves in the barracks and quickly taking hold in the ceiling where the wooden roofing made for a rapid spread. The guards attempted to put the fire out but were hampered by a lack of water and the camp lost another barracks, a different one to last time but just as dramatic.

On the other hand, socialising, and fraternising with those inside and outside of the camp seemed to have really hit its stride in 1918. Arnold speaks of dances, sing songs and the Varieties Theatre concert. Whilst he is not often in the mood for taking part, many others, especially the officers, seem to relish the opportunity to relax and have a bit of fun. Arnold says to Queenie—*"I am sorry your effort to arrange a dance for officers should have met with such little success. It is usually the other way round here."*

There are stories and photographs of the Officers really getting into socialising in the towns and villages where they were based. The Norwegian article sent to me by the descendants of Lieutenant Alltree states, *For the officers, the class differences were also reflected in the fact that a New Year's ball was organised with the district's finer daughters sock guests. Anine Wollebæk Slaatto was among those invited and remembers that she reacted to the strange serving, a kind of sitting buffet* and Deborah Callaghan, the granddaughter of Chief Engineer Charles Nelson, tells of a photo album she had inherited with photos of her grandfather partying with other men and women in houses.

This fraternising may be what led to many of the love affairs, engagements and marriages that occurred between the officers and crew of *HMS India* and the women of the local area. Arnold does not approve of these relationships and writes to Queenie that *Perhaps, I might mention that this week one of the stokers is to be married to a Norwegian girl in Lillehammer. 3 of the officers besides the Commander have all married Norwegian girls recently and five other men are engaged. It doesn't seem right on England anyhow.*

The influx of men into a small Norwegian town had an impact. There are stories of Norwegian guards spending time chasing girls away from the fences of the camp where they were trying to sneak kisses from the interned men. A guard from the camp wrote to a local paper, using the name 'Valdris' and stated that "The biggest task is to remove the girls from the fence, they are very bothered by the English disease."[30] I imagine many of the men must have enjoyed this attention as well!

Through research I have been able to confirm seven marriages and two engagements not including the marriage of Commander Kennedy in 1916.

Ernest Woodburne Alltree married Hedvig Knudsen in 1916 and they had a daughter, Ingrid, born in 1917 (as mentioned earlier, I have been in contact with two of Ernest's great-grandchildren). Lieutenant Alltree, unfortunately, died before the end of the war of Spanish Flu.

Private Norman Harcourt Bolton married Nora Larsen (or Iverson) and they had one son, Sven Norman Bolton, who was born in 1919. Private Bolton may have also served in WW2 as he is listed as having died in Shanghai in 1941.

Norman was unable to remain in Norway as his position as a private in the Royal Marine Light Infantry meant he was obliged to return to England when the war ended before the birth of his son. His records have him being discharged in September 1919 from the RNLI invalided after being wounded in action. It is unclear whether the injury occurred due to the shipwreck or whether it occurred separately. It also appears that Norman may not have returned to Norway, but I cannot be sure on this.

Fireman William Tilley married Agnethe Haugan who was one of the camp cooks. They married on 19 October 1918 and went on to have six or seven children. William died in Norway in 1976.

William Lamb married Anna Roed in 1919 and Arthur Henry Glibbery married Esther Norlie in March 1918.

Tempy Midshipman Harold R Jenkins is said to have married a Norwegian Doctor. An announcement of his marriage was made in the *Aftenposten* paper on 1 June 1918 stating "Marriage will be entered into on the third of this month between Miss Therese Johansen, Kongsvinger and Lieutenant Harold Rhys Jenkins, R.N.R, British Internment Camo, Jørstadmoen. The wedding will take place at the English Church at 1 o'clock, after which there will be lunch at the Grand Hotel." There are, however, no marriage records, so it is very hard to know if the marriage took place.

Jack/John Philip is said to have been engaged Asta Nyhus and Fireman Edward Miller's engagement notice to Emma Halvorsen appeared in the *Lillehammer Tilskuer* in December 1918. Arnold refers to a stoker having got

---

[30] Rønning, O. op cit. p128.

married in the February 1918; this could have been Miller as the title of fireman was sometimes interchangeable with stoker. I can find no marriage records for either of them, so am not sure what happened.

One of the other men who married has a most interesting back story and it was one that took a lot of research to get to the bottom of. Proby Midshipman Ronald Clunies-Ross was known as the Coconut Prince, a name bestowed upon him as he was in the unusual situation of being born on a tropical island. Research revealed that the Clunies-Ross family were the original settlers of an island archipelago in the Indian Ocean known as the Cocos Keeling Islands.

They had settled there in the early 1800s and from 1827 to 1978 ruled is as a private fiefdom. Ronald's enrolment papers have his birthdate listed as the 28 June 1897 and his birthplace the Cocos Keeling Islands. He was a boarder at a school in Margate in 1911 and signed up for the navy in August 1914. Ronald Clunies-Ross married Klara (or Clara) Thygesen (or Larud). An article in the local Lillehammer paper in 1994 sheds further light on Midshipman Clunies-Ross:

"He was popularly called the 'Coconut Prince' probably because he was half white and half coloured. The mother is said to have been a 'queen' on a Malaysian island and the father a British officer named Ross. 'The Coconut Prince' is said to have been a cadet.

Among the twelve officers, this may not have been anyone other than 'Midshipman' Ronald Clunies-Ross, number 11 on the officer list. In Lillehammer, this young officer attracted attention. He seems to have frequented the city a lot, including in artist circles (he fancied himself as a sculptor).

It is said that he fell madly in love with the wife of the painter Rudolph Thygesen. Her name was Klara, they married and had three children. The first year, they lived on the second floor of the villa of the Bjorneby family in Kirkegaten. Later they bought a small on Bergseng where they lived for a few years. Then they went to England. When Ross' mother 'the queen' died, her son inherited the island and the family moved there. The island was later sold to the British."[31]

In my research on Clunies-Ross I found a few things that contradict the findings of the newspaper. The digital archives of Norway (www.digitalarkivet.no) have Clara Marie Larud marrying on 2 February 1918.

---

[31] (1994) 'Detained Officer with expensive habits' *Dangingen*, Thursday 4th March, page 7.

On 27 February 1919, Consular/Overseas record by the British Armed Forces and Overseas Births and Baptisms show that Isobel Clunies-Ross was baptised. This is supported by the local church book from the Brottum parish and mentions that the parents are Klara Marie Larud and Rainold Clunies-Ross.

The 'Coconut Prince' appears to have been granted leave at the beginning of 1919 but was informed that he must return to England after the leave has finished. He commenced two months of repatriation leave in March 1919 and his records show that by October 1920 he states that he has no employment and is studying art with a view to taking up sculpture as a profession. By 1923, Ranald/Ronald/Rainold (depends on which records you look at) and Clara/Klara had found their way to Guernsey where their son, Knut was born. A document outlining Knut's life takes over the story from there:

"Five months after Knut was born, the family goes back to Norway. The father plants vegetables and the mother has the most beautiful stand on the market with his goods. The father also trains sled dogs and little Knut can often see nothing because of the snow."[32]

The document goes on to say that Clara then takes the children to England, whilst Ronald stays in Norway "to earn money for the family in construction. Before he could follow the family, however, he died during gastric surgery." I have seen other records which have Ronald dying or buried in Bromley, Kent. The truth will be a combination of all of these things.

Whilst a few men were lucky in love during their time in Jørstadmoen, records from late March tell the story of poor Acting Sub-Lieutenant Harold Musselwhite who was not lucky. In September 1917, Musselwhite was granted leave to go back to Lewisham to marry Daisy Stotesbury.

Fleet Surgeon R W Stanistreet writes, "He returned to Norway and brought his wife with him. His domestic life was very unhappy and his wife left him after a few weeks and has not returned to him. This caused a nervous breakdown and he came home on leave from Norway at the end of February 1918. On his arrival home he quite lost his mental balance and had to have an attendant night and day. He has improved slightly but suffers from much depression and worries a great deal, brooding over his unhappy domestic affairs. During the interview he quite broke down, bursting into tears."

---

[32]Garrett, V. B. The Movement Academy Project. www.movementacademyproject.com/we-content/uploads/2014/10/Knut-Ross.pdf

Musselwhite's condition is confirmed in late March by Doctor Robert Domullen who begs:

"to recommend the repatriation of Lieutenant H Musselwhite on the grounds of his health.

Owing to domestic trouble with his young wife, he completely lost his mental balance a month ago when I first saw him and was in a condition of acute melancholia. His state was so marked and his depression so great that it was necessary to have a male attendant with him night and day.

I am convinced that there is a great danger of the recurrence of the melancholia if the original conditions are reproduced as they would be by his return to Norway and on these grounds, I recommend his repatriation."

It takes until 28 July before a minster from the Foreign Office confirms that Lieutenant Musselwhite is "quite unfit for service" and is "therefore released under the recognised regulations for the release of interned belligerent sailors who are seriously wounded." This camp and being interned in it obviously played with the minds and mental health of many of the men.

What was the family doing?

1918 was, as I have touched on before, a tragic year for the Clarke family. The 4 February had started out as a normal Monday. In Gravesend, R Feaver had been lucky enough to have Wilfrid home for a few days on leave. He had not seen him since before Christmas 1917, so there must have been a lot to catch up on and Wilfrid, one imagines, would have been full of tales about his flying training and life on the base at Grantham.

Wilfrid having been home over a weekend, Edith or Queenie may have also made the trip back to 9 The Avenue, Gravesend to spend time with their younger brother. After breakfast Wilfrid caught the train back to London and then up to Grantham. That afternoon he was on a training flight and something went horribly wrong. The plane nosedived and Wilfrid and the other man onboard died on impact when the plane crashed into the ground.

R Feaver, being Wilfrid's next-of-kin was informed by the Royal Airforce by telegram and it would have been up to him to break the awful news to his daughters. As Arnold noted it fell to Edith to send a cable to him to let him know but he did not receive that until 3 days after Wilfrid had died. It may have taken a day or two for R Feaver to get the news to all the girls. Wilfrid's death must have come as a real blow to the whole family, from all accounts he was a lovely, well-liked man and the family was very close.

The obituary printed in the local paper ran to almost two columns and was written by John Denny Gedge [33] who was the vicar at St George's, the Gravesend Church attended by the Clarke family. To this day there is a plaque in the church dedicated to Wilfrid and his name is also on a bell as he was a bellringer at the church. Gedge writes glowingly about Wilfrid and shares some of the sympathy letters received by the family.

Wilfrid's squadron commander wrote, "I have remarked that if all pupils were as keen and hard-working as your son, our work would be much easier. Always cheerful, always ready for any work, he set a fine example." The Bishop of Chelmsford praised his "clean and wholesome life" and a friend commented, "So splendid in physique, so courteous, so tender, so genuine, so clean. The world is a loser when such as he is taken, for to know him was to love and respect him."

Wilfrid was buried on the 7 February 1918 in Grantham with his father and Edith and Winnie in attendance, it must have been deemed too far for Queenie and Dorothy to travel.

A few months later the family were grieving again but perhaps not as unexpectedly or as keenly. Aunt Dinah Pearce passed away on the 6 May 1918 at the ripe age of eighty-two. A pious woman, Aunt Di (as she was known to the family) was generous and well-known in the Govan area of Glasgow for her philanthropy.

Dinah sat on school boards, built community centres, and instigated "Fresh Air Fortnights" to get ill children out of the polluted, industrial areas of Glasgow and get them to the country or seaside to assist in their healing and well-being. She was also a dedicated aunt and kept a close eye on her nieces and nephews, of which there were at least twenty, but especially keeping an eye on the Clarke children who had lost their mother so early in their lives.

Clarke family members were often invited to holiday with their aunt and letters to them are at times addressed to St. Brendan's, Aunt Dinah's house in Wimbledon. Arnold had remarked a number of times on the sombre mood that

---

[33] The clipping from the newspaper that features Wilfrid's obituary unfortunately does not include a header so it is impossible to know what paper it was taken from but it has been dated Feb 16th, 1918. It was in the family archives and I suspect it was a local Gravesend publication.

permeated St Brendan's—*It must have been a bit of an effort to bring off a joke at St B. The atmosphere is so strained,* but the family continued to be regular visitors and so the relationship seems to have been a close one and Aunt Di seems to have been in fairly regular correspondence with Arnold and he thanks her through Queenie, at times, for care packages that she has sent to him.

Her death would have amplified to Arnold again how removed he was from home and from those he loved.

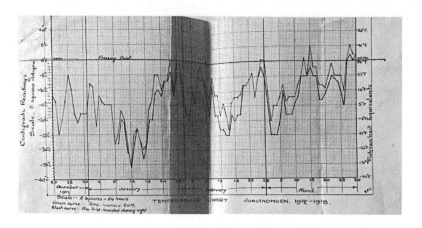

In his typical engineering, mathematical approach to life, Arnold graphed the weather for the first three months of 1918.

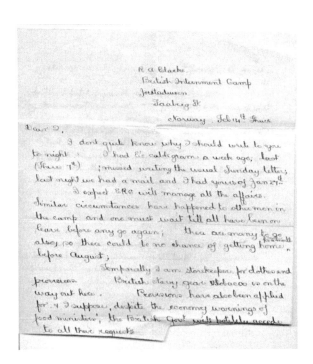

Censored letter written by Arnold seven days after learning of the death of his brother, Wilfrid.

From the collection of Seaman Robert Charles Maynard, this photograph was annotated "Crew around table—wedding." I am not sure whose wedding it was, but a celebration was being had!

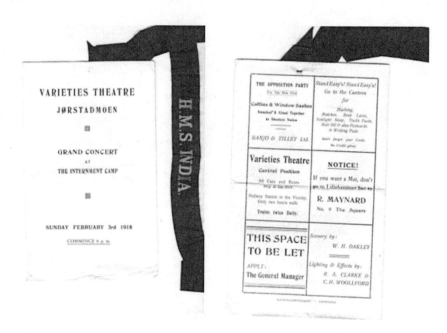
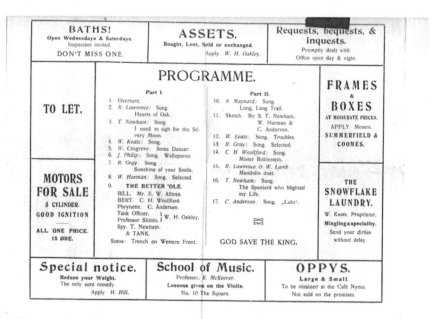

Programme from concert staged by the Officers and Men of HMS India on 3 February 1918 at Jørstadmoen Internment Camp

Wilfrid Randall Clarke 15 June 1891-4 February 1918.

PER ARDUA AD ASTRA.

ON FEBRUARY 4TH, 1918.

ACCIDENTALLY KILLED WHILST FLYING,

WILFRID RANDALL CLARKE,

LIEUTENANT ROYAL FIELD ARTILLERY,

ATTACHED TO ROYAL FLYING CORPS,

AGED 26 YEARS.

INTERRED IN GRANTHAM CEMETERY, FEB. 7TH, 1918.

*Mr R. Feaver Clarke & Family
desire to express their sincere thanks
for the kind sympathy extended
to them.*

*9 The Avenue,
Gravesend.*

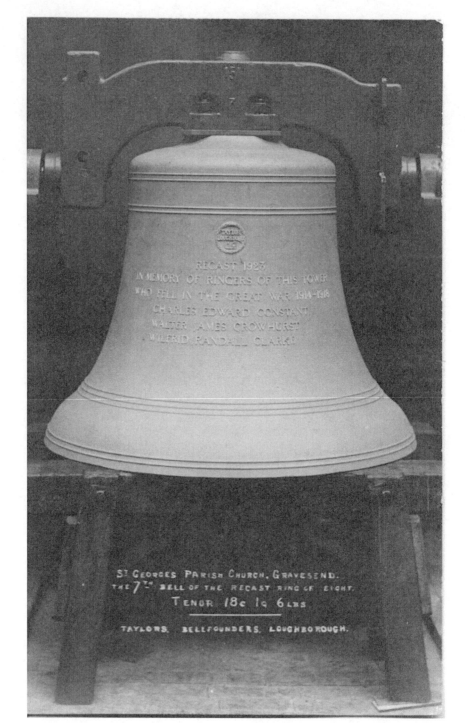

RECAST 1923
IN MEMORY OF RINGERS OF THIS TOWER
WHO FELL IN THE GREAT WAR 1914-1918
CHARLES EDWARD CONSTANT
WALTER JAMES CROWHURST
WILFRID RANDALL CLARKE

ST GEORGES PARISH CHURCH, GRAVESEND.
THE 7TH BELL OF THE RECAST RING OF EIGHT.
TENOR 18c 1q 6LBS

TAYLORS, BELLFOUNDERS, LOUGHBOROUGH.

The Late Lieut. W. R. Clarke,

R.F.A.

Lieutenant Wilfrid Randall Clarke, R.F.A. (attached to Royal Flying Corps), whose death we briefly announced in our last issue, was born on the 15th June, 1891, at Gravesend, and entered upon his school life at St. Lawrence College, Ramsgate, September, 1904, where he remained four years. On leaving the College he was apprenticed at Messrs. Vickers, Ltd., Erith, to learn engineering. Upon the completion of the term of his apprenticeship, this firm retained his services, and while so working he passed his examination, upon which he became an Associate Member of the Inst. C.E. During his residence at Erith he joined the 4th Home Counties Howitzer Brigade as a private, and at St. Lawrence College he was also a private in the Cadet Corps. Upon the outbreak of war in August, 1914, Lieut. Clarke resigned his appointment at Messrs. Vickers to join the colours, selecting the Public Schools Battalion training at Epsom. He was given a commission, and gazetted Second-Lieut., Royal Field Artillery, on November 20th, 1914. Further training followed at Salisbury and Berkhamsted until October, 1915, when he went with his Battery to the front, and during the winter of 1915 was at Ypres and Arras. After being six months at the front he was transferred to the Inspection Department (Carriages), Royal Arsenal, Woolwich, where he remained until September, 1917, when he volunteered for the Royal Flying Corps, and being accepted went into training. He was enthusiastically devoted to this work and made good progress, passing his examinations successfully. He went home on February 1st for two days' leave in the fullest vigour of young healthy manhood, stimulated with the anticipation of taking his final examination at the end of the month to secure qualification for the granting of his "wings." He returned from Gravesend early on the morning of February 4th, and in the evening of the same day his father received the sad intelligence that he had met with a fatal accident whilst flying in the afternoon. He received his promotion to First Lieutenant in the R.F.A. on July 1st, 1917. Lieut. Clarke was buried in Grantham Cemetery on Thursday afternoon of last week with full military honours. His father and two of his sisters, Miss Edith R. Clarke and Miss Winifred S. Clarke, being present.

Mr. Feaver Clarke's younger son is a prisoner of war, interned in Norway. He was one of the survivors of H.M.S. "India," sunk by German submarine in the Arctic Circle on August 8th, 1915. Fortunately he obtained leave for a month on parole in England last November, and arriving had three days with his brother. A singular coincidence occurred in the fact that the two boys joined the colours the same day, one in Kent, the other in Glasgow, without previous communication either to each other or to their father.

The family of Lieut. Clarke have received a large number of letters of sympathy. His words which the Russian novelist puts into the mouth of his escaping prisoner when he falls dying—'Fly on, my soul.' Yes, fly on my soul! The body's work is done, the service rendered, his part in the world, apparently so short and so abruptly ended, fulfilled. Soul, fly on. This lad, as you know, has always been one of us. He used to help us in our Band of Hope, he was a regular communicant, a member, and a fellow-worker. Who shall say what he does for us still? Are they not ministering spirits, those whom God sets free from the trammels of earth? He breaks the clay but sets the spirit free. Why, and for what? Surely for some purpose, some service to be rendered. And so, on the dark cloud of widespread sorrow which now broods over our nation, on the bosom of that dark cloud of anxiety and apprehension which looms so large in the face of the great assault which must soon come and the tremendous sacrifice it must involve, God paints for you and me once more the rainbow of immortal hope. The boy who took with us last Sunday morning the bread of life, the food of immortality, gives this parting message to all—'a moment in the air: another moment in eternity!' So may we learn that to live is Christ; to die is gain."

W.R.C. ob.: FEBRUARY 4, 1918.

With what new joy to-day to God I bring
My Sacrifice of Praise and Thanksgiving!
Thou, Father! at whose feet I all confess,
Dost not disdain Thy creature's happiness!
Thou, who did'st consecrate the wedding-
    feast :
Dost not esteem my cause for joy the least
Amid the satisfactions that impart,
By Thine ordaining, fullness to the heart!
Thou that hast led my life up to this hour
Will still sustain me with Thy gracious
    power,
And will vouchsafe me wisdom to fulfil
All manly parts, submissive to Thy will.
It is Thy mercy o'er us that bestows
Such joys as this wherewith my bosom glows,
To Thee I trust to sanctify always
Our love, our pure affection to upraise
Above the tenderest of earthly ties
And seal them with Thine own eternities.

* * * * *

Dearest! with what new buoyancy this time,
Once I have signed this, up toward heaven I
    climb!
Nay! to what heaven already have I flown
Through this free access to you as my own!
What fuller sense will raise me, as I rise
To make my glorious circuit through the
    skies,
Of a man's duty and a nation's call,
Now that your claim upon me heightens all!

She lifts! she rises up! joy splendid bird!
With what new eagerness my pulse is
    stirred!
What pride assails me as I leave behind
The earth's dull spread to ride upon the
    wind!
I, the so happy one, the man so blest!
Does heaven bear one man happier on its
    breast?

Up! up! what boat on wave, on earth what
    car
Can make of men such conquerors as we are?
As with our tabernacling wings we sweep
The unseen surges of the aerv deep,
As with keen touch we feel the varying flow
Of currents and their hidden dangers know,
Counter with zest the elemental strife
And by triumphant cunning guard our life?
Oh glorious course! oh sweet sublimest swim
On air's broad ocean, with earth's distant
    rim

Fainting from sight around me! Force how
    free
How jubilant, beating this boundless sea!
What sense of mastering skill as swift I
    steer
Upwards and downwards, all ways, without
    fear,
Seize safety still from every turn of fate,
Nor care what new adventure may await!

It cannot be! It is! Courage sublime
Exhilarates all my being! There is time!
Earth is far off! Some opportunity
Is sure to offer! What? Is it so nigh?

J. DENNY GEDGE.

Chatham Empire Theatre.

In Association with the London Coliseum.
Joint Managing Directors:
Mr. Oswald Stoll and Alderman H. E. Davis.
Geo. Piercy, Manager.

6.15.   8.45.
Soldiers and Sailors in uniform at reduced prices at first performance only, except Saturdays

The Lads of the Village,

the famous Musical Comedy Melodrama, in

10 SCENES,

from the Oxford Theatre, London.

BOB STEVENS as "ERB," V.C.

Lyrics by Clifford Harris. Music by James
W. Tate ("That").
Full Company of 50 Artistes. Beauties as
Maids of the Village.

DISCHARGED WOUNDED SOLDIERS

(some of whom have been decorated in the
present war) and realistic battle effect.

TIMES AND PRICES AS USUAL.

THE PICTURE HOUSE,

CHATHAM'S PALATIAL CINEMA,

Adjoining the Empire Theatre, Chatham.
Manager: H. C. Webley, late R.F.C.

Monday, Tuesday and Wednesday, Feb.
18th, 19th and 20th: "Rasputin: The
Power Behind the Throne" (six acts); a
story of the arch-villain whose treachery
brought about the Russian Revolution; the
greatest sensational drama of the day.
Picture-goers: If you miss this great Russian picture you miss a dramatic treat indeed.

Thursday, Friday and Saturday, Feb.
21st, 22nd and 23rd: "The Ragged Messenger" (five acts), featuring Violet Hop-
son and Gerald Ames. "Lovers' Leap,"
11th Episode of "Patria." "Hula Hula
Land" (two parts), a screaming Keystone
comedy.

1,000 Seats. Prices (including tax), 4d., 8d.,
and 1s. 3d. 2.30 to 10.30.

Meat Supply Problems in Gravesend.

(Continued from Page 5).

an examination, and he suggested that if she
called at a house she should be detained in
conversation while the police could be fetched.
The committee had never given any women
or anybody else any leave to make such an
examination.—Councillor Wynn: I am not in
favour of a statement, because it will tell
Alderman Huggins's pals that the Inspector
is coming. Let the public find out. Those
who are not doing wrong need not be fright-
ened.—Councillor Owen thought it was not
desirable for the public to have the information suggested. The Inspector would have
proper credentials.—Alderman Enfield: I
don't know how it will affect the gentleman
mentioned by Councillor Wynn who had 200
cwt. of sugar.—Councillor Wynn: I know
someone who has two ton in his place. I
have told them, and they won't take action.
COMMUNAL KITCHENS.
Councillor Hinkley inquired and was
informed by the Town Clerk that the question
of central kitchens was going forward as
rapidly as possible under the circumstances.

Squadron Commander, R.F.C., writes:—"If
sincere sympathy can take any weight off
such a blow, then the sympathy that the
whole of my squadron has for you may help,
for we all loved him. He was my own pupil,
and I have often remarked that if all pupils
were as keen and hard-working as your son
was, our work would be much easier. Always
cheerful, always ready for any work, he set
a fine example, and his death was a great
shock to us all." The Chaplain, R.F.C.,
writes:—"It is with the greatest regret that
I have heard of your son's death to-day, and
I should like to send you and his family my
deep sympathy. I hear on all sides what a
good fellow he was, keen and plucky. . . . . .
It is a heavy price we have to pay for the
training of the men who serve their country
in the air." The Bishop of Chelmsford sends
the following tribute:—"I know how poor
human words must be at such a time as
this, but you have his memory, which must
be of great value to you now. I well
remember his visit to me at Bethnal Green
and how he delighted us all by his clean and
wholesome life. You must thank God for
what he was, and what he is, for surely he
is in the Service above. . . . . . ." A Friend
writes:—" Poor Will! So splendid in
physique, so courteous, so tender, so genuine,
so clean. The world is a loser when such as
he are taken, for to know him was to love
and respect him."

Preaching at St. George's Church,
Gravesend, on Sunday morning, from the
words, "I do set my bow in the cloud"
(Genesis ix., 13), the Rev. Canon Gedge
alluded to the death of Lieut. Clarke.
"Man's extremity is God's opportunity," he observed, and continued:
"You must be thinking of one whose sudden
death, in a sense, marked the passing of the
last week. Only last Sunday morning, in the
bloom of life and in the flush of youth he
was with us. He would come to his early
Communion, saying that he must always
remember that with him and those with him
it was one moment in the air and the next in
eternity. The words were of singular
significance. It was even so with him in a
few hours. He left us the next morning to
go back to Grantham, to ascend 1,500 feet
and then to fall like a stone. A sudden
faintness must have prevented his releasing
the controls which would automatically have
righted the machine, and thus he went to his
death, probably unconscious. Very early in
the war we lost one of our best, well known
to us here, by a fatal and insidious disease
then little understood. Since then again and
again we have had to face this tragic effect
of this war, costing us our young, and brave
and bright. That is the peculiar effect of
this war. It takes the young. We feel it
to-day and are repeatedly conscious of it.
And yet, who would have it otherwise than
it is. If the cause is sacred, if it is the
cause of God, then by an instinct, which has
prompted men in all ages to make the
sacrifice of the best, we are giving to God
our best and strongest, our youngest and our
bravest. As the Bishop of Chelmsford says,
writing about our young friend, who was
also his friend, and who has worked with him
—'He is serving still.' He is in the service
of God above. In the service! That is what
these young souls are, living and dying. It
is the proud title which indicates their rela-
tion to their sovereign and their country.
Their motto is the motto of the Heir
Apparent—'I serve.' They serve alike in
life and in death. It is the supreme test of
service unto death. So we must not grudge
it. Like another young spirit which fled only
a week or two ago, he would have 'had his
wings.' And he has had them. The
heathen said 'Whom the gods love die
young.' We can but realise that it may be
in great mercy and tenderness they are taken
away from the evil to come. Our young
friend was suddenly dashed to the ground,
broken like the potter's vessel. It might

Second Half of 1918 — "I Am in No Wise over Brimming with Cheerfulness."

The second half of 1918 begins with Arnold working in Oppdal, just over 200Km from Jørstadmoen. After arriving in late May, he remains working there through July and indeed for the rest of the war, not that he, of course, had any idea that the end of the war was near. If he had felt isolated in the camp in Jørstadmoen, this was nothing to compare with the isolation of working on the railway in at the base of the Dovre Mountain ranges where the weather could be challenging and the locals wary.

As Arnold explains, the isolation also meant that contacting his family was made even harder with a two mile walk to get mail and there were challenges dealing with the locals as well. His letters of this time tend to be unusually detailed. As he explains in one of them, there is little for him to do apart from work and walk and so writing long letters, if nothing else, passes the time.

1 July

Am sorry I missed the postman, so must wait three days. It's rather a nuisance, this stoppage of—They can't get sugar,—or anything to this part of the valley.

Had rather a good day yesterday. The schoolmaster borrowed a bike for me and we went first for a cycle ride up round Sundalen. Sondalsoren (40 miles away) lies on a sea fjord; the road lay high up the hillside, so there was a good panoramic view. Some valleys wide, fertile and pleasant, others deep precipitous, v rugged; above all these were the peaks of rock, ice and snow. I'm sick of these scenes. Oh for surburbia and the nine-fifteen, the milkman and the motorbus.

After the ride, we went to Oppdal church and played the organ an hour or so; then we paid a call on the organist. He is something like Bindle,—always in a good humour; he is the local schoolmaster also. He plays the violin and for an hour he treated us to Highland flings, jigs, English waltzes and marches. It was cheering and what memories! He had some good books too, so it was a pleasant Sunday.

I have seen quite a lot of the German sailors now. They pass pretty regularly on their way to the doctor's; plenty also come up this way for a stroll now. Of course, I am always grimy and in civvies but mutual recognition may come; meanwhile the time goes slipping by.

I have been up here over six weeks and it doesn't seem a fortnight. Soon the 3rd anniversary will be round. Oh Lord, how much longer?

I am afraid these letters are not very cheery, but at times one does get a bit homesick.

Meanwhile, best wishes to you all,

Yours A

(Later)

What ho! For democratic Norge. Just had a telegraphic message that 'eight hours working day' has been granted. At 9 hours a day the railway's completion would have taken umpteen years, at 8 hours a day, it will never be finished, so we can die happy but there's a witch lives just alongside the railway. She's anything between 80 & 120 years old and I'm sure she's been casting spells about. She doesn't like railway workers either. It's lucky we don't understand each other when the air is charged with invectives.

2 July 1918 (Oppdal)

My Dear Father,

Just received your letter of 7 June, so am sending you a line at once.

Many thanks for sending the £2. It has not come yet but will doubtless turn up ultimately. The pay on this job is very good, but there is no opportunity of spending, hence one is compelled to save. I pay £2 weekly for lodging and over and above that, have got enough—well to do a lot. I don't know how long the job will last.

There was a big batch of letters for me at the post office tonight so it was worth the 2 hours walk in the rain.

The 8 hours working day has been conceded I started today. I wonder when we shall get our first Labour government. It came very quickly and back the

242

workmen turned up at 6:30, the old time, as they had heard nothing about it. I still knock out 11-12 hours, Sunday included.
No time for more.
Yours ever, A"

To Queenie, Arnold speaks of walking through the rain to collect his treasured mail and being rewarded with "a budget" and a fairly decent sized one at that. It would appear that harsh weather has made the infrequent deliveries of mail even less regular.

4 July 1918
My dear Q,
   Various expedients are being followed to establish communication between Trondhjem and Kristiania—be sea, via Sweden or by state-fuelled motor car over Dorrefjeld.
   Early the other morning I saw a motorcar piled high with mail sacks crawling over the fjeld road, so immediately after work I—me (in the pouring rain) to the post kontor and received a budget. I am deeply indebted for the following:
   RFC's B'th 7 June, ERC's D'd 1 June, DC's Wareham ;8 June, yours of 3 and 10 June. I was very glad to get them. It is immensely cheering to get them.
   We knocked of work today, at dinner time, owing to the rain. Ordinary rain, we work in but when it comes down in a solid mass one knocks off. When a small narrow river drains a huge valley, it doesn't take much to make the river rise a few feet. Ours rose a couple of feet in 2 hours. Luckily it subsides as quick. But people are still talking about the floods of last week. The damage is about 2,000,000 kroner.
   As I was rather garrulous in the last 2 letters, I will close yrs A

Arnold's depression, loneliness and isolation are always close to the surface and Queenie continues to be his main support through the most challenging times but in reward for that she also gets to share in the more interesting stories and the times when he can see the lighter side.

6 July 1918

My dear Q,

Here is the usual Sunday letter, but it is best not to send it round as I am not in the best of spirits.

One naturally is effected by the weather and when you get steady rain and wind for three weeks, one is apt to get depressed. Farmers' seeds suffered from lack of moisture at first; now they are drowned.

However, even the dullest lives have glimpses of humour; such a one occurred this morning; where the railway runs through small holdings, the original farm fences are carried across the track leaving only a width enough for the light railway.

This space is blocked by poles, to prevent the cattle from straying. These poles are removed (by one) during working hours. Early this morning I was shunting the first train full of trucks down to the tip when a coupling broke and 4 waggons rushed down the incline. One could only watch events. Poetry best describes it:

and like a horse unbroken, when first it feels the reigns,

The furious waggons struggled hard and tossed their tawny manes,

And burst the curb and bounded,

Rejoicing to be free

And whirling down in fierce career—

Rushed headlong—

Just at the right moment, the woman of the farm came out of the house to see 4 waggons dash past and hurl the mangled remains of the fence on the pathway at her feet. 'A ten-pound look', by Jove, yes and cheap at the price, however, in less than 2 hours, there was as good a one re-erected.

I don't know what the first matrimonial quarrel is like, but I've just had the first dispute with the landlady. The air is highly charged with electricity, but I do not know how things will pan out.

Out of sheer boredom tonight I went for a 10 mile walk in the pouring rain, but there is nothing to see except the endless fir woods and above, the rock, ice, snow and clouds and waterfalls. How one aches for bricks and mortar. I don't think nature intended for me an engineer; I wish I were a stockjobbers clerk, juggling with figures from 10-4.

Have you ever felt school teaching is not your 'métier'? The workmen talk about jobs they did in 1911—seven years ago. It will be another seventy before the railroad is finished and then they can truly say 'Trondhjem to Kristiania,—warranted handmade'.

I am sorry if these letters are long and uninteresting, but it is so terribly lonely here of an evening, that to stop myself from going mad, I must do something and at present no new newspapers have come along. The old ones I have read and reread from start to finish, including advertisements.

This new 8-hours day is rather democratic. On all public works (i.e., State) married workmen received 10 øre per hour more and 5 øre per hour for each child. I wonder when such will come in England.

No more for now as I must set out for the post office and have the usual Sunday walk.
Best wishes to all.
Ever Yours A

From here on, Arnold's letters take on a downcast tone. He really can see no way out of his current situation and is lonely and dejected enough to write that a *"good dose of strychnine would relieve all, but one is too afraid."* It is hard to know whether, had he been kept in Norway through another winter, he would have ever gone as far as to attempt harm himself or take his own life. I would like to think not and luckily, we never got to find this out, but it is still painful for his family to think, even now over one hundred years later, how desperately despairing he was.

17 July 1918
My dear Q,
Here is the usual mid-weekly letter to let you know how things are going for the last few days have been spent in reading and re-reading all the papers and letters of the last mail.

You had better not seen this around as a circular for it is not in a very cheerful strain.

E's birthday today. It has been awful weather;—a raging wind and a scorching sun and mosquitoes to bite. The former blew all kinds of flies, grasses and smoke into the eyes and mouth and we had more accidents in 8 hours than in the palmiest of the 9 hours day. I append a short sketch of one.

Two whole rails gently collapsed outwards and nearly the whole train sank into the earth. If the Recording Angel takes down all our words—well, my pages won't read wholesome. If paradise is one half of the place we make it out to be, I often wonder there's not a bigger rush for the early doors.

(censored) I grow to—more and more every day. I do wish the war would stop. As well, sigh for the moon. A good dose of strychnine would relieve all, but one is too afraid.
Well, for the time being,
Yours A"

There are only two surviving letters from September. One is a postcard written to Queenie and the other is excerpts from a letter that is one that was in the collection of a member of the Scandinavian Philately Society. Both are written from Oppdal where the weather is getting steadily colder and conditions steadily harsher.

15 Sept 1918
Many thanks indeed for your letters of 18 Aug. Hope you had a good time in London. It is a pity you dislike the folk of a seaside resort. How would you like this place for company? First snowfall yesterday. It is cold up here. Most of the cattle have been brought from the fields and put into the barns. The birds have nearly all gone and the weather makes one feel miserable. Give me trippers and the madding crowd for a bit.
Yours A

22 September 1918 (from Roger Partridge)
Dear Q,
—Well, I shan't be home for your half-term holiday this year—that's certain—it is awfully hard to say goodbye to summer in this climate—it is nice to sit indoors and listen to the wind howling round this farm, but there won't be any leaves on trees very shortly. As we are situated 1800ft up and look down the valley in both directions for many miles, we get every zephyr that blows.
However, I think 21 September is about the time of equinoctial gales, so we must not grumble. I suppose things are jogging on unchanged at home. How is the coal rationing with you? What else can they ration? The majority of men from the camp who were working on the railway down the valley have packed up work and returned back to the camp.

I expect to be here another month; the squirrels have been pretty active latterly and as last winter was very short, one may take it for granted that this winter is going to be long and severe. I would very like to hear from WSC—has she left Homerton? I suppose so by now. In fact, the next mail will be gladly welcomed for it has run 15 days since the last letter came. And now best wishes, Yours Ever A.

Both October letters have both come from collectors. The first one was being sold on a South African site and I was able to transcribe from the scan provided on the website and the second one was from the original Partridge collection and a copy was in the Theisen file that I was fortunate enough to have access to.

Once more, the weather is the main protagonist of each letter, but Arnold also mentions the pay he has received throughout the period of his internment. This can be seen further in the photographs where a scan of an accounting document created by Arnold was found in his papers by his son.

He is right in saying that he was able to save money. Unlike some of the other internees, he limited his socialising and did not spend money on luxuries except for his treasured skis and skates. He was also lucky to have a family regularly furnishing him with food, clothes and art supplies.

10 October 1918
C/o Ødgrard Renning, Opdal
My dear Q,

Many thanks indeed for your letter of 22 September. By the same post came "..." the Graphic of 28 September. This post came entirely unexpected, as I had received a post only 14 days previous.

I regret, I did not write a O (I am pretty sure that this means a circular) last Sunday, but no doubt the daily newspapers will be more interesting. Sunday is an ordinary working day for me and the past few days have been strenuous.

The other day the first wagon jumped the rails, pulled the engine off the track, smashed sleepers and ripped up the rails for 20 metres. Even William the silent might have lost his reputation.

We have had fairly fine weather here. No rain, but a double allowance of wind; the other morning a train of wagons had disappeared from the siding, we found them a 1/4 mile down the line—the wind having blown them all the way. By Jove the wind is strong up here—it comes up the valley like a tidal wave.

I hope the job will not be long in packing up now. When you have to take a coal hammer to break your water supply, it is time all Christians took up indoor work, leaving the heathens to their inheritance.

I hope you have a successful term.

Please excuse more but my lamp has run dry (no more for some day) and I am dog-tired.

Best wishes. Yrs A

26 October 1918 (Thiesen)

Dear F, N and all,

This is rather an auspicious day to write a letter and my wishes that a satisfactory dwelling comes along in due course. "Blembie" sounds too much like an illness.

This week has been lucky in bringing a mail. There were R F C's letters of 29 Sept and 6 Oct, DC's letter of 6 Oct, AVG's letters of 29 Sept and 6 Oct, WSC's letter of 6 Oct also Punches, Observers, Nations and the 'Reporter' all up to date; it was most welcome and entirely drove away a touch of Spanish sickness. At least one calls it this, to be in the fashion, but it was only a cold in the head plus dieting.

I was greatly amused at WSC's sardonic description of luggage transport.

I am glad to hear that the cheques have been paid. It must be curious to have money and make use of the applied mathematics one learnt at school. Just at present, I am fixed with more money than I have ever had in my life before and I can't spend it. The local shop has even a cap!

It is not so much use talking about current events or Dovrebanen. Suffice it to say, we have made fairly good progress and swung right into winter—the motors have stopped and probably farmers will be using sleighs next week. There is eighteen degrees of frost tonight. The underparts of the engine are covered in ice. Life is cheerful.

The latest addition to the household is a young pig and a very lively one. He is quite one of the household (he lives indoors) and looks very peaceful when sleeping between the two cats under the stoves hearth.

We have got paraffin. Farms get 4-6 litres per month according to size. I had 1 litre from the railway and one has to be extra sparing with it, to make it last.

Optimism doesn't pay. I sold my skates and skis last year and now have to purchase again at greatly enhanced prices.

Many thanks indeed to WSC's for the 'Lord of the World' I have scanned it and it certainly is sensational but I have not time nor light to read it up here, so will wait till I go back to the camp again.
Meanwhile, best wishes to all.
Ever Yrs, A"

The final letter in the collection is written eight days before the Allies claimed victory over the Germans and the Alliance. The letter shows absolutely no clue to what is to happen in just over a week. He does write, however, of the arrival of the "*Spanish sykdom*" which must refer to the Spanish Flu.

He writes of two Germans dying of it but by this time, unbeknownst to Arnold, Lieutenant Alltree had died of the virus and Leading Seaman W J Beynon was to die on 2 November. The disease was spreading through the camp. In fact, there were several men who did not make it back to the United Kingdom until early 1919 due to contracting the virus and needing to recover before they went home—this would have been a bitter pill to swallow.

3 November 1918
My dear Q,

It is only the very sternest sense of duty which induces me to write a Sunday letter. Things are not interesting up here and I am in no wise over brimming with cheerfulness, just at present.

I was greatly pleased to receive this week—RFC's letter from Grav 12 Oct, ERC's of 12 Oct, WSC's letter of 12 Oct, also a Graphic and the Observer of 5 Oct.

It is not much use talking of outside events—they move too rapidly. Dovrebanen home truths would be too much for the Norwegian censor—so, what is there to say.

It is comforting to know from WSC's letter that a ford car can beat them (It would beat me at present) but from the papers one gathers that all works and jobs are an open book to women; only recently in an English provincial paper I saw the writer referred to 'the thousands of motor cars driven by reckless young women.

The weather has not been at all bad recently, but the winds up here are terrible. There is no variety between all or none. When there is all, the house rocks and groans and at work, one's face is stung by gravel, coal dust and soot.

1 November was a Saints Day holiday up here—a 'bedsdag'. I went for a long walk along the railway workings to the next station and back on the road, about 16 kilometres; I met 4 people and saw 4 in the distance, otherwise there was only the sound of the wind in the trees, the everlasting—of mountain streams, far and near and now and again the faint tinkle of a cow bell. It would be a change to see a policeman whistling—dogs barking etc.

'Spanish sykdom' is going all through this district. I don't know whether one can be sick of Norway and sick of Spain at the same time. I think they have got it in the camp; one or two of the German interned have died of it recently.
There is not space for more.
Best wishes to all. Yrs A.

After this letter I have no idea of what happened with Arnold until late November where when looking at his Statement of Accounts he has listed at the bottom of the page, under 1918 "Arrived Ripon, 27 November". Arnold's war was over. I imagine that he spent a bit of time at Ripon which was a repatriation camp as well as an army base. I, unfortunately, do not know when he finally managed to make it home to his father and sisters, but I am sure it was one of the happiest moments of his life when he did.

What was happening in the camp?

I think that the short answer to this question at this stage of the war was not a lot! The numbers in the camp had decreased again with at least two more men being repatriated home, several more working outside of camp or at the Legation and some up at Oppdal with Arnold.

There are letters in the Scandinavian Prisoner of War files from the Missions to Seaman concerned for the spiritual welfare of the men still in internment and with offers to provide the services of a chaplain or two.

The letters begin with a bit of a dig at Commander Kennedy with the 24 July letter stating, "The captain, they told me, has married a Norwegian and has settled at Lillehammer and does nothing whatever for the men in the camp. The other officers have been allowed to accept various posts in other places, so that there is now no one in the camp to take any interest in the men or organise any recreation or instruction for them. Neither is any provision whatever made for their spiritual needs."

The Legation and the Admiralty are quick to refute the claims made by the anonymous sailors who made the complaints, whilst on leave. Mr Findlay assures the Mission that an "incorrect representation" of the situation has been made by the men on leave and that "Reverend Messers Mooney and Slater visit camp and periodically hold services which are sparsely attended."

The Admiralty agree that the "men on leave from Norway have given a misleading impression of their treatment and privations" and say that an independent observer would be needed to confirm whether conditions were as reported.

One particular miserable internee tried to pull off a very inventive escape from camp with the help of his brother. Trimmer William H Oakley was finding life at Jørstadmoen very difficult and whilst on leave in July 1918, a plan was concocted whereby William would remain at home and his brother, Albert, would take his place in camp.

All was going well until the return to camp in Norway when the returning men were called to muster and the ruse was blown as Albert was instantly recognised as not being William. Albert was handcuffed and taken to Akershus prison and William was made to return to camp. William was well known at camp as he had found life there very challenging and had been known to cause trouble, even to the point of being gaoled himself in 1917. Fortunately for William, the war was to end in a few short months!

The Spanish Flu made its impact on the camp too, as mentioned earlier, with a couple of deaths and about 16 men kept behind in Norway to recover before heading back to the United Kingdom.

The official files on *HMS India* conclude with letter of commendation written by the Norwegian Minister and forwarded by the Norwegian Legation.[34]

1 January 1919
Norwegian Legation
The Norwegian Minister presents his compliments to the Secretary of State for Foreign Affairs and has the honour to ask that through the kind intermediary of the Right Honourable A J Balfour the British Government's attention may be called to the deserving behaviour of Commander Kennedy, of the British vessel "India."

---

[34] This document can be found at The National Archives FO 383/527

The rest of the British Forces who were interned at Jørstadmoen, Norway, have now been sent home. The Norwegian military authorities emphasise that the whole internment has taken place without any serious and durable frictions is due principally to the English officers and in the first place to Commander Kennedy.

The circumstances were from the beginning very difficult because a great deal of the interned men were without any military discipline. The situation at the Jørstadmoen being, especially at the beginning, little suitable for internment during a longer period, it was not to be avoided that during the internment which lasted more than three years various difficulties and frictions arose.

Under these circumstances, it was of greatest importance for the maintenance of the good order at the camp that Commander Kennedy resided near the Jørstadmoen and that he could at his continuous inspections exert his influence. Through his tactful and understanding behaviour Commander Kennedy has in a more effectful degree than any other man been able to contribute to the satisfactory conducting of the service at the camp.

The Norwegian military authorities have, therefore, thought it their duty to call the attention of the British military authorities interested to this matter and have applied for the assistance of the Norwegian Government in order that through diplomatic channels the British Government may learn of Commander Kennedy's behaviour.

London, 31 December 1918
No. 71/1230/P

The Secretary of State for Foreign Affairs presents his compliments to the Norwegian minister and has the honour to acknowledge with thanks the receipt of Monsieur Vogt's note of the 31st ultimo, in which he is good enough to convey the appreciation of the Norwegian Government of the services of Commander Kennedy in connection with British prisoners of war interned in Norway.

The matter has been brought to the notice of the competent authorities.

Foreign Office,
8 January 1919
Admiralty

22 January 1919

Sir, (Secretary, Prisoners of War department)

I am commanded by my Lord's Commissioners of the Admiralty to acknowledge the receipt of your letter, No.71/1919/P 1230 of the 9th instant and to acquaint you that the Norwegian Minister's recommendation of Commander William G A Kennedy, R N, has been Notre in this Officer's favour.

I am, Sir,

Your obedient Servant.

JWS Anderson

What was the family doing?

Once again there is not a lot to report from the family. R Feaver was in the process of making the decision and then finally moving out of Gravesend and over to New Milton to live near Queenie who was still teaching at Branksome College. A house called Henbury was bought and Nurse and R Feaver had moved in by the time Arnold returned to them. Both Edith and Winnie were teaching at Dartford and Dorothy was still perfecting her chicken and dairy handling skills.

A postcard from September 1918 sent from Opdal (sic) to Queenie

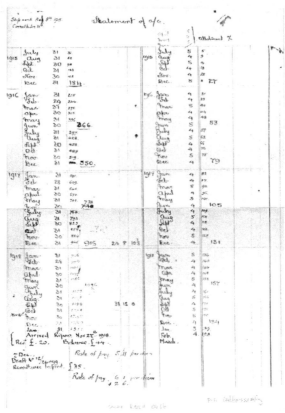

Arnold's Statement of Accounts from July 1915 to February 1919. Expenditure was exceptionally low for a few years!

Below a package form for a quantity of tobacco sent to Arnold in March of 1918.

Kriegsgefangenensendung.

Packed and despatched by ... LLOYD & SONS ...

under authority granted by the Central Prisoners of War Committee of the British Red Cross Society and the Order of St. John of Jerusalem in England.

Verpackt und versendet mit der Autorisirung des Central Komité für Kriegsgefangene des Britischen Roten Kreuzes und der Vereinigung St. Johannes von Jerusalem in England.

CONTENTS. INHALT.

Parcel No. and Date of Despatch

BRITISCHER KRIEGSGEFANGENER.

TOBACCO.

B.P.O.W. INTERNED IN NORWAY.

R. Arnold Clarke. E. R. A.
British Internment Camp.
c/o Vaktchefen.
Jørstadmoen.
Faaberg Jernbanestation.

N O R W A Y.

A censored letter with enclosed censor notes from the British censors and another one of Arnold's beautiful pen and ink drawings.

255

collapsed outwards & the whole train sank
into the earth. If the Recording Angel
takes down all our words — well my
pages wont read wholesome.. If Paradise
is one half the place we make it out to
be, I often wonder there's not a bigger
rush for the early doors.

I grow to
more & more every day I
do wish the war would stop. as well
sigh for the moon. A good dose of
strychnine would relieve all, but one is
too afraid. Well for the time being

Yrs C

Photos of the crew working in Oppdal. The first one on the previous page may be from 1917 with a crew from an earlier job. The gentleman on the far right is Able Seaman George Ward. The other two photos are from Arnold's personal album. The last photo has Arnold looking out from the cabin of the train.

I need to thank Rolf Scharning for assisting me in translating these two documents that were found in a photo album of Arnold's. The letter on the left reads "Engineer A. Clarke is given permission to travel on the train from Ulsberg til Støren Thursday the 14 November 1918." This was written 3 days after the war ended and may have had something to do with getting Arnold to the place he needed to be to be repatriated back to the United Kingdom. Rolf writes that the document on the righthand side "was sent through the railways internal telegram service, between employees" and that the "text says that he is offered a job". "Arnold Clarke, Internee, Fåberg. Position as locomotive driver at Ulsberg Dovrebanen. starting 22 May/ wages 12 kroner per working day."

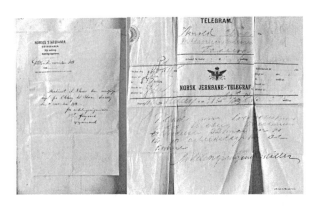

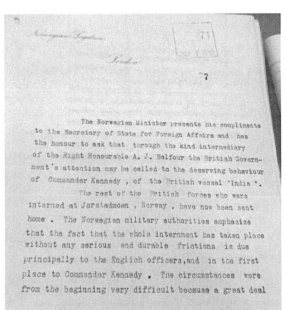

The first page of the commendation written about Commander Kennedy.

A Caricaturist's View – "A Great Humourist Has Obviously Not Let this Opportunity Go."

Drawing, etching and woodwork seemed to be common and shared pursuits amongst the Jørstadmoen internees. Arnold wrote in one of his letters that he would have submitted to Punch magazine had he been better at faces. Someone who did make a bit of a name for himself as an artist and caricaturist was Lieutenant Ernest Woodburne Alltree.

Ernest Alltree was born in Atcham, Shropshire in 1888, the son of an ironmonger. He attended school as a day pupil at Shrewsbury School and joined the Royal Navy as a midshipman in 1907. He was a career Naval man and by the time war broke out he had risen to the rank of an Acting Sub-Lieutenant.

It was in this role that he worked on the *India* (although records have him as a Sub-Lieutenant at this stage) and it was he who was responsible for providing written records of the sinking to the Admiralty having also been one of the minorities who scored a place in the ships rescue craft. Lieutenant Alltree was an Officer and so did not have to live in the Internment camp after the start of 1916.

Life in Norway suited him as on 7 August 1916, he married Hedvig Knudsen at the Church of St. Edmund in Christiania and then in 1917, Ernest and Hedvig had a daughter, Ingrid. The Scandinavia files from the War Office at the National Archives have a letter dated 21 November 1917, from the British Legation concerning Lieutenant Alltree, his wife, and their young child.

It reads that Lieutenant Alltree "wishes his sister to come out from England to reside with him during the winter months. He states that his wife is suffering from ill-health and is in an extremely nervous state, as a result of a severe illness during last summer and he wishes his sister to assist his wife with the house and young baby during the winter months. He has produced a certificate from Dr

Konow of Lillehammer stating that such assistance is necessary in the present state of Mrs Alltree's health."

This letter is followed a few weeks later by a letter from Charles Walker at the Foreign Office asking that the Admiralty consider granting permission for "her passage in an Admiralty vessel." The paper trail runs cold after this an unfortunately we never learn if Dorothy Alltree got to travel to Norway to help her brother or whether the young Alltree family had to muddle through on their own.

Unfortunately, Ernest's story does not get much brighter after this and does not come with a happy conclusion as although he seemed to have started to set up a life for himself and his family in Norway, he was one of the unlucky men to die of the Spanish Flu. He died on the 29 October 1918, thirteen days before the war ended.

Whilst he was alive and living in Norway, Lieutenant Alltree became a proficient artist and caricaturist and the local papers appear to have really enjoyed including his art in their publications and, thanks to his family, many examples of his art survive. They provide a humorous and pictorial view of the goings-on within the camp and tie in beautifully with some of the experiences Arnold wrote about to Queenie.

Many of the sketches are not dated but all provide another insight into camp life and looking at the descriptions in some of the skiing and skating sketches and thinking of Arnold's descriptions of his escapades, it makes me wonder if perhaps Lieutenant Alltree had seen Arnold trying to perfect his skills!

The Interned British
Return from the mountains.

Lieutenant Alltree and Hedvig Knudsen on their wedding day in 1916.

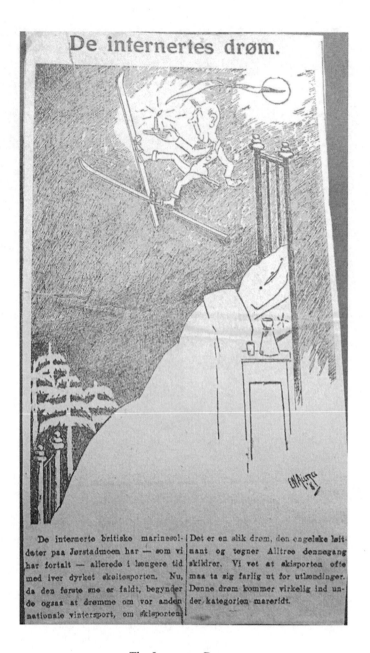

De internertes drøm.

De internerte britiske marinesoldater paa Jørstadmoen har — som vi har fortalt — allerede i længere tid med iver dyrket skøitesporten. Nu, da den første sne er faldt, begynder de ogsaa at drømme om vor anden nationale vintersport, om skisporten. Det er en slik drøm, den engelske løitnant og tegner Alltree dennegang skildrer. Vi vet at skisporten ofte maa ta sig farlig ut for utlændinger. Denne drøm kommer virkelig ind under kategorien mareridt.

The Internees Dream

The interned British sailors at Jørstadmoen have—as we have been told—already for a long time eagerly drank the skating sport. Now that the first snow has fallen, they are also starting to dream about our second national winter sport, skiing. It is such a dream, the English Lieutenant and cartoonist Alltree once depicts. We know that skiing often must be dangerous for foreigners. This dream really comes under the category of nightmares.

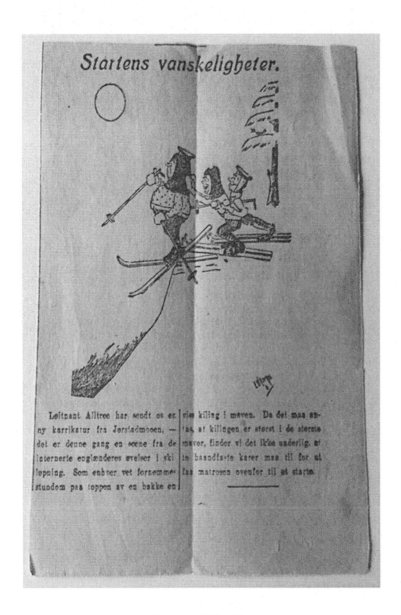

Starting Difficulties

Lieutenant Alltree has sent us a new caricature from Jørstadmoen, this time being a scene from the interned English drills in skiing. As everyone knows, sometimes the top of a hill fits a nasty tickling in the stomach. Since it is believed that the tickling is the largest in the largest stomachs, we find it no wonder that two strap-on vessels must be taken to phase the sailor above to start.

Connection between Fåberg and Jørstadmoen.
A suggestion of one English Officer

Av årets saga

To britiske rømlinger fra Jørstadmoen.

28/5. To matroser er rømt fra Jørstadmoen, hvor det engelske mannskap fra «India» er internert. En ung løytnant, mr. E. W. Alltree, som morer seg selv og de andre internerte med å tegne, har laget denne tegningen av rømningen. Her gir han en forklaring på hvordan de to matrosene kom seg bort fra moen.

Of this year's saga
Two sailors have escaped from Jørstadmoen where the English crew from "India" are interned. Lieutenant Mr W Alltree, who amuses himself and the others interned with drawing, has made this drawing of the escape. Here, he explains how the two sailors got away from the camp.

When the rope broke

As is well known, the traffic conditions at Fåberg have become quite heavy, after the Bridge was struck by the flood a few months ago. A ridge now provides the crossing. But the other day, the ferry, which our correspondent has already announced, was in an accident, as the steel wire rope broke and the boat drifted down the river until it finally got anchor.

The interned English Sea Officer at Jørstadmoen, Lieutenant Alltree, who, as you know, is a great humourist, has obviously not let this opportunity go. He sends us the above from the dramatic moment when the rope broke. When the event appears to one man, who has seen the danger with his eyes, then it must have affected the peaceful inhabitants of Gudbrandsdalen.

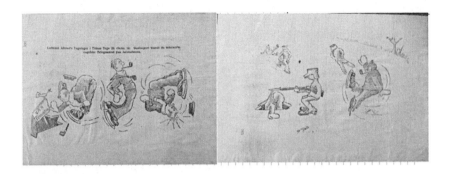

Lieutenant Alltree's drawings of the times 29 October 1916: Shooting sport among the interned English warriors at Jørstadmoen.

How one of the interned Englishmen, Mr Alltree, assumes the conditions are in a normal Norwegian home nowadays.

New Year's Recital at the Prison camp at Jørstadmoen.
We have received the picture above as a small greeting from the British camp at
Jørstadmoen. Lieutenant Alltree, who performed the drawing, accompanies the picture
with some gloomy considerations on the change of the year. It is a heavy heart that the
interns now think that the time inside the steel wire fence is beginning to feed long. As
it turns out the Lieutenant is already looking into that time, when both the prisoners
and the guard must get a grey beard.

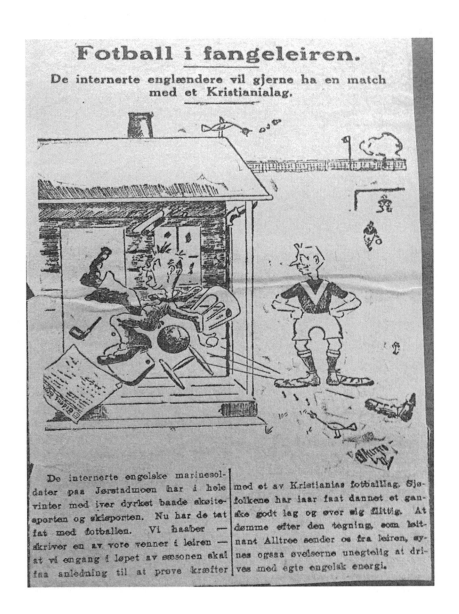

Football in the Prison Camp

The Interned English would like to have a match with the Christiania team.

The interned English sailors at Jørstadmoen have been practicing both skating and skiing all winter long with eagerness. Now, they have a grip on football. We hope, writes one of our friends in the camp, that sometime during the season we will have the opportunity to try our hand at one of Kristiania's football teams. The seafarers have for years been able to form a good team and practice diligently. Judging from the drawing that Lieutenant Alltree sends us from the camp, the exercises also seem to undeniably run with genuine English energy.

— Luk døren ialfald!

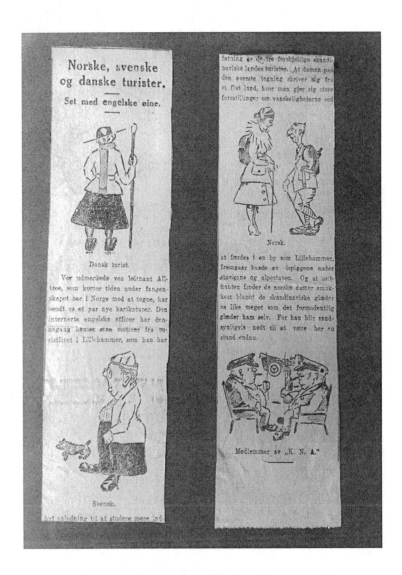

Norwegian, Swedish and Danish tourists
Seen with English eyes
Our distinguished friend Lieutenant Alltree, who is drawing during time in captivity here in Norway, has sent us a few new cartoons. The interned English Officer has then retrieved his motifs from the unrestricted Lillehammer, whom he has taken to study more about the three different Scandinavian countries tourists. That lady in the earliest drawing comes from a flat country where great ideas are made about the difficulties of traveling in a city like Lillehammer are evidenced by both the ice spikes under the shoes and the alpine rod. And that the Lieutenant finds the Norwegian ladies most beautiful among the Scandinavian delights as much as he pleases himself for, he will probably have to be here for a while yet.

This is a bit of a joke about the Chief of Staff, Charles Nelson. The rough translation says that Engineer-Lieutenant-Commander Nelson has paid a principle for 16 days of 6.12kr making a total of 97,92kr.

What Next? What Are the Stories of and What Happened to some of the HMS India Crew?

Arnold was one of 107 men who survived the sinking of *HMS India* and were subsequently sent to an internment camp in Norway. He was one of approximately seventy men and maybe ten or more officers who were repatriated in November 1918 and were able to return to Britain to their families. They all have stories to tell and here are a few of them that I have gathered from descendants I have met through my research and extensive Google searches!

Charles William Nelson

I have touched on Charles Nelson's story much earlier in the book in the chapter concerning the sinking of *India*. Charles was the officer who had his leg injured and subsequently, after the war, had to have his left leg amputated. Much of this story is told by his granddaughter, Deborah, who has shared his and her story with me.

She wrote that he had been serving on the *India* since 1913 when the vessel was still being used by P & O. He was one of the older members of the *India* crew and was 38 years old when the vessel was lost. Twenty-two days later, Deborah's mother was born. Charles Nelson was allowed two periods of Leave of Absence, the first over Christmas in 1916 and the second from September to October in 1918 and so he would have seen his young family a couple of times across the three years he was interned.

Deborah was unaware that the officers had lived outside of the camp and she said that it made the photographs that she had found of her grandfather's make more sense as they were often of parties or socialising. Deborah wrote in detail about the trauma her grandfather went through upon returning to Britain.

"In Norway, it (his leg) had not caused him much pain or discomfort, but after the end of the war and his release, he was advised that the lump had become gangrenous. The following year, almost to the day, he was admitted to Lady Whittaker's Private Hospital at Pylewell Park to have his left leg amputated.

The postcard he sent to my grandmother appears to have been written on the evening following his arrival there. It is postmarked 9:55 p.m., 22 November 1920. The postcard shows the exterior of the hospital.[35] A window is indicated by an inked cross and the inscription reads, *I slept here in room with 7 beds. I live under the X and very nice too. I think that is one of the best views I have seen. Yours C.*

To me this seems so amazingly understated from a man who had been in an internment camp for four years and who had his leg cut off. Four months later, 16 March 1921, he was back at sea.

She goes on to describe the leg he then wore for the rest of his life and her memories of him.

"It was some early form of hard articulated plastic with leather straps, hung on a hook from the top of the wardrobe together with its sock and shoe and I being just a child, was curiously fascinated by it. I have often wondered how he negotiated the stairways board ship with a false leg. The engine room would have been well below decks and quite difficult to manoeuvre.

Grandfather died in March of 1957 having lived through the turmoil of two world wars. I can remember him musing to me that the daffodils would be out soon. They bloomed a day or two after he died.

He had been athletic and had been a fine swimmer and a competent skier. He had brought his wooden skis and poles back with him from Norway but, of course, never used them again after the amputation. They remained thereafter in the garage of our Essex home until I used them playing on a local street slope in the bitter winter of 1962/3 and managed to snap one of the skis."

One mystery remains from Charles Nelson and his photograph album. There is a single photo of a noticeably young boy, only one year old. Deborah was always at a loss as to why, amongst photos of skiing, socialising and internee life there was this one photo of this young child.

---

[35] Note, Pylewell Park is an exclusive and vast country house in Hampshire near Lymington. The top floor of the house was taken over as a hospital for officers during and just after the First World War. The house has its own private beach and views across the Solent to the Isle of Wight as well as acres of private grounds.

Since finding out the officers did not live-in camp and that many of them married and had children, Deborah has found herself with more questions than answers. Questions about a photograph of a little boy that will probably never be answered.

John Tindling

During my lockdown research period I had spent some time trawling the various chatrooms and had left posts requesting that anyone who had relatives or information on *HMS India* contact me. I did not get many replies, but one that I did receive was from the granddaughter of John Tindling, Kerry, who wrote that she had spent time trying to research the *India* and was extremely interested in my research.

Her story is similar to others I have heard, including our personal family story, in that her grandfather never spoke of the torpedoing or of his WW1 experiences. John Tindling was one of the many men on *HMS India*, who had grown up in the East End of London. Unable to read and write, his story represents the story of many of the men who went to sea at this time.

He was employed to work in some of the harshest conditions in the bowels of the ship as a fireman. His job would have been to keep the huge fires that created the steam for the engines going. He may have been down in the engine rooms for hours at a time in all conditions, day or night. We will never know where he was when the ship was torpedoed but we do know that John Tindling managed to escape the sinking vessel and was rescued by the *Gotaland,* which meant that after a brief period in Narvik, he was able to return home to his wife and go on to father eight children.

His wife was aware that the ship her husband was on had been torpedoed and Kerry writes "my nan had always said that she was informed that grandad was missing, presumed dead and passed out when he turned up on the doorstep!"

As far as his family knows, John returned to the war after recuperating from injuries sustained during the sinking of the India, although he was physically scarred for life with marks and a noticeable bump left on his head that was said to have been inflicted by debris from the wreck of the vessel he had been serving on. John Tindling lived a full life after his near-death experience in the North Sea and died in 1968 at the age of 75.

William Tilley

William Tilley was one of the many firemen on board the *HMS India* and his job, along with the others, would have been to tend to the massive coal-stoked fires that would have run continuously to keep the steam engines that drove the boat running.

William was 21 when the ship was torpedoed but had been onboard since 1914, before the war, when the ship was still a member of the P & O fleet. He was one of the many that was rescued by the *Trawler Saxon*. William Tilley can be seen in several photographs from Jørstadmoen including the one of all the crew sitting on the hill where he can be seen with his head poking through the *HMS India* life ring. He can also be seen in many of the football photographs.

Tilley was one of the small group of men who married a Norwegian lady. William and Agnethe Haugen, one of the camp's cooks and a native of Fåberg, were married on 19 October 1918 and had only a brief time together before William was repatriated and sent back to Britain. His certificate of discharge from the Royal Navy is dated 28 January 1919 and from there he went back to his hometown, London and investigated joining the police force.

On returning to Norway to collect Agnethe he changed his mind and decided that he and his wife should remain in Norway and with a recommendation from Commander Kennedy, he applied for and was given a job on the Norwegian State Railways. After gaining Norwegian citizenship in October 1921, William and Agnethe settled into married life and had seven children.

But things were not to remain settled for long. William became involved in the Second World War after the Germans invaded in 1940 and this is where his story becomes more interesting. He was still working with the railways and was given the job (with several other men) of moving the engines to Lillehammer. This was achieved even though the Germans attacked several times during the move.

Soon after the English troops arrived and William Tilley was asked to assist as interpreter and guide. Late in April 1940, William was given the task of driving the engine of a train that was taking a Norwegian major to Hjerkinn on the Dovrebanen right through the section that Arnold and his other fellow internees had helped to build.

They never made it to their destination due to German bombing raids, but William's skill and affinity with the English language led to him being promoted to locomotive-foreman and he worked in transporting the troops before escaping to London. A document he wrote outlines the work he did during this time, but I will hand over to Roger Partridge to tell more of the story.

When he eventually escaped to London, he wrote a seven-page report on his activities during this period, but some of these were a lot less detailed than others and I (R.P) suspect he was not only helping the British troops but was also involved in the train movements that enabled the Norwegian Government to rescue its Gold reserves and get them to the coast at Åndalsnes, from which a Royal Navy cruiser carried them over to Scotland.

Tilley and a companion reached Åndalsnes on May 1st and although they had been promised passage on a ship, they soon found themselves held under armed guard by nervous troops who thought they were spies. Luckily, they were spotted by a major who they had helped earlier and were taken to General Paget, the Officer commanding, who strongly recommended that Tilley should leave Norway and his family as the Germans would certainly shoot him if he was captured.

So, he sailed away from Norway on board *H.M.S Calcutta* on 2 May and reached Scapa Flow the following day.

Roger Partridge's research uncovered that William returned to his hometown in London (West Ham) and assumed the role of an air raid warden, but this was not to last for long as in January 1942 he is released from this role to take up the position of Head Porter and senior fire guard at the Shaftesbury Hotel.

The Shaftesbury Hotel was in central London and was managed by the Norwegian Government. Roger Partridge questions whether William was working in the jobs he was listed as doing or whether this was a cover for some other military or undercover work, but by April 1943, William has left London and has joined the Norwegian Army. He was certainly having a busier war the second time around than he did the first time and it still was not over.

William survived an emergency landing in a plane in Sweden in 1945, where he lost everything but his life. Luckily for him and everyone else, the war was over about a week later and William was able to return to his wife and children in Norway. He had not seen them for five long years and had only been in contact through Red Cross Mail.

It must have been such a relief to finally settle down to family life again. William Tilley spent the rest of his working life on the Norwegian State Railways and died in 1976 and is buried in the Hamar valley region—not too far from Jørstadmoen.

Late in the writing of this book I was contacted by Linn Tilley Brandt, one of William Tilley's grandchildren, seeking information on her grandfather. I forwarded her the passage I had written using Roger Partridges research which provided me with the bulk of my information.

I asked Linn to corroborate the research Roger had done and to alert me to any inaccuracies in the story. She wrote that "all the information seems to be correct" and then went on to say that "World War Two was extra difficult for the family because William was English and they would not talk about it, so my father could not tell much. He did not know anything about his English relatives, the only contact he got was birthday cards from his grandmother."

I was also contacted by Kjell-Arne, one of William's other grandchildren and he reassured me "your story seems to be close to my walk down the memory lane." Interestingly, Kjell-Arne had spent time with Roger Partridge and was instrumental in assisting in the unearthing of the documents belonging to Commander Kennedy.

There were a handful of men who petitioned to be allowed to remain in Norway for the purposes of employment as well as some for love. Upon being able to visit the National Archives in Kew, London again (they had been closed through the first Covid-19 lockdown of 2020) I found a telegraph dated 19 November 1918 and sent from the Legation at Christiania. It requested:

"Following interned Prisoners of War are willing to remain in Norway under present conditions of pay and allowance.

Eng. Lieut F W Tims is employed as Registrar and S J Perry Officers Servant as messenger.

D F Trinder Private RMLI and R Maynard are employed as messengers at Consulate in Bergen.

W Lamb Officers Servant is employed as messenger at the Naval Vice-Consulate at Bergen.

Services still "urgently required."

I decided to try and do more research on the men who had been petitioning to remain in Norway. Frederick Tims was an engineer on board the *HMS India* and his records have him returning to England in May 1919 to work in administration and that is all I have found on him.

I was able to find out a bit more about Private David Trinder who also returned to England in 1919 and then records show him emigrating to Brooklyn,

New York in 1942. The internees I found most about were William Lamb and Robert Charles Maynard whose stories were told to me by their respective grandsons.

William Knight Lamb

William Knight Lamb was an Officers Steward on HMS India and my early research had shown that he was born in 1892, was mentioned in the 1917 tally of interned men and had performed in the 1918 Varieties Concert. Research by Roger Partridge had also revealed that he had married a Norwegian woman by the name of Anna Roed.

After seeing that he had petitioned to remain in Norway after the war, I attempted to research him more thoroughly and came across an article in the Henley Standard. The article, written in May 2020, outlined the work being done by Mike Willoughby to get Henley men recognised for their involvement in WW1 or 2 and have them listed in the Commonwealth War Graves registry.

Mike had not only been researching the life and war involvement of William Lamb (or William Knight Lamb) but also that of Lieutenant John Henry Biggs. I managed to find a way to email Mike and in September 2020, we enjoyed a lengthy telephone conversation about our research.

In that conversation, Mike mentioned that he was in contact with William Knight Lamb's grandson and would I be happy for him to pass on my contact information—of course, I was and, to cut a long story short, Peter Lamb lives 15 minutes from my front door and we have since met in a pub on the banks of the Thames and shared stories about our ancestors.

William Knight Lamb was born in Brixton and signed up to the navy at the age of sixteen. After onshore training he first set sail in 1910 and then was at sea until 1913. The 1911 census has him as an Officers Steward in the Royal Navy at Sea and in Ports Abroad.

Peter Lamb writes, "In 1913 his name appears in a number of police gazettes in Australia and New Zealand. They might relate to something that occurred that was related to me by my Great Aunt Nellie (William Knight Lamb's sister). This concerned the death of a petty officer that had tormented and bullied my grandfather and other junior sailors. It is possible that he and others dealt with the matter which resulted in the death of the officer. According to Aunt Nellie, he received a King's Pardon for the offence."

William Knight Lamb's official records note that he had "Run 11.4.13 'Pyramus' Sydney" which I can only assume meant that he had absconded from his ship on the same day that the Brisbane Telegraph and The Sun newspapers have the ship leaving Sydney for New Zealand.

I have since found records in Australian Police gazettes advertising the missing man and offering a reward. The Tasmanian Police Gazette from 25 April 1913, states, "Absent without leave. On the 11th instant ~ William Knight Lamb, Officers Steward, native of England, age 21 years, height 5 feet 6 ½ inches, brown hair and eyes and dark complexion. A reward of £1 is offered for the arrest of this absentee."

The South Australian Police Gazette of 30 April of the same year states "From HMS Penguin, at Sydney on the 11th instant. William Knight Lamb, Officers Steward, 21 years of age, English, 5ft 6 ½ inches, brown hair, high forehead, brown eyes, clean teeth, round face, dark complexion, £1 reward on arrest."

Comparable listings were also found in the New Zealand Police Gazette and the Victorian one. One way or another, he found himself back in the UK by the start of the war.

By 1915, William was back on ships and was one of the men that was on *HMS India* when it was torpedoed. Whilst the records have him mentioned in the 1917 camp list and on the 1918 Varieties Concert programme, William was afforded the opportunity to work outside of the camp. This is unsurprising considering that William was an Officers Steward and all the Officers lived out of the camp for much of the time.

The telegram that requests the permission for William to remain in Norway has his position listed as a messenger for the Naval Vice-Consulate in Bergen. Bergen is almost 450Km from the camp at Jørstadmoen so if he was working there before the end of the war it is unlikely that he spent much of his time at the camp.

The first record we have of William post-WW1 is his marriage certificate. He is married in May of 1919 to Anna Roed, a local 21-year-old woman from Bergen. Mike Willoughby's research led him to record that Anna was "a member of a local concert party who played at the camp to entertain the internees." Whilst I agree that there were likely to be musicians visiting the camp every now and then, I think that there might also be the possibility that Anna and William met in Bergen, whilst he was working there. It would seem to be a long way for Anna to travel to entertain British internees, but I've no solid proof either way. Anna and William were back in England residing in Henley-upon-Thames by 1920 when their first child, Raymond was born. William returned to sea and their second child, Daphne, was born in 1934.

At the commencement of the Second World War, William was still serving in the merchant navy and this is where his story ends. Records show that William Knight Lamb died and was buried at sea, in the Red Sea, on 2nd October 1941. He was serving on the *SS Strathnever* and was reported to have died of heat stroke and exhaustion and was buried, coincidentally, in the same sea as his father was.

I found over twenty-five links on family trees on genealogy sites and sent out enquiries to all of them. Most have not replied yet (maybe that is for the second edition of the book!) but of those who did, Christopher Elston has provided new information and photographs and consequently sent me back to the keyboard to include the story of his grandfather, Robert Charles Maynard— "a very funny, caring man who was much loved by our family."

Robert Charles Maynard

I have written about Robert Charles Maynard briefly in other sections of the book. I touched on his love affair with Florence Baker, as seen in the lovely letter she wrote him in 1917. I also mentioned that Robert was granted permission to remain in Norway at the conclusion of the war to continue his work as a messenger for the Consulate in Bergen. Robert has proved to be the owner and taker of one of the best collections of photography from the camp.

His great grandson, Christopher, writes, "My great grandfather loved using his little Brownie box camera" and relates how Robert Maynard came to be a seaman saying:

"He ran away to sea at thirteen after his father died and the story is, he found a sailor's 'ticket' on the ground at the docks and pretended he had experience joining the crew of a Norwegian sailing ship. On the voyage, they were rough with him, breaking his nose with a belaying pin. The captain's wife, who apparently sailed with her husband, was kind to him."

Christopher was also able to relate some of the stories told to him that put a different spin on the situations I was aware of and had written about. My research had concluded that the men were in Norwegian uniforms as they had lost their own uniforms during the wrecking of *HMS India*, Robert Maynard related that they also played around with the uniforms that they had managed to save saying "they swapped clothes so the Norwegians would not initially know their names."

Christopher also tells of a different side of the story to the cabin fire of 1917, saying that the story he was told was that "it was deliberately set on fire over the bad quality of the food." There is nothing in the official file about the fire and although Arnold mentions it in his writings to Queenie, he does not go into much detail. It also could be that he was very aware of the censors and so did not divulge too much. The photos Robert Maynard took and kept are an amazing record of a dramatic event in camp.

Able Seaman George Ward

George's granddaughter, Helen, replied to a request I left on her blog about her grandfather being in the bath when *HMS India* was torpedoed. She happily provided photographs and wrote, "My grandfather, George Ward (1884-1970) was originally from Goole, West Yorkshire. He joined the Royal Navy as a Boy, training as a naval gunner and leaving in early 1914 only to be recalled in September of that year following the outbreak of war. At some point during his internment, he was given leave to travel to the UK to attend a family funeral before returning to Norway. After the war, he settled in Nelson, Lancashire where he became a postman."

Blacksmith's Mate William Gardiner

I was able to find Ian, William Gardiner's grandson, through an article he had written on the internet regarding his grandfather. Ian informed me that William's family were one of the families who were incorrectly informed that their son had been killed in the torpedo attack, only to be informed days later that he was safe and well.

Ian writes, "As far as stories, the best I can relay is that when he talked about his time as a 'POW' in Norway, it was more like a vacation since they were allowed freedom and as he said, they were even taught to ski."

He then recounts a quirky taste that his grandfather developed in Norway saying, "To the day he passed away, he always had a desire for a Norwegian cheese and bought it here in Canada when he could." I found the recollection of feeling like internment was a vacation interesting but wonder whether when compared to years in the smoky, fiery furnaces in the bowels of a ship, life in camp at Jørstadmoen might have been preferable.

Able Seaman/Gunner Will Keats

One of the last descendants I contacted was Bill Anstead, the grandson of Will Keats. Bill had undertaken extensive research of his own in the early 2000s and had completed the massive feat of sailing 3000km from Scotland to Bodø in 2007 and visited Helligvaer Islands and dropped flowers over the wreck site. He had been in contact with the relatives of Commander Kennedy and they were kind enough to introduce him to me. Bill's research has been a fantastic addition to my own.

Will Keats was a career sailor who had joined the navy at the age of 17 as a cadet and two years later was promoted to Able Seaman. He was trained as a gunner and proved to be a very talented one, winning various competitions. He left the navy in 1908 but was retained as a member of the Royal Fleet Reserves and was then recalled as an Able Seaman to serve during WW1.

He left on *HMS India* in 1915, leaving a pregnant wife and three children behind. His daughter, Agnes, was born four weeks after the torpedo attack and in honour of the time Will spent in hospital in Bodø, she was given the middle name and was known as, Bodø. Her full name was Agnes India Bodø Keats.

Will had suffered back injuries during the sinking and rescuing and was hospitalised in Bodø for a time and did not accompany the rest of the crew in their journey to Jørstadmoen but joined them once he had been discharged from hospital.

Grandson Bill reports that Will Keats is not thought to have participated much in sports activities but he was a central figure in arranging and participating in self-made entertainment within the camp. The programme for the 1918 concert lists him singing songs in parts I and II. His sense of humour shows in the advert for Snowflake Laundry— "Mingling a specialty, send your dirties without delay."

Will waited three long years before being granted leave to return to England and finally meet the daughter who was born four weeks after the torpedo attack. He left Norway on the 4 October 1918 with the conditions that he was to return in 45 days. War ending on the 11 November meant that Will never had to return, although he did maintain fifty years of contact with the local Hammershaug family with whom he had built a friendship during his time in internment.

Commander William G A Kennedy

I found it exceedingly difficult to work out when my research was finished and wondered that if I kept digging, I would keep finding more descendants and more stories to tell and I would have to stop somewhere, but I knew that there was one contact that I wanted to make and that was with Marie Barltrop.

I had seen her name mentioned a few times on different documents and believed that she had been heavily involved in the creation of the now defunct *HMS India* website and was perhaps related to Commander Kennedy. It was December 2020 when I finally had a breakthrough. During yet another lockdown and whilst researching Commander Kennedy, I came across a reference to Ken Barltrop on an incomplete website written by K Groenha (www.kgroenha.net).

The website was about a relative of Commander Kennedy's who had spent considerable time, coincidentally, in Norway in the nineteenth-century and it also made mention of the Kennedy family home in Ulverston, Stone Cross. I swiftly googled Ken and Marie Barltrop and a few pages in, I found an email address. Without knowing if these were the people I was looking for I hastily typed out an email introducing myself and explaining that I was wishing to contact the descendants of Commander Kennedy.

A mere two hours later I had a reply and bingo! I had found Marie and her husband Ken and through them, Marie's brother, Bill. Not only had I found them, but they were happy to talk and share resources with me and I in turn shared things for the website that Ken was endeavouring to get published once more.

William George Ainslie Kennedy was born in 1873, the son of a very wealthy Cumberland mine owner. He was an experienced and decorated naval officer who had been promoted to Lieutenant at the age of 25 and then to Commander at age 34 whilst serving in the Mediterranean. It was during this period that he was awarded the Commander of the Order of the Crown of Italy owing to the work he had done to assist in the rescuing of civilians following the Messina earthquake of 1908.

Commander Kennedy took over the command of *HMS India* after her refitting and was in command when she was torpedoed. It was he who decided that his men would be better served remaining in Norway instead of risking placing near drowned, unclothed men on unsatisfactory vessels to try and get them back to England and it was he who stayed with them. I have written earlier about some of the external views of Commander Kennedy and unfortunately, neither Marie nor Bill got to meet their grandfather as he died before they were born.

They did, however, spend time with their grandmother, Alice Fedora Kennedy (nee Lundh) who, herself, was the daughter of a Norwegian Naval commander and had married the commander in Norway in February 1916. Bill writes— "There is only one story that my grand-mother repeated from time to time and that was about my grand-father having "gone down with the ship', only to resurface amidst the turmoil and turbulence to be rescued and to become one of those fortunate to survive the sinking."

Bill and Marie's father, Myles Harold William Kennedy, was born in Norway in April 1917. The descriptions given by the Norwegians of Commander Kennedy seem to be of a larger-than-life man, who had a taste for the good life but the family and the family biographer, Stuart Allison, give the impression that the Commander was a "true gentleman."[36]

As I mentioned, I had huge difficulties in deciding when my research was finished but whilst waiting to hear back from publishers, four other descendants contacted me I had attempted to contact. Theresa Trinder, the great granddaughter of David Trinder, Roland Adams, the grandson of John Roland Adams, John and Gordon Musselwhite, the grandsons of Harold Musselwhite and Clare, the great-granddaughter of Thomas Joseph Sanders.

I had left a message on Theresa, John and Clare's Ancestry pages and I had attempted to contact Roland through a chatroom. Theresa did contact me and although she was unable to add anything to her great-grandfather's story, she was so interested in the story of the camp that her encouraging words spurred me on. Then John and Clare answered my posts and told me that whilst they knew little, they were happy to do some digging and would get back to me. Roland was a fantastic source of added information and the stories his grandfather had told were reminiscent of the letters Arnold wrote.

---

[36] Allison, Stuart. The Kennedys of Stone Cross Mansion. Pixeltweaks Publications, Ulverston, Cumbria. 2014 p64

Harold Musselwhite

John and Gordon Musselwhite were able to tell a bit more about Harold and his time in the Navy, especially just after the torpedo attack.

"When HMS India was torpedoed in the North Sea during the Great War, Sub-Lieut. Harold Musselwhite went down with her and was half-an-hour in the water. Swimming to an upturned boat, he remained there for an hour and a half, being amongst the last to be picked up.

He received his early nautical training on H.M. Training Ship Worcester, being the cadet captain and winning the Worcester Silver Medal and a nomination as midshipman in the R.S.R. He was rescued by a Norwegian fisherman and interned in Norway for much of the war."

Harold wasn't mentioned in the list compiled in 1917 but being an officer, he would have lived out of the camp. I was able to share with Harold's descendants the sad story of his ill-fated marriage to Daisy and the troubles he went through after it. Happily, Harold married again in 1924 and went on to have a long life, dying in 1984.

Thomas Joseph Sanders

Chief Armourer (Pens) Thomas Joseph Sanders was a career sailor who had been at sea since 1888 after spending his early working years as a blacksmith. He came out of retirement to join the crew on *HMS India* and would have been responsible for maintenance of the weaponry onboard the boat. His conduct as a sailor was always ranked as good and his character was considered very good. Clare and I find it funny that his official records mention that he is a pipe smoker!

John Roland Adams

John Roland Adams was a part of the Carpenters Crew on *HMS India*. He was born in Newcastle-Upon-Tyne in 1891 and signed up as R.N.V.R in Tyne. He was interned for the whole period of the war. Roland, his grandson, states emphatically that "he hated the camp and soon after being taken there was given piece work (work output measured against time) to keep busy."

Roland's mother had related to him that John felt that "the Norwegian prison guards sympathies seemed to be with the Germans and that the guards would taunt the internees telling them that "you won't win the war." He then wonders "that the longer the war went on, they began to treat the prisoners a bit better."

John Roland Adams was one of the men who was reported missing after the torpedo strike and Roland relates that "distressed his future bride, Louise Fairbairn, very much. I understand he had to swim for it and eventually made it to a lifeboat." Adams was counted as one of the men rescued by one of *India's* boats. He was granted leave at the very end of 1917 and "was married on New Year's Day 1918." His daughter was born on 29 October 1918 and was named Olive— "the universal sign of peace".

Two photographs supplied by the Kennedy family. Above is Fedora's mother, Alice with baby Myles in 1917 in Norway. To the right is Commander Kennedy and Myles in 1921 outside the family home in Ulverstone, Stone Cross.

Various papers from the archives of Charles William Nelson, Chief Engineer and Chief of Staff. They include his appointment to Senior Engineer dated 22 March 1915. There is also a copy of a letter granting Leave of Absence from Jørstadmoen for December 1916.

The Internment Camp,

Jørstadmoen,

Faaberg,

Norway.

I hereby certify that *Engineer Lieutenant Commander. C. W. Nelson. RNR* has been granted one month's leave of absence in order to proceed to England to visit his relations. The leave has been granted on the conditions that he should return to the Internment Camp in Norway and should not be employed on any military work during his leave.

Commander, R. N.
late in command of H.M.S. "India".

The document below is a Certificate for Wounds and Hurts which details the damage done to Charles Nelson's leg. This damage eventuated in him having his leg amputated.

Charles Nelson received what looks to be a handwritten letter from King George acknowledging his "miseries and hardships" and being pleased that he can now "enjoy the happiness of a home." Charles was forced to wait a bit more for this as he had to endure having his leg amputated and the subsequent recovery and rehabilitation period which was spent in the officers' hospital at Pylewell Park as seen in the postcard below.

BUCKINGHAM PALACE

1918.

The Queen joins me in welcoming
you on your release from the
miseries & hardships, which you have
endured with so much patience &
courage.

During these many months of trial,
the early rescue of our gallant Officers
& Men from the cruelties of their captivity
has been uppermost in our thoughts.

We are thankful that this longed
for day has arrived, & that back in
the old Country you will be able
once more to enjoy the happiness of
a home & to see good days among
those who anxiously look for your
return.

George R.I.

1917

Photographs on previous pages from the album of Charles Nelson —the young Nelson before WW1 and HMS India. In 1917 in Norway. Partaking in one of his favourite activities, swimming. Nelson had the lower half of his left leg amputated after the war.

A photograph of William Knight Lamb and Anna Roed on their wedding day in 1919 before moving back to Britain to set up home in Henley-on-Thames.

William Tilley and his bride, Agnethe Haugen on their wedding day, 19 October 1918 in Fåberg and William in the camp.

A caricature of Commander Kennedy as drawn by Lieutenant Alltree.

*—William Tilley with memorabilia from HMS India and his son Christian.
Dated about 1920.*

From the descendants of Able Seaman George Ward, it is hard to know who the other men in the photo are but George is the sailor on the right-hand side with a pipe in his hand. The sailor on the right has HMS India on his cap.

Right—a young William Gardiner before he took his place as Blacksmith's Mate on HMS India.

Page 337—Fedora Kennedy and her mother 1918, an article from a local Cumbrian newspaper published on the 100th anniversary of WW1 Page 338 Bill and Fedora Kennedy from 1918.

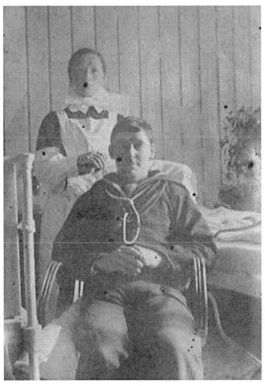

Able Seaman Will Keats spent longer in Bodø in hospital due to a back injury (seen on previous page) and had to join the rest of the crew at a couple of weeks later at Jørstadmoen. Once there he especially enjoyed when he was able to walk into the neighbouring village and meet the Hammershaug family for afternoon tea. He maintained contact with them for almost 50 years.

Ordinary Seaman Constantine Laggan on his wedding day. His wife was informed of his death only to quickly receive updated news that he was alive and interned in Norway. Photo supplied by his family.

JOHN ROWLAND,
Royal Navy, of Newcastle.
(Lost on H.M.S. India).

On the left, John Roland Anderson, as sent to me by his grandson. On the right is a clipping from a paper that I had found online. It had confused me as it clearly stated that the sailor was from HMS India (it was reporting that this sailor was missing), but the name did not match any of my records. It was not until chatting to Roland that it dawned on me that the paper had got the name wrong!

A collection of photos of Seaman Robert Charles Maynard from his family archives.

Rogues Gallery

I thoroughly enjoyed the process of hunting out other descendants and relatives of *HMS India* crew and many of them have found themselves in the same situation of knowing little about the boat and the crew and their misfortunes. I wanted, however, to still pay homage to as many of the men involved as possible so this chapter is a gallery of all the photos I could muster of the crew of *HMS India*.

Included are a collection of photographs of the football teams that were formed in the camp and who gained a reputation as being highly skilled and hard to beat by the local teams. Hearsay tells that football was not played in the region until the English arrived, I am not sure if this is true or not, but the English players certainly made an impact and a few were even given permission to play with local teams and the 1918 season became a highly successful one for the local team Fremed with the help of internees Trimmers Albert Jolley and George Barber.

The team were so successful that the Hamar football team made a formal protest to the Norwegian Football Association regarding the use of foreign players and after a tough fight in the courts, the Fremed team were allowed to keep their British players and continue their winning ways until the end of the war.

Selected members of the crew of HMS India. Back row, second from left is John William Perkins.

John William Perkins was a shipwright born in 1888. He was interned but is not mentioned in the 1917 camp list. He may have been repatriated or on leave at the time. He returned to civilian life after the war but his granddaughter, Lizzy, writes "Unfortunately, he disappeared in 1929. He went to work one day and never came home. No one in the family has ever seen him again. He was traumatised by the war and used to wander and sometimes sleep rough, but usually he would come home. But that day he did not."

THE LATE SUB-LIEUT. C. J. BALE.

Sub-Lieutenant Claude John Bale survived the torpedo attack but died from a 'sub phial haemorrhage' on 7 December 1915 aged 25. He died at the internment camp leaving his widow, Mary, in London. He is buried in the churchyard in Fåberg. Just under three years later, Leading Seaman Walter James Beynon was buried next to him after dying of pneumonia, (maybe Spanish Flu) only 9 days before the war ended.

Photograph from Kennedy archives. I am assuming that Mr Byrne is Chief Gunner Charles James Byrne. I have been able to find very little information on him.

From the Kennedy archives, Fedora Kennedy with Lieutenant John H Biggs, an officer who was second in command.

Below are photographs of work on the railway at Hjerkinn in 1917. I assume that these are HMS India crew working but cannot manage to identify any of them. This is from the Kennedy archives.

Photographs from the album of Charles Nelson. Top photograph shows Nelson, Midshipman Jenkins and two others trying out golf. The bottom photograph shows Nelson and Jenkins again with one of the Norwegian officers. Jenkins was one of the other officers and is rumoured to have married a Norwegian doctor. Considering he was only twenty years old when the war ended this seems unlikely but may have happened.

Below one of the football teams created during time spent in Jørstadmoen. The English were respected for their fine football playing. Joseph Vincent Mahood Magill is in the front on the left. This is the 1916 team.

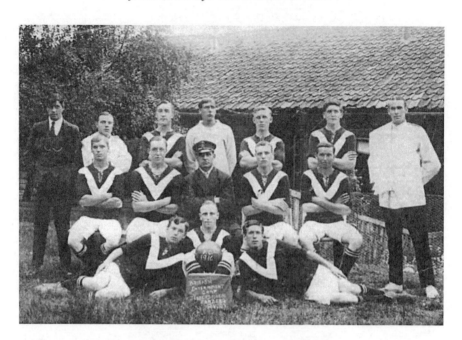

this snak was
taken after a
very fast game
with Gjovik. I
was taken prisoon-
er in the first
half. one chap
tried to kick
me in the net.
I never reached
it, although I
reached the
bunk quick.

result- Indians won
6 - 3

Interned Force
versus
Lillehammer

result win
for the
Indians by
5 - 1

A collection of photographs of various football teams from the Jørstadmoen camp.
These photographs are from the collection of Seaman Robert Charles Maynard a
feature a couple of postcards written by Maynard that mention the final scoreboards.
The internees seemed hard to defeat! The photograph of the attempt at goal is from the
collection of William Tilley as shared by his grandson, Kjell-Arne Tilley.

The Officers of HMS India taken prior to the torpedo attack. Commander Kennedy is seated in the middle of the second row. I am having real difficulty recognising anyone else! About ten officers died in the torpedo attack.

Photographs from the collection (on previous page as well) of Seaman Robert Charles Maynard and Fireman William Tilley, they show a sports day (I am confident that the photos are from the same day although I have no proof). The number of spectators makes me think it was a public festival that internees were invited to or a camp event that the local folk were invited to.

Reginald (Reg) Antliffe Parsons marrying Dorothy (Dora) Fuller in 1917 when on leave from internment in Norway. Photo supplied by family member Carly Harris.

These photographs of accordion players are from two sources. The black and white one is from Roger Partridge's papers and he mentions that Norman Bolton is on the right and trimmer George Barber is on the left. The players positions are reversed in the sepia photo and that Norman Bolton is on the left with the hatless with no pipe. I am sure they are the same men—how many accordion players would one camp have?

The Rest of Arnold's Life

My hunt through the family archives has unfortunately not resulting in finding any mention of Arnold returning home. I know that he arrived in Britain on 28 November 1918 and was taken immediately to Ripon Camp, Yorkshire which was not only a training camp but also a military hospital and repatriation centre. I do not know how long he stayed at Ripon but deeply hope that he was home with his father and sisters for Christmas 1918. What a bittersweet Christmas that would have been. The first Christmas without Wilfrid but the first Christmas in years with Arnold.

Arnold did not stay a landlubber for long, as he had predicted in his letter to Queenie on 16 June 1918—"*I don't think I should stop at home though—After all, the fascination of the Wanderlust is almost as great or greater than any others.*"

His Mercantile Marine service records show that he was back at sea working for Union-Castle line early in 1919. On the 4 March 1919, Arnold's logbook shows him leaving on his first voyage with Union-Castle Line on the *Dunvegan Castle* as 8th Engineer. He sailed from Southampton to Poplar and his report of character has him rated as very good for both ability and general conduct—a rating that never changes throughout his time at sea.

In May of 1919, Arnold departs on the *Llanstephan Castle* for the mail run to South Africa. He had already been promoted to 6th Engineer and over the next few years he makes the same trip many, many times. At the same time, he completed his engineering certificates and had worked his way up to being a First-Class Engineer by the end of 1922.

Arnold worked for Union-Castle Line for his whole mercantile shipping career and during that time worked on some of the most well-known and advanced ships of the time. Richard, Arnold's son writes:

"The *Arundel Castle* was the largest ship built in 1921 and Arnold was on her maiden voyage. She was powered by coal and had eleven boilers which were feeding two steam turbines and driving two propellors. The vessel consumed about t tonnes of coal per day or 8,000 tonnes for a return trip to South Africa. The work in the boiler room was extremely dirty and heavy and this influenced Arnold to persuade his son to become a navigating officer—a much cleaner job!"

Arnold was also on the maiden voyage of the Union-Castle Lines first motor ship, the *Carnarvon Castle*, in 1926. He had spent six months familiarising himself with the diesel engines operations and during his time aboard her he obtained his First-Class Motor Certificate.

During the early 1930s, Arnold spent time on the building of new ships in Belfast as a resident engineer for Harland & Wolff (builders of the Titanic) as well as time at sea but at the end of 1934 Arnold came ashore for the longest period since leaving Norway. Around this time, he met Isabella (Isa) Woods who was working as a secretary in the Harland & Wolff offices in Belfast and they soon married—he was over forty at the time but a life at sea had not seemed to have left much time for romance.

In October 1936, Isa and Arnold had their first child, Arnold Richard Clarke, known as Richard. By 1939, World War Two had broken out and Arnold decided to move his wife and young son to New Milton to stay with his sisters. They would be safer there than in Belfast which was a target for the Germans due its large shipbuilding facilities. They would also be closer to Arnold who was based in Southampton but working across the country repairing damaged war ships in places like London, Glasgow, Liverpool as well as in Southampton.

Isa's and Arnold's second child, Christine, was born in 1940, whilst Arnold was at sea and he did not meet her until she was over two months old. It was after WW2 had ended that the family made a long term move to Belfast, where Arnold worked as a resident ship engineer.

He was transferred one more time before his retirement and the family (minus Richard much of the time as he was often at sea) moved to West London whilst Arnold worked in the London offices of Union-Castle Line until his retirement in 1958. He liaised between the ship owner and the shipbuilder on matters such as design, fitting out and building of the ships.

On his retirement, Arnold and Isa were gifted a free first-class voyage to South Africa aboard the *Athlone Castle*, the very same ship their son was Junior 4th Officer on. After a brief holiday in Durban, they returned to Southampton on the final voyage of the *Arundel Castle* for obvious nostalgic reasons. They then returned to Belfast and assumed residence in Lisburn for the rest of their lives.

Arnold always kept in regular contact with his sisters, especially Anne/Queenie and Winifred. He would visit them whenever he was in Southampton and they made the occasional visit to Belfast. Arnold outlived Isa by eight years and died in 1978 in Belfast at the grand age of eighty-five. He is survived and remembered with love by his children and his grandchildren.

Crossing the⁺ Line

An undated photograph from the family archives. Arnold is second from the left. His son comments that "I don't think that he ever wore his hat correctly!"

Edith, Anne, and Arnold at Henbury. The dog is named Lucky as he was rescued after being thrown from a car.

Isa Beggs Woods. Arnold met her in Belfast in the early 1930s. This photograph was taken in Southampton.

Arnold introducing his baby son to Anne (left) and Winifred (far right) in Belfast in 1936

Above—the family enjoying time on the beach at Barton-on-Sea close to where they were living at the time. Around 1938.
And Arnold and Isa on top of Great Orme in Wales.

Arnold and his children with Anne and Winifred at Ballyholme Beach

Epilogue

This book was written during a time when much of the world was sent into an enforced isolation. Just over one hundred years since the end of WW1 and since the scourge of the Spanish Flu, the inhabitants of planet earth were universally sent another challenge—the Covid-19 pandemic. Being considered "at risk," I spent much time in my family home isolated from much of the world. Like Arnold, I relied on communication from loved ones.

Unlike Arnold, my ability to make contact was more immediate due to the modern luxuries of the internet. My father died in November of 2020 and just like Arnold, I was unable to return to my homeland to say my goodbyes and it was then that, I suppose, I felt close to the desperation Arnold had felt over the three years he was kept from his homeland and from his loved ones.

I have often questioned myself as to the importance of Arnold's story when so many other young men were fighting in the trenches and dying awful deaths but now, after experiencing only a taste of what Arnold experienced, I can say with confidence that his story and that of the other crew of *HMS India*, is a story that deserves to be told. The other thing I grappled with during the writing of this book was the differences in experience for many of the men who were interned in Norway. Not only the obvious demarcation between the officers and the crew but even the differences between the men who were in the camp.

Some of the men seemed to quite enjoy their time in Norway and may indeed have been grateful not to be fighting. I chose to primarily tell Arnold's story and supplement it with experiences and events that included the other men. The fact that I have a story right from the mouth (or pen) of the man who lived it makes it more the poignant and interesting to me. These letters have survived for a reason and they needed to be shared.

The deeper I researched, the more I was enthusiastic I became and that conviction was supported through the relationships I was building with the other relatives of survivors and crew who had lost their lives. One person who gave me a great deal of support was Deborah Callaghan.

We struck up an email-based friendship in the early days of my research and Deborah's generosity in sharing of her grandfather's documents was touching. Being unable to scan the documents in herself, Deborah waited until the first Covid-19 lockdown had finished and took them all down to a shop in her local village where they scanned the photographs and documents for her and sent them to me.

Deborah, like me, could see the value in getting this story to a wider audience. Similarly, Mette Fruergaard and her brother, Lars Fruergård-Jensen, were equally generous with the sharing of their grandfather's sketches and stories and family photos. As my research deepened more relatives and descendants so generously shared their time and the stories they had been told or researched themselves.

I give huge thanks, in no particular order, to Peter Lamb, Sindre Torp, Linn Tilley Brandt, Bill Anstead, Kerry Toulson, Ian Morris, Helen Ward, Steven Filmer, Joe Ryder, Roland Adams, Theresa Trinder, Christopher Elston, Wicher (Vince) Feenstra, Kjell-Arne Tilley and Marie and Ken Barltrop and Bill Kennedy. I was so happy to include the stories of the other crew, survivors and internees and I feel we are all somehow connected.

The other angle, of course, was that of the philatelists. The many I contacted were incredibly helpful. Patricia Adams from the Scandinavian Philately Society was also a wonderful help and so generous in sharing her resources. Rolf Scharning not only shared an interesting letter but assisted in translations that I could not work out on my own!

I wish that I had the opportunity to meet Roger Partridge. Receiving the completed chapters work from his unpublished book was extremely exciting as it filled in so many gaps and introduced me to even more mail that I did not have copies of.

Alan Totten was another person who went out of his way to copy and send me Roger's writing, I could not have found it on my own. Roger's writing shows someone who was becoming interested in more than the philately side of the letters and envelopes from Jørstadmoen. He was starting to tell the story of the people behind the letters. I like to think that he would have liked this book and what I have been able to uncover. I am sure he would like my collection of envelopes! I think the two of us would have had a lot to talk about.

The international philately community has been truly kind to me. The more I searched and left messages with sellers and with societies, the more information was sent my way. It was through them that I was put in touch with author John Thiesen, who graciously sent a selection of incredibly useful documents and letters from Denmark to London for me.

He had accumulated such a wealth of information on the camp and so much of it was to do with Arnold. This book would be half the size without his contribution. Other collectors were equally as generous and as my collection grew, so did my enthusiasm, my awareness that others would be interested in this story and my determination to get it told.

I am also indebted to Nick Messenger who comes to the story through his interest in P & O and was happy to share information and contacts in the early stages of my research.

I also wish to extend thanks to the wider Clarke family for allowing me, an interloper, to write this story. Arnold's daughter, Christine, gave me her blessing to use the letters and her sons, David and Philip have been equally supportive. As has my sister-in-law, Kate. I also must thank my mum, Heather, for being my proof-reader in the preliminary stages—her support gave me the courage to keep writing as did that of my children, Phoebe, Lucy and Seamus.

I never got to meet Arnold. I met James in 1986, eight years after Arnold died. James is the spitting image, in personality more than looks but in looks to a certain extent, of his father. My mother-in-law and I continually joke or complain, that the Clarke male gene runs so strong that James is like a clone of his father.

Our son, Seamus, seems to have inherited many of these shared characteristics. The Clarke men I know are indescribably kind, genuine, friendly, gentle, family orientated men. I think that they may have all inherited a great many of these characteristics from Arnold.

The unravelling of this story has been intensely personal for Richard, my father-in-law and Arnold's only son. I have tried to keep him actively involved and chapters were read by him. This became an emotional process and tears were shed. I know that Richard had read many of the letters before but perhaps not in a chronological order with all the background information supplied. I could understand why it was hard for Richard to read some of what his father had written.

I wanted this story told. I wanted it for Arnold, but I also wanted it for Richard. He is a man I admire and love dearly. A fantastic dad and grandfather himself, I knew that he was interested in knowing about this part of his father's life in more detail and that there was a sense of regret that he had never taken the time to try and talk to his father about it.

Arnold had certainly never willingly offered up the information himself. I think that maybe, overall, it is Aunt Anne or Queenie who I really need to thank. She had the foresight—or the hoarder's instinct—to hold on to these letters. These wonderful letters that paint such a vivid picture of thirty-nine months of isolation. Thirty-nine months of a "bare chronicle of existence."

Marie Barltrop and Bill Anstead leaving flowers at the wreck site of HMS India in the North Sea off Norway.

References

Files From the National Archives, Kew, London

ADM 1/8429/227
ADM 116/1440
ADM 137/1911A
ADM 53/44343
ADM 53/44825
ADM 53/44826
FO 383/212
FO 383/327
FO 383/449
FO 383/527
WO 339/14533

Websites

Air of Authority—A History of RAF Organisation—www.rafweb.org

Ancestry—www.ancestry.co.uk

Australian War Memorial—www.awm.gov.au

The Auxiliary Division of the Royal Irish Constabulary—www.theauxiliaries.com

Bath Postal Museum—www.bathpostalmuseum.co.uk

British Maritime History—www.barnettmaritime.co.uk

The British Newspaper Archive—www.britishnewspaperarchive.co.uk

The Commonwealth War Graves Commission—www.cwgc.org

The Dreadnought Project—www.dreadnoughtproject.org

Drill Hall Library—www.campus.medway.ac.uk

Find My Past—www.findmypast.co.uk

Forgotten Wrecks of the First World War—

www.forgottenwrecks.maritimearcheologytrust.org

Forces War Records—www.forces-war-records.co.uk

The Great War 1914-1918—www.greatwar.co.uk

Great War Forum—www.greatwarforum.org

Imperial War Museum Lives of the First World War—
www.livesofthefirstworldwar.iwm.org.uk

Imperial War Museum Stories—www.history/voices-of-the-first-world-war-the-submarine-war.

Karl-Ludwig's Page—www.kgroenha.net

Margate Civic Society—www.margatecivicsociety.org.uk

The Mail, Cumbria—www.nwemail.co.uk

The Movement Academy Project—

www.movementacademyproject.com/we-content/uploads/2014/10/Knut-Ross.pdf

My Heritage—www.myheritage.com

The National Archives of Norway—www.digitalarkivet.no

The National Archives UK—www.nationalarchives.gov.uk

Naval-History.Net—www.naval-history.net

Newport Pagnell Remembers—
www.doverwartimememorialproject.org.uk

Northwich Philatelic Society—www.northwichphilatelicsociety.co.uk

Pages of the Sea—www.pagesofthesea.org.uk

The Old Peninsular & Oriental Steam Navigation Company c1835-1972.
www.pandosnco.co.uk

Royal Museums Greenwich—www.rmg.uk

Royal Sussex Living History Group—www.royalsussex.org.uk

Scottish Maritime Museum—www.scottishmaritimemuseum.org

St. Mary's Island History Group—www.stmarysislandhistorygroup.co.uk

Tom Morgan's Hellfire Corner—www.hellfirecorner.co.uk

The Wartime Memories Project—www.wartimememoriesproject.com
Weatherby War Memorial—The Great War 1914-1918—
www.weatherbywarmemorial.com

Wrecksite—www.wrecksite.eu

Books and papers

(1967) 'Detention post for Norway during World War 1'. Evensen, E Norwegian
Philatelic Journal.

(1994) 'Detained Officer with expensive habits' *Dangingen*, Thursday 4 March, page 7.

(2014) *World War One: How did 12 million letters a week reach soldiers?* BBC News Magazine. 31 January 2014. www.bbc.com/news/magazine-25934407

(1995) 'Briter bak piggtråd' Pryser, T and Olstad, I. Faberg og Lillehammer, ye Lokalskrift av Faberg Historielag. Vol 15, 1995.

Allison, S. *The Kennedy's of Stone Cross Mansion.* Pixel Tweaks Publications. 2014

Chatterton, E.K. *The Big Blockade.* Hurst and Blackett Ltd, London. 1930

Dawson Lilley, T. 2012. *Operations of the Tenth Cruiser Squadron. A challenge for the Royal Navy and its reserves.* Greenwich Academic Literature Archive (www.gala.gre.ac.uk)

Hashagen, E. (translated by Celestino Corraliza) *U-Boats Westward! My voyages to England 1914-1918 (Great War at Sea).* Trident Publishing. 2019

Hurd, A. *The Merchant Navy, Volume 1.* London, John Murray, Albemarle Street W. 1921

Hurd, A. *The Merchant Navy, Volume 2.* London, John Murray, Albemarle Street W. 1924

Janicki, D. 2014. *The British Blockade During WW1: The weapon of deprivation.* Inquiries Journal. Vol 6. No 06. P1/51.

Osborne, E.W. *Cruisers and Battle Cruisers: An illustrated history of their impact.* ABD-CLIO. 2004

Partridge, R. *The postal history of Scandinavia in WW1.* Unpublished

Rønning, O. (Husemoen, O & Hosar, K). *Fra dragon og musketeer til elektronik og data: eServer plassen Jørstadmoen.* Lillehammer Thorsud Lokalhistorisk fori. 1998

Thiesen, J. *Prisoners of war and internees in Norway WW1 1914-1919. A postal history.* War and Philabooks Ltd AS, Oslo. 2006.

Thompson, J. *Imperial War Museum—Book of the War at Sea 1914-1918.* Pan Macmillan, 2011.

People

Philatelists
Patricia Adams
Harold Krische
Dann Mayo
Bjorn Muggerud
Susan Oliver
Roger Partridge (posthumously)
Rolf Scharning
Alan Totten

Descendants and family members
Roland Adams—grandson of Carpenters Crew John Roland Adams
Bill Anstead—grandson of Able Seaman Will Keats
Ken Barltrop—grandson-in-law of Commander William G A Kennedy
Marie Barltrop—granddaughter of Commander William G A Kennedy
Melanie Bennett—granddaughter of Able Seaman John Shirley Attwood
Linn Tilley Brandt—granddaughter of fireman William Tilley
Deborah Callaghan—granddaughter of Chief Engineer/Chief of staff Charles Nelson
Richard Clarke—son of ERA R Arnold Clarke
Christopher Elston—great grandson of Seaman Robert Charles Maynard
Mike Farrier—great nephew of trimmer Walter Farrier
Wicher (Vince) Feentsra—Nephew-in-Law of Ordinary Seaman Constantine Laggan
Steven Filmer—great nephew of Lieutenant Robert Nelson

Mette Fruergaard—granddaughter of Sub-Lieutenant Ernest Alltree

Lars Fruergaard-Jensen—grandson of Sub-Lieutenant Ernest Alltree

Carly Harris—descendant of Private Reginald Parsons

Peter Lamb—grandson of steward William Knight Lamb

Bill Kennedy—grandson of Commander William G A Kennedy

Ian Morris—grandson of blacksmiths mate William Gardiner

Gordon Musselwhite—grandson of Acting Sub-Lieutenant

John Musselwhite—grandson of Acting Sub-Lieutenant Harold Musselwhite

Lizzy Perkins—granddaughter of shipwright John William Perkins

Joe Ryder—grandson of Boy First Class Joseph Vincent Mahood Magill

Kjell-Arne Tilley—grandson of fireman William Tilley

Kerry Toulson—granddaughter of fireman John Tindling

Theresa Trinder—granddaughter of Private David Trinder

Helen Ward—granddaughter of able seaman George Ward

Miscellaneous

Nick Messinger

Sindre Torp

Appendix

Potted History of R Feaver Clarke and his six children

The Clarke Family

Richard Arnold Clarke was the youngest of the six living children of R Feaver and Rebecca Clarke. The youngest of a close knit, lively, well-educated, and loving family.

Richard Feaver Clarke was the son of a town clerk and registrar who was born, educated, and trained in Somerset. The family plan had been to send R Feaver to sea, like his brother Robert Feaver, however during a period when his brother was missing at sea in 1860, it was decided he would not become a sailor but stay land bound and become apprentice to a local chemist.

The family were sure that they had lost one son and I do not think they were prepared to lose another, luckily Robert turned up after only a few months. The pharmaceutical profession ended up suiting R Feaver and though the chemist he was training with died before Richard's indentures were complete, he was able to secure himself a position in a chemist in Torquay where he was supported to complete his exams and in 1876, he took possession of a pharmacy in Gravesend, Kent.

It was there he met Rebecca Sowter (1853–1906), the youngest daughter of a licensed victualler and one of six sisters. They married in 1881 and in 1882 they became guardians of Bessie Ella, after her father and mother died within a year of each other. Bessie's father had been R Feaver's only brother, Robert. Around the same time, they had their first child, a daughter, Elizabeth Mary. What was a happy start to a marriage was quickly saddened by the deaths of both Bessie and Elizabeth in August/September 1883.

In late 1884 they were blessed with the birth of another daughter, Dorothy and over the next eight years they had five more children—Edith Rebecca

(1887), Anne Victoria (1888), Winifred Sowter (1890), Wilfrid Randall (1891) and Richard Arnold (1893).

The family lived in Gravesend, Kent above the shop where R Feaver had his pharmacy. They lived a comfortable life in a house large enough to accommodate the family, two chemists' assistants, Nurse and at least one domestic servant. Highly involved in the life of the town, the Clarke's were on various school boards and involved in local theatre and sports.

Education was a high priority in the Clarke household with all girls attending the newly formed Rochester Grammar School for Girls. Rebecca was noted to be in huge support of educating her girls as mentioned in a letter from Father to Annie in 1907 on the announcement of her gaining a scholarship to Cambridge University, which was deemed to be a "hallowed tribute to the ever-watchful care and devotion which dear mother ever expressed to help bring about the cherished idea for you to have the privilege of a University Education."

Rochester Grammar was being progressive and the girls all thrived and came through with distinctions. It was a great pity that Rebecca did not live to see the success her girls made of their academic lives. She died in 1906 from a reported brain haemorrhage and so never saw Queenie or Winnie get to Cambridge or Edith become a well-known sports star. Her influence, however, stayed with her girls their whole lives. All four girls benefited from their education but three of them thrived because of it and threw themselves into lives as educators.

Dorothy did not move straight into further education like her sisters but remained at home and then completed secretarial studies before gaining employment at the King Edward VII Sanatorium at Midhurst as a typist. She remained there a few years before following her passion and studying farming methods, specialising in chickens and dairy, at Reading College before working in Devon for a while. She appears to have been back with father in New Milton around the end of WW1.

Edith moved straight into a two-year Diploma course at the Bergman-Österberg Physical Training College, Dartford and then into a work placement, organised by Madam Bergman-Österberg, at Roedean School in Brighton. She was invited back to the college in 1910 as a member of staff and at the request of Madam was send abroad in 1913 to study Eurhythmics and Dalcroze at the Dalcroze Institute, Hellerau, Dresden, where she gained a further diploma.

Her time in Dresden was cut short by the outbreak of WW1. In the event of the sudden death of Madam in 1915, Edith returned to the college and taught there for another four years. Edith was also extremely busy as an athlete and became quite renowned as a hockey, lacrosse, cricket and tennis player. She was regularly mentioned in newspaper articles as her prowess on the game's fields became well known. She participated in international hockey in 1912–1913 and was the captain of the England International Lacrosse team from 1912–1922.

Annie (or Queenie as she was known by family and friends) studied for her Imperial Institute, London University matriculation in 1905 which she passed successfully. This led her to apply and be granted the Kent County Scholarship in 1907 allowing her to enroll in Newnham College, Cambridge to study Mathematics and then gaining her BA (Mathematical Tripos) in 1910.

An impressive feat as this course was and is known to be one of the most challenging of mathematical university courses. She went straight from university into a teacher career starting at St Elphin School, Darley Dale before moving to the New Forest to become a senior mistress at Branksome College and then forming Fernhill Manor School with her life-long friend and companion, Irene Macnamara, the beginnings of the founding of this school can be read in the diaries of 1915.

Winifred followed in the steps of her elder sister, Edith and studied at both Bergman-Österberg Physical Training College and the Dalcroze Institute before beginning a long teaching career in Physical Education that would see her teach in schools across England before moving into tertiary education teaching in both the U.K and the U.S.A but being based at Manchester University.

Her first teaching job was at Halifax High School, this was found for her by Madam Bergman-Österberg. Throughout the war years she also taught at Greycoat Hospital School, Westminster before returning to Dartford to teach in the college again with her sister and then to Cambridge University to study early forms of sports psychology.

The two boys were educated locally at The Gravesend Municipal Day School and then sent to boarding school, Arnold firstly at Steyne School in Worthing and then both boys at St Lawrence College, Ramsgate. Being more interested in practical work than academics, they both then moved into apprenticeships, Wilfrid in Erith at the Vickers Munitions factory and Arnold at the Yarrow Shipbuilder yards in Glasgow, owned by Fairfield Boatbuilding which had close ties to the family.

Both boys enlisted to fight WW1 on the same day, Wilfrid being sent to the front and fighting at Ypres and Arnold joining the Royal Navy Volunteer

Reserves as a Leading Seaman/Engineer. Wilfrid did not live to see the conclusion of the war (see chapter 10) and his death was felt deeply by the whole of his family.

As I mentioned earlier, they were a very close-knit family who, even as adults, holidayed together and kept in constant contact with each other through their frequent letter writing. A letter written to Queenie by Evelyn Gedge, the daughter of the local vicar, after Wilfrid's death comments on the family unit thus— *"You have always been such a very united family that the blow will be really the bitterer for you all and the wrench of separation more hard to face."*

Hms India Casualties

Name	First name	DOB	Role	Service number	Buried Norway or Sea	Other info	In contact with family
Aers	Frank Ernest	19/04/1872 – 43 years old	Able Seaman	CG PO142921	Narvik Old Cemetery	Wife Edith Aers 1901. Had three children Dorothy, William and Frederick. Dover. In Royal Patriotic Asylum for Boys 1881. Listed as missing.	
Allison	Thomas	1881-34 years old	Greaser	MMR 781351	Sea	Born Poplar. Married to Minnie, Canning Town. Body not recovered for burial. Commemorated on Plymouth Naval Memorial	
Anthony	Thomas Robert	1887 – 38 years old	Storekeeper	MMR 243701	Sea	Commemorated on Plymouth Naval Memorial.	
Barrell	James William	26/11/1889 – 26 years old	Leading signalman	CH237068	Sea	From Swanley Junction, Kent. Enlisted 1906. Commemorated on Chatham Naval Memorial	

Name	First name	DOB	Role	Service number	Buried Norway or Sea	Other info	In contact with family
Barrett	Charles Reginald	17 years old	Private RMLI	CH/19075	Sea	Streatham. Signed up 14/09/1914. Listed as missing. Listed as killed in action. Adopted son. Born Wells. Norfolk. Commemorated on Chatham Naval Memorial	
Barry	James	31 years old	Trimmer	MMR	Sea	Body not recovered for burial. Commemorated on Plymouth Naval Memorial	
Bethell	Edwin	22/08/1867 – 54 years old	Chief Engineer	RNR	Sea	Wife Elizabeth Bethell, Lewisham. Born Sutton Saint Helens, Lancashire. Enlisted 1892. Commemorated at Chatham Naval Memorial	
Boyle	William		Trimmer	MMR	Sea	Commemorated at Plymouth Naval Memorial	
Brooks	Albert Ernest	05/05/1883 – 33 years old	Able seaman	CH/201160	Sea	Hertingfordbury. Commemorated on Chatham Naval Memorial	
Brooman	William W	15/10/1871 – 45 years old	Leading Seaman	138931	Sea	Havant. Married Lily. Born St Michaels Sussex. Commemorated on Portsmouth Naval Memorial.	
Butler	William	04/08/1890 – 25 years old	Stoker, 1st Class	SS/107934	Sea	Northampton. Listed as missing. Commemorated on Plymouth Naval Memorial	

Name	First name	DOB	Role	Service number	Buried Norway or Sea	Other info	In contact with family
Brown	John	21 years old	Steward	MMR	sea	Commemorated on Plymouth Naval Memorial	
Bungard	William	21 years old	Leading Seaman/Steward	MMR 796977	Sea	From Thornton Heath, Surrey. Body not recovered for burial. Commemorated on Plymouth Naval Memorial.	
Cairns	John		Fireman	MMR		Mother lived Dennistoun. Body not recovered for burial. Commemorated on Plymouth Naval Memorial.	
Carey	Herbert	27/11/1883 - 32 years old	Able seaman	212125	Narvik Old Cemetery	Born Holloway, London. Enlisted 1900.	
Chandler	William Richard	26 years old	Leading seaman	London 10/2698	Sea	Woodside, London. Promoted to Leading Seaman 1912. Enlisted 25/10/1912. Commemorated on Chatham Naval Memorial	
Charles	William A		Fireman	MMR	Bodo Cemetery		
Church	Frederick		Donkeyman	MMR		Commemorated on Plymouth Naval Memorial.	
Clark	Sydney Broford	32 years old	Lieutenant	RNR	Sea	Monkseaton, Northumberland. Sub-Lieutenant 1912. Killed in action. Commemorated on Chatham Naval Memorial.	

Name	First name	DOB	Role	Service number	Buried Norway or Sea	Other info	In contact with family
Clarke	Charles William		Trimmer	MMR	Sea	Commemorated on Plymouth Naval Memorial.	
Clarke	Felix William	27/03/1878, Suffolk - 37 when died	Able Seaman	CH/B5010 or 184591	Fredrikstad Military Cemetery - moved from Lodingen Churchyard		
Cook	George	01/11/1877 - 38 when died	Able seaman	178504/RFR 4789	Bodo Cemetery	Sutton, Suffolk. Married Mary J. Listed as missing	
Cotton	William	26 years old	Fireman	MMR	Sea	Commemorated on Plymouth Naval Memorial.	
Crowley	Desmond Joseph	13/04/1891 - 24 when died	Able Seaman	London 4/2958	Sea	Born Hampstead. Enlisted 1913. Killed in action. Listed as missing. Commemorated on Chatham Naval Memorial.	
Culhane	Patrick	28/12/1872 - 42 when died	Petty Officer 1st Class	146034	Sea	Wife Kate Culhane. Gillingham, Kent. Bally Longford, Kerry. Commemorated on Chatham Naval Memorial.	
Daubney	Lionel H	23 years old	Steward	MMR	Sea	Listed as missing. Mother Bridport. Commemorated on Plymouth Naval Memorial	
Davies	Norries		Fireman	MMR 794323	Sea	Commemorated on Plymouth Naval Memorial.	

Name	First name	DOB	Role	Service number	Buried Norway or Sea	Other info	In contact with family
Dennison	James	39 years old	Fireman	MMR 681183	Sea	Married to Agnes, Bradford. Body not recovered for burial. Commemorated on Plymouth Naval Memorial.	
Dent	Walter	42 years old	Greaser	MMR	Bodø Cemetery	Widow Rosina.	
Devine	John	48 years old	Fireman	MMR 735685	Sea	Daughter Annie. Body not recovered for burial. Native of Canning Town. Commemorated on Plymouth Naval Memorial.	
Dickson	Andrew Ferguson	24 years old	Sub-Lieutenant	RNR	Sea	Glasgow. Temp Sub-Lieut 1914. Killed in action. Commemorated on Chatham Naval Memorial.	
Dipple	Henry	02/06/1885, 30 years old	Fireman	MMR 747471	Sea	Enlisted 1903. Married Alice. Daughter born 12/10/1915. Commemorated on Plymouth Naval Memorial.	
Divine	William Marshall	29/12/1888, 27 years old	Seaman	7913A RNR	Sea	Commemorated on Chatham Naval Memorial.	
Doggett	Michael		Greaser	MMR 398917	Sea	Listed as missing. Sister Annie. Body not recovered for burial. Commemorated on Plymouth Naval Memorial.	
Duncan	James	50 years old	Donkeyman	MMR	Sea	Sister Elizabeth. Body not recovered for burial. Commemorated on Plymouth Naval Memorial.	

Name	First name	DOB	Role	Service number	Buried Norway or Sea	Other info	In contact with family
Dunn	Robert		Fireman	MMR	Sea	Wife M.A. Glasgow. Body not recovered for burial. Commemorated on Plymouth Naval Memorial.	
Farrier	Walter James	11/06/1885 – 30 years old	Trimmer	801188	Sea	Hastings. Brothers also fell – Albert and Thomas. Listed as missing. Commemorated on Plymouth Naval Memorial.	yes, great nephew Mike
Fisher	John Henry Lawson	20 years old	Trimmer	MMR 790066	Sea	Custom House, London. Commemorated on Plymouth Naval Memorial.	
Flegg	Joseph	27 years old	Trimmer	MMR 679132	Sea	Married to Mary, Canning Town. Commemorated on Plymouth Naval Memorial.	
Freeman	Thomas	29 years old	Fireman	MMR	Sea	Widow Emily. Commemorated on Plymouth Naval Memorial.	
Fry	Thomas		Fireman	MMR	Sea	Mother Margaret. London. Commemorated on Plymouth Naval Memorial.	
Fryer	Henry William Joseph	26/03/1891 - 24 years old	Able seaman	SS/2901	Sea	Camberwell. London. Wife. Commemorated on Chatham Naval Memorial.	
Gallagher	Neal		Fireman	MMR	Sea	Listed as missing. Mother Margaret. Letterkenny, Ireland. Commemorated on Plymouth Naval Memorial.	

Name	First name	DOB	Role	Service number	Buried Norway or Sea	Other info	In contact with family
Gibson	Charles	18/01/1897 – 19 years old	Private	CH/19088	Sea	Glasgow. Enlisted 09/09/1914. Listed as missing. Killed in action. Commemorated on Chatham Naval Memorial.	
Gibson	George William		Greaser	MMR	Narvik Old Cemetery	Widow. Tidal Basin.	
Gilbert	John	08/07/1874 – 38 years old	Stoker 1st Class	174381	Sea	Wife Emma. Cattedown, Plymouth. Listed as missing. Commemorated on Plymouth Naval Memorial.	
Gladwell	Charles		Fireman	MMR	Sea	Widow Alice, East Ham. Commemorated on Plymouth Naval Memorial.	
Goodwin	Charles William	13/09/1882 – 33 years old	Able Seaman	206685	Sea	Wife Annie. Langley Kent. Born Maidstone, Kent. Listed as missing. Commemorated on Chatham Naval Memorial.	
Gunn	William	26/06/1884 – 31 years old	Private	CH/14409	Sea	Enlisted 02/02/1904. Listed as missing. Killed in action. Commemorated on Chatham Naval Memorial.	
Haggerty	George		Trimmer	MMR	Narvik Old Cemetery		
Haigh	Louis		Fireman	MMR 47850	Sea	Listed as missing. Commemorated on Plymouth Naval Memorial	

Name	First name	DOB	Role	Service number	Buried Norway or Sea	Other info	In contact with family
Halliday	George		Trimmer/Fireman	MMR	Sea	Brother J Halliday Glasgow. Commemorated on Plymouth Naval Memorial.	
Harding	Samuel Arthur	30/01/1899 – 16 years old	Boy first class	J/34328	Narvik Old Cemetery	Truro	
Hawkes	Albert Edward	15/12/1896 – 19 years old	Private	CH/19204	Sea	Enlisted 29/09/1914. Listed as missing. Killed in action. Commemorated on Chatham Naval Memorial.	
Hodges	Cyril Shirley	18 years old	Seaman	8400A	Sea	Listed as missing. Commemorated on Chatham Naval Memorial.	
Holloway	Leonard	25/11/1879 – 36 years old	Able seaman	183337	Sea	Richmond, Surrey. Listed as missing. Died in active service. Commemorated on Chatham Naval Memorial.	
Hornby	George James (served as Charles Haggerty)	39 years old	Trimmer	MMR	Narvik Old Cemetery		
James	Albert Marcus	40 years old	Petty Officer 1st Class	156090	Sea	Wife Helen. Portsmouth. Listed as missing. Commemorated on Portsmouth Naval Memorial.	

Name	First name	DOB	Role	Service number	Buried Norway or Sea	Other info	In contact with family
Jellis	Charles William	31/01/1872 – 39 years old	Private	CH/14274	Sea	Wife Ada. Chatham. Enlisted 31/01/1890. Killed in action. HMS Duncan 1909 - Italian earthquake. Listed as missing. Commemorated on Chatham Naval Memorial.	
Jennings	Stanley John		Steward	MMR	Sea	Brother F.H Jennings. Maida Vale. Commemorated on Plymouth Naval Memorial.	
Jones	Herbert Owen	20/07/1882 – 33 years old	Asst Paymaster		Narvik Old Cemetery	Temp assistant paymaster 1914.	
Kingdon	James John	20/08/1869 – 45 years old	Petty Officer	PO/128972	Narvik Old Cemetery	Enlisted 1884. Born Portsea. Listed as missing.	
Leach	Dick		Steward	MMR	Sea	Widow Beatrice, Fulham. Commemorated on Plymouth Naval Memorial.	
Logie	Daniel		Steward/Trimmer	MMR 787247	Sea	Commemorated on Plymouth Naval Memorial.	
Lovett	Frederick John	26 years old	Warrant Telegraphist	RNR	Narvik Old Cemetery	Temp. warrant Telegraphist 1914.	
Maloney	Maurice	30 years old	Trimmer	MMR	Sea	Wife Edith, Stepney. Commemorated on Plymouth Naval Memorial.	

Name	First name	DOB	Role	Service number	Buried Norway or Sea	Other info	In contact with family
Marks	Lewis	08/01/1869 – 48 years old	Private	CH/5339	Bodo	Listed as missing. Mother Amelia, Wile End	
Mathews	Henry Joseph Johns	35 years old	Head Steward	MMR	Sea	Wife Edith, Upminster. Commemorated on Plymouth Naval Memorial.	
MacRitchie	Roderick	38 years old	Leading Seaman	3398B	Sea	Wife Catherine. Stornoway. Listed as missing. Commemorated on Chatham Naval Memorial.	
McCarty	James		Boatswain	MMR	Sea	Commemorated on Plymouth Naval Memorial.	
McKay	Duncan		Fireman	MMR	Narvik Cemetery	Listed as missing. Father William, Glasgow	
McKeever	Thomas		Fireman	MMR	Sea	Listed as missing. Commemorated on Plymouth Naval Memorial.	
Moffat	Frederick J	08/12/1881 – 34 years old	Able Seaman	194815	Narvik Cemetery	Shoreditch. Enlisted 1897. Listed as missing.	
Neill	William		Fireman	559895	Sea	Wife Elizabeth, Canning Town. Commemorated on Plymouth Naval Memorial.	

Name	First name	DOB	Role	Service number	Buried Norway or Sea	Other info	In contact with family
Nelson	Robert	28 years old.	Lieutenant-Officer	RNR	Sea	South Shields. Proby Sub-Lieutenant 1914. Listed as lost with HMS India. Son of Alfred. From Cunard Line. Commemorated on Chatham Naval Memorial.	yes, great nephew Steven
Nightingale	William		Fireman	MMR	Sea	°Commemorated on Plymouth Naval Memorial.	
Noble	Edward James	31 years old	Carpenter	MMR	Narvik Old Cemetery		
Oiller	William Richard	15/09/1884 – 31 years old	Leading Seaman	219400	Sea	Dungeness, Kent. Enlisted 1902. Commemorated on Portsmouth Naval Memorial.	
Osborne	Henry Walter	31/10/1884 – 31 years old	Able Seaman	218175	Sea	Wife Louisa. Swanley. Listed as missing. Hextable. Commemorated on Chatham Naval Memorial.	
Patterson	John	18/01/1876 – 39 years old.	Able Seaman	165672	Sea	Hebburn-on-Tyne, Durham. Listed as missing. Commemorated on Chatham Naval Memorial.	
Pattison	Thomas	23/12/1876 – 38 years old.	Able Seaman	172668	Sea	Wife Charlotte. Stockton-on-Tees. Listed as missing. Enlisted 1893. Medal issued to HMS Widow 1918. Commemorated on Chatham Naval Memorial.	

Name	First name	DOB	Role	Service number	Buried Norway or Sea	Other info	In contact with family
Peacock	John William	04/05/1878 – 38 years old.	Able seaman	178585	Sea	Wife Isabel. Sunderland. Listed as missing. Enlisted 1894. Born Durham. Commemorated on Chatham Naval Memorial.	
Pengelly	James	02/12/1883 – 30 years old.	Leading Seaman	205236	Sea	Wife Leah. Sandhurst. Enlisted 12/07/1899. Listed as missing. Commemorated on Portsmouth Naval Memorial.	
Pollard	Charles Edward Livermore	23 years old	Fireman	MMR	Sea	°Commemorated on Plymouth Naval Memorial.	
Potter	Percival Barber	19 years old	Midshipman		Sea	Wavertree, Liverpool. Temp Midshipman 1914. Killed in action. Commemorated on Chatham Naval Memorial.	
Prior	John Henry	21/01/1870 – 45 years old	Petty Officer 1st Class/Private	137246	Bodo Cemetery	Listed as missing. Born Wantage, Berkshire.	
Radley	William		Fireman	724798	Sea	Brother Thomas. Commemorated on Plymouth Naval Memorial.	
Rayner	Alfred Herbert	35 years old	Able Seaman	196193	Sea	Wife Maud. Stamford Hill London. Listed as missing. Commemorated on Chatham Naval Memorial.	

Name	First name	DOB	Role	Service number	Buried Norway or Sea	Other info	In contact with family
Reveley	Frank	28/12/1894 – 21 years old	Able seaman	204690	Sea	Malton, Yorkshire. Enlisted 1899. Listed as missing. Commemorated on Chatham Naval Memorial.	
Ring	Andrew		Fireman	MMR 767798	Sea	Sister Mary. Commemorated on Plymouth Naval Memorial.	
Robbins	Edward William	29 years old	Fireman	MMR 624597	Sea	Mother Elizabeth Bethnal Green. Commemorated Plymouth Naval Memorial.	
Roberts	Henry		Fireman	MMR	Sea	Wife Alice from Plumstead. Commemorated on Plymouth Naval Memorial.	
Robinson	Sidney	06/05/1884, 31 years old	Able seaman	CH/B5098/ 205032	Fredrikstad Military Cemetery, Narvik	Listed as missing. Born Greenwich. Wife Florence.	
Rouse	Bert	24 years old	Fireman	MMR 731142	Sea	Wife Martha. Commemorated on Plymouth Naval Memorial.	
Salter	Edwin Charles	24/07/1880 – 35 years old	Able Seaman	187300	Sea	Enlisted 1896. Listed as missing. Commemorated on Chatham Naval Memorial.	
Saunders	Wilfred Arthur	10/04/1894 – 21 years old	Corporal	CH/17005	Sea	Sandwich, Kent. Enlisted 22/04/1911. Killed in action. Commemorated at Chatham Naval Memorial.	
Scott	Charles H		Trimmer	MMR	Sea	Mother, Tidal Basin. Commemorated on Plymouth Naval Memorial.	

Name	First name	DOB	Role	Service number	Buried Norway or Sea	Other info	In contact with family
Seddon	William Charles Joseph	05/04/1894 – 21 years old	Leading Seaman	Z/453	Sea	Killed in action. Commemorated on Chatham Naval Memorial	
Shackell	Frederick		Butchers Mate		Fredricksta d Military Cemetery	Executor Richard Shackell. Acton	
Simmendinge r	William	28/08/1879 – 36 years old	Able Seaman	188747	Sea	Enlisted 1896. Listed as missing. Commemorated on Chatham Naval Memorial.	
Smith	Harold George	16/10/1880 – 35 years old	Able Seaman	192680	Sea	Enlisted 1897. From Poplar, London. Listed as missing. Commemorated at Chatham Naval Memorial.	
Stampton	Henry	14/11/1871 – 44 years old	Chief Petty Officer	143378	Sea	Listed as missing. Born Bethersden. Wife Harriet, Hackney. Commemorated on Chatham Naval Memorial.	
Stanley	Robert	05/03/1881 – 34 years old	Able Seaman	190580	Sea	West Norwood, London. Wife Mary A. Listed as missing. Enlisted 1896. Died in active service. Commemorated on Chatham Naval Memorial.	
Staples	Thomas	16/02/1889 – 26 years old	Leading Seaman	Z/62	Sea	Upper Tooting, London. Listed as missing. Killed in action. Commemorated on Chatham Naval Memorial	

Name	First name	DOB	Role	Service number	Buried Norway or Sea	Other info	In contact with family
Stenson	Joseph	18 years old	Fireman	MMR	Sea	Mother Rachael. Canning Town. Commemorated on Plymouth Naval Memorial.	°
Stone	Robert Benjamin	05/04/1875 - 40 years old	ERA	121EC	Sea	Listed as missing. Born in Jarrow. Widow Margaret, South Shields. Commemorated on Chatham Naval Memorial.	°
Sullivan	Patrick	20 years old	Fireman	MMR	Sea	Mother Hannah. Commemorated on Plymouth Naval Memorial.	°
Thackara	Roy Arthur	25 years old	Assistant Engineer	°	°Sea	Portsmouth. 1914 temp ass engineer. Killed in action. Commemorated on Chatham Naval Memorial.	°
Townrow	Wilfred John	47 years old	Canteen Steward	682556	Sea	Wife Minnie from Gravesend. Commemorated on Plymouth Naval Memorial.	°
Trounson	Samuel Percival	23 years old	Assistant Engineer	°	Narvik Old Cemetery	Temp Ass Engineer 1914. Killed in action.	°
Walsh	James Patrick	°	Fireman	MMR 397759	Sea	Wife Canning Town. Commemorated on Plymouth Naval Memorial.	°
Ward	Henry Albert	°	Fireman	MMR	Sea	Wife Alice. Commemorated on Plymouth Naval Memorial.	°

Name	First name	DOB	Role	Service number	Buried Norway or Sea	Other info	In contact with family
West	Arthur Henry	27/03/1879 - 36 years old	Able Seaman	181486	Sea	Born Pirton, Worcestershire. Enlisted 1894. Listed as missing. Commemorated on Chatham Naval Memorial.	°
Whatley	Frank	21/03/1884 - 31 years old	Stoker 1st Class	300924	Sea	Bristol. Enlisted 1902. Listed as missing. Died in active service. Commemorated on Plymouth Naval Memorial.	°
White	James	°	Writer	MMR	Narvik Cemetery	Relative C.S Taylor Thornton Heath.	°
Wigley	Albert Patrick	26 years old	Trimmer	MMR	Sea	Son of Henry and Margaret. Commemorated on Plymouth Naval Memorial.	°
Wood	Eli Arthur	27/09/1874 - 41 years old	Petty Officer 2nd Class -	151369	Sea	Born Minster, Sheerness. Enlisted 1889. Listed as missing. ?Bullet wound 1894. Commemorated on Chatham Naval Memorial.	°
Wood	Fred	24/10/1881 - 34 years old	Able Seaman	195048	Sea	Born Teddington, London. Enlisted 1897. Commemorated on Chatham Naval Memorial.	°
Wood	George Douglas Harry	18 years old	Midshipman	°	Sea	1914 - Temp Midshipman. Article in Jedburgh Gazette. Commemorated on Chatham Naval Memorial.	°

Name	First name	DOB	Role	Service number	Buried Norway or Sea	Other info	In contact with family
Woodstock	Robert James	°	Refrigerating Mechanic	MMR	Sea	Wife Beatrice, Plaistow. Commemorated on Plymouth Naval Memorial.	°
Wooldridge	Walter	11/08/1897 - 18 years old	Private	CH/19097	Sea	Enlisted 10/09/1914. Listed as missing. Commemorated on Chatham Naval Memorial.	°
Wren	Ernest Frederick	19/08/1897 - 18 years old	Private	CH/19259	Sea	Enlisted 08/10/14. Listed as missing. Commemorated on Chatham Naval Memorial.	°

Name	First name	D.O.B	Role	Service number	Info	In contact with descendants	
Akerman	Andrew Simon Read	°	Temp Warrant telegraphist RNR. Officer		After *India* joined Chatham on shore. Demobilized 21/05/19. Signed up 08/04/1915	°	°
Atkins	John	°	Greaser	°	°	°	°
Baker	Arthur W	°	Signalman	RN Chatham 235983	On *HMS Hyacinth* prior to 1914	°	°
Bentley	William L	°	Baker's Mate	°	°	°	°

Name	First name	D.O.B	Role	Service number	Info	In contact with descendants	
Binney	Charles	23/11/1888 Islington	Able seaman	RN Chatham SS2214	Orderly on *HMS Lancaster* 1909. 1918 medal issued directly to man	°	°
Brown	George A	28/08/1883 Lambeth	Able Seaman	RN Chatham 208652	Joined at age 17. 1918 medal issued directly to man.	°	°
Bruce	Alex	°	Leading Fireman	°	°	°	°
Carpenter	Henry	°	Able seaman	RN Chatham 207208	°	°	°
Churcher	Algernon A	°	Steward/ordinary Seaman	°	Article in newspaper.	°	°
Clarke	John	°	Fireman	°	°	°	°
Cooper	George	°	Leading Fireman	°	°	°	°
Cruikshank	Robert Dick	°	Prob. Midshipman Officer	RNR	Signed up 1914. 1916 Promoted to acting Sub-Lieutenant *HMS Victorian.* 1917 Sub-Lieutenant. 1918 Lieutenant	°	°
Daly	William	°	Fireman	°	°	°	°

Name	First name	D.O.B	Role	Service number	Info	In contact with descendants	
Davies	W. T	°	trimmer	°	°	°	°
Dockree	Walter	30/06/1871 St Albans. Died 1951	M.A.A (Pens)	RN Chatham 350132	1901 Ships Corporal. *HMS Dominion* 1911. 1918 medal issued directly to man.	°	°
Dunt	William C	°	Able seaman	RN Chatham 182308	1918 medal issued directly to man.	°	°
Eade	Alfred Freding	01/11/1871	M.A.A (Pens)	RN Chatham 139520	1914 Chief MAA. 1917 Acting Chief MAA. 1918 Chief MAA	°	°
Evans	Clarence T	°	Private	RMLI Chatham 19126	°	°	°
Farley	Ed J	°	Jun. Res. Attdt	M99910	°	°	°
Fielding	Geo H	°	Chief writer	°	°	°	°
Flynn	Timothy	°	Fireman	°	°	°	°
Franklin	Jas. T	°	Greaser	°	°	°	°
Frost	Alfred C	°	trimmer	°	? Service number 87. 1916 Silver War badge	°	°
Furniss	Chas. M	°	Able seaman	RN Chatham 162226	Medals issued	°	°

Name	First name	D.O.B	Role	Service number	Info	In contact with descendants	
Fury	Alfred E		Greaser				
German	George		Steward				
Gilchrist	Alan A		Able seaman	RN Chatham S.S 2893	1918 medal issued to man.		
Gill	Alfred T		Trimmer				
Gomes	Francis		Pantryman				
Goodman	John J		Fireman				
Gowers	Reg. Chas	01/08/1897	Private	RMLI Chatham 19151	Enrolled 21/09/1914. Enlisted again 3/03/1920		
Gross	Charles				Listed in local Ramsgate news		
Groundwater	Richard G	13/06/1879 Aberdeen	Lieutenant Officer	RNR	1916 Lieutenant Commander. Made Lieutenant 1908		
Guiness	Francis		Fireman				
Henay	David		Fireman				
Hennessey	Dan		Trimmer				

Name	First name	D.O.B	Role	Service number	Info	In contact with descendants	
Hole	Sidney P	21/06/1890 Hampstead	Able Seaman	RN Chatham 236285	1908 *HMS Barham.* Survived active service medal issued to man.		
Hood	Fred J		Hydraulic Winchman				
Howlett	Thomas		Able seaman	RN Chatham 172508	1918 medal issued directly to man		
Hyde	Thomas H		Greaser				
Irwin	William		Able seaman	RN Chatham 191440	1918 medal issued directly to man		
Jackson	William G		Chief Cook		Medalled 1918		
Johnson	Gerald S	22/04/1891	Lieutenant engineer Officer	RNR	1914 - awarded 1914/15 Star. 1914 Temp Engineer & Temp Assist Engineer. 1918 Engineer Lieutenant. 1919 Temp Lieutenant with IWT		
Johnson	Henry F		Storekeeper				
Johnston	James T		Proby surgeon	RNVR			

Name	First name	D.O.B	Role	Service number	Info	In contact with descendants	
Malarn	William		Fireman				
MacDiarmid	John Malcolm		Ass. engineer - Officer	RNR	1914 Temp Ass Engineer. 1918 Engineer Sub-Lieutenant		
Marchington	Edward		Trimmer				
McCreary	Ernest Jas.	13/01/1897	Private	RMLI Chatham 19222	Enlisted 2/10/1914		
McKay	John		Engineer officer - Officer	RNR	1914 - Temp engineer. 1918 - Engineer Lieutenant		
McKeag	Ernest L	1896 - Newcastle-on-Tyne	Temp Midshipman Officer	RNR	1914 - Temp Midshipman. 1918 - Sub-Lieutenant		
McKee	John		Fireman				
Moore	Chas.		Trimmer				
Moore	David		P.O 1st class	RN Chatham 134222	1918 medal issued to man		
Moss	Geo. V	01/02/1888	Able seaman	228500	Medal issued to mother. Index casualty number 1283/1922		
Nahar	John	1/02/1891 Chiswick?	Steward				

Name	First name	D.O.B	Role	Service number	Info	In contact with descendants	
Norton	Frank H		Fireman				
O'Connor	Nicolas		Private	RMLI Chatham 19107			
Peters	Arthur W		Steward				
Pipkin	Ernest		Ass. storekeeper				
Revell	John L	1893 Great Clacton	Temp warrant telegraphist - officer	RNR	1914 - Temp Warr Telegraphist. 1915 - Temp Senior Warr Telegraph. 1918 - Warr Telegraphist		
Robertson	Albert H		Trimmer				
Skelton	Arthur J	1890 - Nottingham	ERA	RNR 1741	Medalled 1918		
Smart	William	25/11/1888	Ordinary Seaman	RNVR Clyde Z/11493	1914 - Able Seaman		
Smith	Thomas H		Private	RMLI Chatham 16368			
Thompson	Chas Stephen		Private	RMLI Chatham 19243			
Tindling	John	1893 - 1968, born in Poplar	Fireman	698143	contact with granddaughter, Kerry	yes, granddaughter Kerry	

Name	First name	D.O.B	Role	Service number	Info	In contact with descendants		
Tothill	John H	03/01/1888 Plymouth	Stoker, 1st Class	RN Devonport 102744	Survived active service medal issued to man			
Travis	William	1891 South Shields?	Able Seaman	RN Chatham 201860	Survived active service medal issued to man			
Turner	Louis Cecil	21/05/1891 Willesden	Arm. crew	RN Chatham M8470	Survived active service. *HMS Dragon* 1918			
Walker	Charles P		Bugler	RMLI Chatham 18305				
Walker	H. J		Leading Seaman	Rn Chatham 177263	Survived active service medal issued to man			
Wallis	Charles E		Able Seaman	RN Chatham 180600	Survived active service medal issued to man			
Ward	Arthur		Butcher					
Watkins	William H		Greaser					
White	Arthur		Trimmer					
White	Charles		Able Seaman	Rn Chatham 181578	Survived active service medal issued to man			
Williams	Thomas	28/10/1896	Private	RMLI Chatham 18239	Joined up 6/11/13			

Name	First name	D.O.B	Role	Service number	Info	In contact with descendants		
Wilson	Charles R		Steward		From Ramsgate. Name in local news			
Worrow	Thomas		Fireman					
Wyatt	William H		Able Seaman	RN Chatham 184268				
80 men								

Surname	First names	Birth and death dates	Rank	R. N/R.N. R/R.NV. R	What happened after	Rescue mode	Any other interesting info	Interned and number given in camp	Description of role	Mentioned in Jørstad moen camp list 17 July, 1917	Contact with descendants
Allen	Henry John	15/04/1891 - Ramsgate. Died 1963	Cook's mate	R.N. Chatham M2749		India's boats	Reported missing - letter safe		Assistant to cook	Yes	
Alltree	Ernest Woodburne	14/08/1888 - Atcham, Shropshire. Died 29/10/1918	Acting Sub-Lieutenant - Officer	R.N. R	Died 29th October 1918 Spanish Flu. Married Norwegian lady - Hedvig	Lifeboat	Officer on watch when sunk. Wrote report for Sir E Grey October 1915. On no.2 cutter. Performed at 1918 Varieties Concert. Had one daughter born in 1917.	Yes, but allowed to live out of camp	Subordinate officer who had gained role by order not commission.		Yes

Surname	First names	Birth and death dates	Rank	R. N/R.N. R/R.NV. R	What happened after	Rescue mode	Any other interesting info	Interned and number given in camp	Description of role	Mentioned in Jørstad moen camp list 17 July, 1917	Contact with descendants
Anderson	Carl	21	Plumber		In forces-war-records. co.uk - same name, carpenter on S.S Grelhead in 1941.	India's boats	Half-Norwegian (father). Performed at 1918 Varieties Concert.	Yes		Yes	
Anderson	John Roland	04/07/1891 - Newcastle-on-Tyne. Died 1965/66	Carpenter's crew	R.N.V.R Tyne 6/137	Allowed leave in December 1917 to marry fiancé then returned to Norway for the	India's boats	"My grandfather described internment as pretty ghastly - men were set to piece work. the guards were not friendly and several sailors went mad." greatwarforum.org	Yes	Junior ranking	Yes	Yes

Surname	First names	Birth and death dates	Rank	R. N/R.N. R/R.NV. R	What happened after	Rescue mode	Any other interesting info	Interned and number given in camp	Description of role	Mentioned in Jørstadmoen camp list 17 July, 1917	Contact with descendants
					rest of the war.						
Arkell	Albert James William	02/10/1878 Saint Ebbe, Oxfordshire. Died 1952	A. B	R.N Chatham 178423	°	India's boats	°	°	A seaman with more than two years' experience.	Yes	°
Attwood	John Shirley	10/01/1892 Brockley, London. Died	A. B	R.N.V.R London 1/2680	°	Saxon	Nickname Mr Lofty. From Brockley	°	°	Yes	°Yes

Surname	First names	Birth and death dates	Rank	R. N/R.N. R/R.NV. R	What happened after	Rescue mode	Any other interesting info	Interned and number given in camp	Description of role	Mentioned in Jørstadmoen camp list 17 July, 1917	Contact with descendants
		1982, Slough									
Baile	Benjamin C	11/11/1890 Poplar. Died 1964, Hampstead.	Painter	°	°	India's boats	Repatriated. In Royal Artillery in 1912. Listed as missing.	Yes, 53	°	No	°
Bale	Claude John	06/09/1890	Tempy. Sub-Lieutenant Officer	R.N. R	Died 7/12/15	Saxon	°	°	°	No	°
Barber	George	°	Trimmer	?1024562	°	Saxon	°	Yes. 93	Position in engineering department of a coal-fired ship involve	Yes	°

Surname	First names	Birth and death dates	Rank	R. N/R.N. R/R.NV. R	What happened after	Rescue mode	Any other interesting info	Interned and number given in camp	Description of role	Mentioned in Jorstadmoen camp list 17 July, 1917	Contact with descendants
									s coal handling tasks.		
Basketfield	John William	28/02/1879 Kennington. London. Died 1958	A.B/Private	R.N Chatham 192224	Medically unfit for further service. Discharged December 1916.	India's boats	Recognized in the National Roll of the Great War. Married to Ada Emily Colman	Yes		No	
Beynon	Walter James	11/11/1880	Leading Seaman	C.G Portsmouth 201889	Died 2/11/1918 of Spanish Flu	India's boats	Article in Portsmouth Evening News on dead/alive scenario	Yes	Senior to able seaman.	Yes	
Biggs	John Henry	21/12/1883, Wiltshire. Died	Act. Lieutenant - Officer	R.N. R	1918 on his naval record	Saxon	Got 1 month leave. Second in command	Yes, but Officer -			

Surname	First names	Birth and death dates	Rank	R. N/R.N. R/R.NV. R	What happened after	Rescue mode	Any other interesting info	Interned and number given in camp	Description of role	Mentioned in Jorstadmoen camp list 17 July, 1917	Contact with descendants
		1976, Norfolk.			there is note of "H.M Ministry at Christiania has brought to the boards notice the highly satisfactory manner in which this officer performed his duties at H.M Legation			second in command. Lived out of camp.			

Surname	First names	Birth and death dates	Rank	R.N/R.N. R/R.NV.R	What happened after	Rescue mode	Any other interesting info	Interned and number given in camp	Description of role	Mentioned in Jørstad moen camp list 17 July, 1917	Contact with descendants
					while interned in Norway. Lieutenant Commander in 1923						
Bolton	Norman Harcourt	06/10/1895	Private	R.M.L.I Chatham 19119	Married Nora Iverson. Listed as being a fish porter/heavy worker in 1939 register and living in a boarding	Saxon	Had one son with Nora. Died in Shanghai in 1941.	Yes.¶ 7		Yes	

Surname	First names	Birth and death dates	Rank	R.N/R.N. R/R.NV.R	What happened after	Rescue mode	Any other interesting info	Interned and number given in camp	Description of role	Mentioned in Jørstad moen camp list 17 July, 1917	Contact with descendants
					house in Tower Hamlets,						
Bryant	Edward William	°15/03/1878 - Chatham, Kent	Steward	1013238		Saxon		°Yes.¶ 2	Maintain standards of service the equal of a good hotel. For officers ?	Yes	
Byrne	Charles James	°?11/06/1875, Stoke Damerel, Devon	Chief gunner - Officer	R.N - RMA/15 075?		Saxon		Yes, but Officer so lived out of camp	Worked with artillery		

356

Surname	First names	Birth and death dates	Rank	R. N/R.N. R/R.NV. R	What happened after	Rescue mode	Any other interesting info	Interned and number given in camp	Description of role	Mentioned in Jorstadmoen camp list 17 July, 1917	Contact with descendants	
Buck	Alfred Lewis	O2/10/1883. Ayesham, Norfolk. Died 1967, Middlesex	A. B	R.N Chatham 209482	Policeman in Kew London	India's boats	Article in Surrey Mirror on dead/alive scenario. Married	Yes		Yes		
Carnes	John Henry	28/01/1877. Sculcoats Hull, Yorkshire. Died 1957, Yorkshire	A. B	R.N Chatham 166541		Saxon		Yes		Yes		
Chircop	Lawrence (Lorenzo)	19/02/1888. Vittoria, Malta. Died 1969, Malta	Captain's Valet	Y27089/ L1185		Saxon	Repatriated. Maltese. Roomed with RA at Jorstadmoen. Captains Steward 1st Class Medal 1917. Official file states "can count 1 year, 127 days service in HMS	Yes. 47		No		

Surname	First names	Birth and death dates	Rank	R. N/R.N. R/R.NV. R	What happened after	Rescue mode	Any other interesting info	Interned and number given in camp	Description of role	Mentioned in Jorstadmoen camp list 17 July, 1917	Contact with descendants	
							India whilst interned in Norway to GCB under Art 749."					
Clark	William James	26/09/1891. Stonehouse, Devon. Died 1977, Devon.	Fireman			Saxon	Repatriated	Yes		No		
Clarke	R. Arnold		E.R. A	R.N.V.R Clyde z/16		Saxon	Listed in 1918 Varieties Concert programme. Arrived in Ripon 27.11.18. In room V at Jorstadmoen	Yes. 43	Able to read and write - fitter, turner, boilermaker, coppers	Yes	yes	

357

Surname	First names	Birth and death dates	Rank	R. N/R.N. R/R.NV. R	What happened after	Rescue mode	Any other interesting info	Interned and number given in camp	Description of role	Mentioned in Jørstad moen camp list 17 July, 1917	Contact with descendants
									mith or engine smith		
Clinton	Charles	21/05/18 91. Died 1974, Argyll	Shipwright	R.N.V.R Clyde 4/1700	Escaped 19th May, 1916	India's boats	Scottish Maritime Museum letter. Parents informed of death and then letter of rescue.	Yes. 49	Responsible for building and repairs	No	
Cole	Thomas William		Trimmer			India's boats	Received letter from sister 08/01/1917 brother had died at the front. Envelope in Theisen book.	Yes		Yes	
Connor	James	03/05/18 94	Trimmer	557/ST		Saxon		Yes		No	
Coomes	George Alexander	01/08/18 86	A. B	R.N.V.R London Z/860		India's boats	Listed in 1918 Varieties programme. Enrolled 16/11/1914	Yes		Yes	Yes

Surname	First names	Birth and death dates	Rank	R. N/R.N. R/R.NV. R	What happened after	Rescue mode	Any other interesting info	Interned and number given in camp	Description of role	Mentioned in Jørstad moen camp list 17 July, 1917	Contact with descendants
Cox	Charles Philip	06/02/18 79, West Ham, London	A. B	R.N Chatham 184801		India's boats		Yes		Yes	
Davies	Hugh	30/03/18 87	A. B	R.N.V.R Bristol Z/251		Saxon	Invalided our 1916? Enrolled 2/11/1914. Demobilization March 1919.	Yes		Yes	
Dunn	Richard		Storekeeper			Saxon	Speaks Japanese. Roomed with RA at Jørstadmoen	Yes. 45	Maintaining ship supply stores	Yes	
Fisher	James Tambling	05/11/18 85. Cardiff	Stoker 1st class	R.N Devonport 101059		Saxon	Signed up 19/10/14	Yes	Specialized in engine room duties shifted coal	Yes	
Gardiner	William	03/12/19 82	Blacksmith's Mate	R.N.V.R Clyde Z/71271		India's boats	Photo at camp. Scotsman	Yes	Responsible for all welding	Yes	Yes

358

Surname	First names	Birth and death dates	Rank	R. N/R.N. R/R.NV. R	What happened after	Rescue mode	Any other interesting info	Interned and number given in camp	Description of role	Mentioned in Jorstadmoen camp list 17 July, 1917	Contact with descendants
									forging parts, chains, etc.		
Gillon	William	30/09/18 92 Ibrox	E.R.A. 2nd class	R.N.V.R Clyde 1/1765		Saxon	Roomed with RA when at Jorstadmoen. Mother informed of death.	Yes. 42		Yes	
Glibbery	Arthur H	1890	Fireman			Saxon	Discharged 1918 719152	Yes		Yes	
Green	Arthur William		Cooper			India's boats	maybe listed as victualler's assistant service number M.26379	Yes. 52	Made and repaired barrels, casks and buckets	Yes	

Surname	First names	Birth and death dates	Rank	R. N/R.N. R/R.NV. R	What happened after	Rescue mode	Any other interesting info	Interned and number given in camp	Description of role	Mentioned in Jorstadmoen camp list 17 July, 1917	Contact with descendants
Grigson	J.W. B	26/01/18 93. Died 1943	A. B	R.N.V.R London 9/2866	Escaped to Britain, 19th May 1916	India's boats	Transferred to Royal Naval Air Service in 1916. Flew for the rest of WW1.	Yes		No	Yes
Hackett	William	15/09/18 77 Liverpool. Died 1942?	A. B	R.N Chatham 173676		Saxon		Yes		Yes	
Haddow	Frederick A	Born 1894. Died 1967	Trimmer			Saxon	For a time at Kongsberg and Kongsvinger prisons	Yes		Yes	
Hammond	William		Donkeyman			India's boats	Letters collected by Scandinavian Philately society. Roomed with RA at Jorstadmoen. Letter from wife in Thiesen 09/01/1917. Wife is sick, father broke rib.	Yes. 44	In charge of the donkey engine - a small engine that was	Yes	

Surname	First names	Birth and death dates	Rank	R. N/R.N. R/R.NV. R	What happen ed after	Rescue mode	Any other interesting info	Interned and number given in camp	Descrip tion of role	Mentio ned in Jorstad moen camp list 17 July, 1917	Contac t with descen dants
									used to propel coal into the main engine. Also operated and maintained the small engines on board		
Handover	Alfred Ernest	08/02/1879 Croydon. Died 1967, Chichester.	A. B	R.N Chatham 184538		India's boats		Yes		Yes	

Surname	First names	Birth and death dates	Rank	R. N/R.N. R/R.NV. R	What happen ed after	Rescue mode	Any other interesting info	Interned and number given in camp	Descrip tion of role	Mentio ned in Jorstad moen camp list 17 July, 1917	Contac t with descen dants
Harrison	Herbert	09/12/1877 Faversham. Died 1953, Kent.	A. B	R.N Chatham 174177		India's boats	Article in East Kent gazette reporting on dead but alive story.	Yes		Yes	
Hawes	Sidney		Fireman			Saxon		Yes		Yes	
Hill	Henry George	21/12/1895	A. B	R.N.V.R Bristol 2/130		Saxon	Enrolled 06/03/1912	Yes		Yes	
Hines	Fred	30/08/1879, Aston, Warwickshire. Died 1941, Warwick.	P.O 1st Class	R.N Chatham 190736		Saxon	Requests for Lillehammer excursions or leave had to be submitted to him. Survived active service	Yes		Yes	

Surname	First names	Birth and death dates	Rank	R. N/R.N. R/R.NV. R	What happened after	Rescue mode	Any other interesting info	Interned and number given in camp	Description of role	Mentioned in Jørstad moen camp list 17 July, 1917	Contact with descendants	
Hopkins	Albert North	28/10/1877. Hackney, London. Died 1939?	Private	R.N. Chatham 9865	Repatriated on health grounds. Enlisted 24/06/1894.	India's boats	Imprisoned for three days for disorder and intoxication. Wrote letter complaining about the conditions at camp - at TNA. Re-enlisted 03/10/14. Discharged invalided 27/03/1918. Service from 24/06/1897	Yes	°	Yes	°	
James	William	11/09/1878, Birmingham	Carpenters crew	R.N. Chatham 345686	Reported lost but amended on 24/08/1915 to found	India's boats	°		Yes	°	Yes	°	
Jeffrey	Charles Hastings	°	Cook	M 10848	°	India's boats	°	Yes	°	Yes	°	

Surname	First names	Birth and death dates	Rank	R. N/R.N. R/R.NV. R	What happened after	Rescue mode	Any other interesting info	Interned and number given in camp	Description of role	Mentioned in Jørstad moen camp list 17 July, 1917	Contact with descendants	
Jenkins	Harold Rhys	14/05/1898. Haverfordwest, Pembrokeshire. Died 27/05/1948 at sea from vessel Stanlodge	Tempy. Mid	R.N. R	°	India's boats	Got 6 days leave, married a doctor in Norway. Wrote report for Sir E Grey October 1915. Escaped in 2nd cutter. Officer lived out of camp	Yes	°	No	°Yes	
Johnstone	Andrew	30/06/1891. Linlithgow. Died 1968	Carpenters crew	R.N.V.R Clyde Z/496	°	India's boats	From Linlithgow. Article in Dundee Evening Telegraph reporting dead/alive scenario.	Yes	°	Yes	°	
Jolley	Albert Edward	°July 1895, St. Giles, London. Died 1967.	Trimmer	°	°	Saxon	°	Yes	°	Yes	°	

361

Surname	First names	Birth and death dates	Rank	R. N/R.N. R/R.NV. R	What happened after	Rescue mode	Any other interesting info	Interned and number given in camp	Description of role	Mentioned in Jørstadmoen camp list 17 July, 1917	Contact with descendants
		Hertfordshire.									
Jones	Albert	06/02/1891	Shipwright	R.N.V.R·Mersey·7/75		India's boats	From·Rock·Ferry	Yes.··50		Yes	
Jones	William·G.·A	01/01/1879·-·Liverpool, Lancashire	A.·B	R.N·Chatham·178144		Saxon	21·days·imprisonment·in·early·1915·for·absence.··Career·sailor.	Yes		Yes	
Keats	William·Thomas	16/02/1884·-··Southport.·Died·1968	A.·B	R.N·Chatham·210396	Daughter·named·India·Bodo.··Granted·leave·October·1918	India's boats	Performed·at·1918·Varieties·Concert.··In·hospital·in·Bodo.··Good·shooting·medal·awarded·on·HMS·Pegasus·1905	Yes		Yes	°Yes
Kennedy	William·G.·A	16/09/1873.·Cumberland.··Died·	Commander·-·Officer	R.·N		Saxon	Lived·outside·of·the·camp.··Married·Theodora·Lundh·28.02.16	Yes		No	Yes

Surname	First names	Birth and death dates	Rank	R. N/R.N. R/R.NV. R	What happened after	Rescue mode	Any other interesting info	Interned and number given in camp	Description of role	Mentioned in Jørstadmoen camp list 17 July, 1917	Contact with descendants
		25/11/1938									
Laggan	Constantine	21/03/1884.··Died·1955,·Brisbane,·Australia	Ordinary·Seaman	R.N.V.R·Clyde·Z/191		India's boats	From·Alexandria,·Scotland.··Wife·informed·of·death·and·then·received·letter	Yes		Yes	°Yes
Lamb	William	22/07/1892.··Died·1941,·Red·Sea	Steward	MMR	Stayed·in·Norway·until·1919·and·then·moved·to·Henley.··Died·at·sea·in·1941.	Saxon	Married·Anna·Roed·in·1919.··She·was·a·member·of·a·local·concert·band·who·came·to·camp·to·entertain·the·internees.··Mentioned·in·Henley·Times·article·by·Mike·Willoughby.	Yes.¶1		Yes	Yes

362

Surname	First names	Birth and death dates	Rank	R. N/R.N. R/R.NV. R	What happened after	Rescue mode	Any other interesting info	Interned and number given in camp	Description of role	Mentioned in Jørstadmoen camp list 17 July, 1917	Contact with descendants	
Lawrence	Robert T	°	Baker	MMR	Performed at 1918 Varieties concert	Saxon	Roomed with RA at Jorstadmoen. Mentioned in 1918 letters from Kennedy re: using electric baking plant. °	Yes. 46	°	Yes	°	
Lawson	Frank W	°	Tempy surgeon - Officer	R. N	°	Saxon	Repatriated 15/1/1916	Yes	°	°	°	
Magill	Joseph Vincent Mahood	08/05/1897. Belfast. Died 1927	Boy 1st class	R.N J.34313	°	Saxon	Promoted to Ordinary Seaman by end of WW1	Yes	Like a cadet	Yes	°Yes	
Maynard	Robert Charles	13/01/1892. London. Died 1967?	Seaman	R.N.R 5690A	°	India's boats	Performed at 1918 Varieties Concert. Enrolled 14/03/1914. Initially reported missing. Married Florence D Baker in 1917, 3rd quarter. Tattoos - ILAA on left forearm and roses on	Yes	°	Yes	°Yes	

Surname	First names	Birth and death dates	Rank	R. N/R.N. R/R.NV. R	What happened after	Rescue mode	Any other interesting info	Interned and number given in camp	Description of role	Mentioned in Jørstadmoen camp list 17 July, 1917	Contact with descendants	
							right forearm. Letter with Partridge collection					
McBain	Alex	18/12/1893 - Pitsligo, Aberdeenshire	Stoker	°	°	Saxon	°	Yes	°	Yes	°	
McCan	James	°	Stoker	°	°	Saxon	°	Yes	°	Yes	°	
McKinnon	John	°	Stoker	MMR ?285394	°	Saxon	Repatriated - bad eyes	Yes	°	No	°	
McKeever	Edward	°	Stoker	MMR	°	Saxon	Listed in 1918 Varieties Concert programme.	Yes	°	Yes	°	
Miller	Edwin	°	Fireman	MMR	°	Saxon	Engaged to Emma Halvorsen	Yes	°	Yes	°	
Milligan	Matthew	28/08/1895	Ordinary Seaman	R.N Chatham J.41004	°	Saxon	°	Yes	°	Yes	°	
Mortimer	William Robert	25/11/1873. Died 1958.	A. B	R.N Chatham 187489	°	India's boats	°Signed up at 12 years of age. °	Yes	°	Yes	°	

Surname	First names	Birth and death dates	Rank	R. N/R.N. R/R.NV. R	What happened after	Rescue mode	Any other interesting info	Interned and number given in camp	Description of role	Mentioned in Jørstad moen camp list 17 July, 1917	Contact with descendants
		York, Yorkshire.									
Musselwhite	Harold	Maybe 28/05/1893. Died 1984, Dunstable, Bedfordshire.	Acting sub-Lieutenant - Officer	R.N. R	Request for repatriation whilst on leave in UK - granted	Saxon	Officer - lived out of camp	Yes	°	No	°Yes
Nelson	Charles William	°27/05/1877, Sunderland. Died March 1957.	Senior Engineer/ Chief of staff - Officer	R.N. R	°	Saxon	Chief of Staff, in number 3 boat. Letters collected by Scandinavian Philately Society. Officer - lived out of camp. Deborah granddaughter - sustained injury to his leg whilst in the water and had leg amputated on return to UK.	Yes	°	No	Yes

Surname	First names	Birth and death dates	Rank	R. N/R.N. R/R.NV. R	What happened after	Rescue mode	Any other interesting info	Interned and number given in camp	Description of role	Mentioned in Jørstad moen camp list 17 July, 1917	Contact with descendants
Oakley	William H	°	Trimmer	MMR Oakby	°	°	Performed at 1918 Varieties Concert. Australian	Yes	°	Yes	°
Parsons	Reginald Antliffe	02/06/1892, Lewisham, Kent. Died 1981, Bedford, Bedfordshire.	Seaman/Private	R.N.R 7745A	°	India's boats	Signed up to RNR 16/01/1913. Arrested 24/01/1915 charged with being a deserter from RNR - remanded until 01/02/1915 and then taken to Chatham under police escort.	Yes	°	Yes	Yes
Patmore	Francis William	27/06/1883, Bromley, Middlesex. Died 1960, East Ham, Essex.	Assist Engineer - Officer	R.N. R	°	India's boats	Wrote report for Sir E. Grey October 1915. Officer lived out of camp	Yes	°	Yes	°

Surname	First names	Birth and death dates	Rank	R. N/R.N. R/R.NV. R	What happened after	Rescue mode	Any other interesting info	Interned and number given in camp	Description of role	Mentioned in Jorstadmoen camp list 17 July, 1917	Contact with descendants
Penton	Edward Isaac	27/11/1874 – Hyde. Died 1932, Hastings.	Leading seaman	C.G Portsmouth 152245	Allowed leave in UK, 1916 for 1 month with 2 months extension for ill wife	India's boats		Yes		Yes	
Perkins	John William	Born 1888. Death unknown, disappeared.	Shipwright			India's boats	Photo on livesofthefirstworldwar.iwm.org.uk	Yes. 51		No	Yes
Perry	Samuel J		Steward	MMR		Saxon		Yes. 4		Yes	

Surname	First names	Birth and death dates	Rank	R. N/R.N. R/R.NV. R	What happened after	Rescue mode	Any other interesting info	Interned and number given in camp	Description of role	Mentioned in Jorstadmoen camp list 17 July, 1917	Contact with descendants
Philip	Jack/John	17/10/1892	Private - Corporal	R.M.L.I Chatham 16956		India's boats	Engaged to Asta Nyhus. March 17, 1917, involved in fracas with guard after returning from Akershus drunk. Imprisoned. Performed at 1918 Varieties Concert.	Yes		Yes	
Pidduck	Bernard Fitness	29/12/1893, Whitstable, Kent. Died 1977, Seasalter, Kent.	Seaman	R.N.R 6629A		India's boats		Yes		Yes	
Pike	Frederick	02/06/1881	Corporal	R.M.L.I. Chatham 11417		Saxon	Enrolled 05/02/1900. Hospital in Narvik	Yes		Yes	
Price	William		Fireman			India's boats	Imprisoned for 3 days for disorder and intoxication	Yes		Yes	

365

Surname	First names	Birth and death dates	Rank	R. N/R.N. R/R.NV. R	What happened after	Rescue mode	Any other interesting info	Interned and number given in camp	Description of role	Mentioned in Jørstadmoen camp list 17 July, 1917	Contact with descendants
Quinton	R	06/10/1896	Pro-2nd Cooks mate	R.N Chatham M10850	Repatriated - "invalided home 27/07/16"	India's boats		Yes		No	
Rex	Cyril	26/10/1896, Tadcaster, York.	Private	R.M.L.I 19118		Saxon		Yes. 8		Yes	
Riley	Henry		Stoker			Saxon		Yes		Yes	
Ripley	Herbert Charles	1876, Walmer Kent. Died 1940, Sussex, England.	Colour Sargeant	R.M.L.I Chatham 7437	"Invalided home 1/06/1916"	Saxon	Postcards in open market from start of 1916. In hospital in Narvik.	Yes	Protected the ensigns	No	
Rodriguez	Marian o		Steward			Saxon	Maybe repatriated	Yes. 5		No	
Ross	Charles		Steward			Saxon		Yes. 3		Yes	

Surname	First names	Birth and death dates	Rank	R. N/R.N. R/R.NV. R	What happened after	Rescue mode	Any other interesting info	Interned and number given in camp	Description of role	Mentioned in Jørstadmoen camp list 17 July, 1917	Contact with descendants
Clunies-Ross	Ronald	28/06/1897 - Cocos Keeling Islands. Died 1935 Bromley, Kent	Proby mid - Officer	R.N. R		Saxon	Coconut prince. Married Klara Thygsen (Klara Marie Larud, also known as Clara Marie) Had daughter Isabel in 1919 and Knut in 1924. HMS Victorian in 1914. Acting Sub-Lieut Aug 1914.	Yes		No	
Sampson	Frederick Ernest	31/12/1877 - Wangford, Suffolk. Died 1953.	A. B	R.N Chatham 171702		Saxon	Postcards in open market	Yes		Yes	
Sanders	Thomas Joseph	09/08/1865 - Portsea, Hampshire. Died 1943,	Ch. Arm (Pens)	R.N Chatham 145068	"Invalided home 13/08/1916"	India's boats	Roomed with RA at Jorstadmoen.	Yes. 41		No	°Yes

366

Surname	First names	Birth and death dates	Rank	R. N/R.N. R/R.NV. R	What happened after	Rescue mode	Any other interesting info	Interned and number given in camp	Description of role	Mentioned in Jorstadmoen camp list 17 July, 1917	Contact with descendants
		Portsmouth.									
Simmonds	Charles	21/11/95 - Hounslow	2nd Cooks mate	R.N Chatham M10756	¤	India's boats	Medalled to *HMS Actaeon*. Reported missing but telegram announcing safety	Yes	¤	Yes	¤
Smith	Henry	¤	Fireman	¤	¤	Saxon	¤	Yes	¤	Yes	¤
Spiteri	Felice	1890?	Fireman	¤	¤	Saxon	Maltese	Yes	¤	Yes	¤
Stock	Sidney George	04/08/1881 - Bedford. Died 1950, Bedford.	A.B	R.N Chatham 191684	¤	India's boats	¤	Yes	¤	Yes	¤
Stone	Francis John	10/01/1886 - Dorset. Died 1968, Weymouth, Dorset.	Ship's cook	R.N Chatham 347740	¤	India's boats	Cooks Mate Minerva 1908	Yes	¤	Yes	¤

Surname	First names	Birth and death dates	Rank	R. N/R.N. R/R.NV. R	What happened after	Rescue mode	Any other interesting info	Interned and number given in camp	Description of role	Mentioned in Jorstadmoen camp list 17 July, 1917	Contact with descendants
Summerfield	Samuel Edward	31/12/1875 - Shoreditch. Died Hackney 1920	A.B	R.N Chatham 164464	¤	Saxon	Listed in 1918 Varieties Concert programme	Yes	¤	Yes	¤
Tanner	Arthur Charles	31/10/1882 - Reading. Died 1977, Brighton, Sussex.	P.O 1st class	R.N Portsmouth 201416	¤	Saxon	¤	Yes	¤	Yes	Yes
Taylor	Elvy	05/11/1884 - Meopham, Kent. Died 1973, Dartford, Kent.	A.B	R.N Chatham 210140	¤	India's boats	¤	Yes	¤	Yes	¤

Surname	First names	Birth and death dates	Rank	R. N/R.N. R/R.NV. R	What happened after	Rescue mode	Any other interesting info	Interned and number given in camp	Description of role	Mentioned in Jorstadmoen camp list 17 July, 1917	Contact with descendants	
Temple	Charles Albert	Maybe 1888, Middlesex. Died 1973, Dartford, Kent.	Fireman	¤	¤	India's boats	In Dombås for a period. Written about in National Roll of Great War. Volunteered April 1915. Wounded in sinking. Demobilized December 1918.	Yes	¤	Yes	¤	
Tilley	William M	07/04/1894. Died 1976 in Norway	Fireman	¤	¤	Saxon	Married Agnethe Haugen - camp cook. Listed in 1918 Varieties Concert programme. Had 6 children with Agnethe.	Yes. 78	¤	Yes	Yes	
Tims	Frederick William	18/08/1884, Woolwich, Kent. Died 1934, Woolwich	Engineer Officer	R.N. R	¤	Saxon	Got one week leave. Officer lived out of camp. Listed in the London Gazette. Temp Engineer Lieut March 1915.	Yes	¤	No	¤	

Surname	First names	Birth and death dates	Rank	R. N/R.N. R/R.NV. R	What happened after	Rescue mode	Any other interesting info	Interned and number given in camp	Description of role	Mentioned in Jorstad moen camp list 17 July, 1917	Contact with descendants	
Trinder	David Francis	28/06/1896. Died 1934	Private	R.M.L.I Chatham 18228	Applied to stay in Norway. Listed as on Pembroke until 16/03/1919. Moved to U.S. Petition filed for naturalization in 1942 in Brooklyn.	¤	Enrolled 27/10/1913.	Yes. 6	¤	Yes	Yes	
Wadham	Albert Ernest	01/03/1876. East Preston, Sussex.	Shipwright 1st class	R.N Chatham M11129	¤	India's boats	¤		Yes. 48.	¤	Yes	¤	

Surname	First names	Birth and death dates	Rank	R. N/R.N. R/R.NV. R	What happened after	Rescue mode	Any other interesting info	Interned and number given in camp	Description of role	Mentioned in Jørstadmoen camp list 17 July, 1917	Contact with descendants
		Died 1944									
Ward	George	01/04/1884, Goole, Yorkshire. Died 1943	A. B	R.N Chatham 213827	Allowed leave	India's boats		Yes		Yes	
Ward	William James	28/05/1868	P.O 1st class	R.N Chatham 125843		Saxon	Listed as died on active service	Yes		No	
Ware	Albert Charles	18/08/1876, Portishead, Somerset	Leading seaman	R.N Chatham 170330		Saxon	Made official complaint about food rations	Yes		Yes	

Surname	First names	Birth and death dates	Rank	R. N/R.N. R/R.NV. R	What happened after	Rescue mode	Any other interesting info	Interned and number given in camp	Description of role	Mentioned in Jørstadmoen camp list 17 July, 1917	Contact with descendants
Wells	John Thomas	Aged 38. Born 1879	A. B	R.N Chatham 187303	Died 20/10/1917, buried at Gjovik on October 25th.	Saxon	Died at Prestestæter Asylum - psychiatric hospital Four of his shipmates accompanied by a sergeant of the guard were allowed to attend the funeral	Yes		Yes	
White	Charles Henry	09/08/1882, Portsea, Hampshire	Leading seaman	C.G Portsmouth 197760		India's boats		Yes		Yes	
Wood	George Arthur	22/06/1889, Rainham, Kent	Jun R. A	M. 9723		Saxon	Repatriated 15.01.16	Yes. 55		No	
Woollford	Cyril Horatio	25/03/1895, London. Died 1976	Ordinary Signalman	R.N Chatham J.11615		India's boats	Letter in Bath Postal Museum. Performed at 1918 Varieties Concert.	Yes		Yes	

Surname	First names	Birth and death dates	Rank	R. N/R.N. R/R.NV. R	What happened after	Rescue mode	Any other interesting info	Interned and number given in camp	Description of role	Mentioned in Jorstad moen camp list 17 July, 1917	Contact with descendants
Wright	John Thomas		A. B	R.N Chatham 167868		India's boats		Yes		Yes	
Zwink	Henry George Otto		A. B	R.N Chatham SS 2209		Saxon		Yes		Yes	
108 men on arrival at Jorstad moen. ... 85/6 men remained by the end of the war.											
Abbreviations											
R. N	Royal Navy										

Surname	First names	Birth and death dates	Rank	R. N/R.N. R/R.NV. R	What happened after	Rescue mode	Any other interesting info	Interned and number given in camp	Description of role	Mentioned in Jorstad moen camp list 17 July, 1917	Contact with descendants
R.N. R	Royal Navy Reserve										
R.N.V. R	Royal Navy Volunteer Reserve										
R.F. R	Royal Fleet Reserve										
R.M.L. I	Royal Marine Light Infantry										
C.G	Coastguard										
A. B	Able Seaman										
A. R	Armament crew?										
Assist	Assistant										

Surname	First names	Birth and death dates	Rank	R. N/R.N. R/R.NV. R	What happened after	Rescue mode	Any other interesting info	Interned and number given in camp	Description of role	Mentioned in Jørstadmoen camp list 17 July, 1917	Contact with descendants	
Ch Armr	Chief Armourer	°	°	°	°	°	°	°	°	°	°	
E.R. A	Engine room artificer	°	°	°	°	°	°	°	°	°	°	
Hyd winchman n	Hydraulic winchman an	°	°	°	°	°	°	°	°	°	°	
Jun R. A	Junior radio artificer	°	°	°	°	°	°	°	°	°	°	
Pens	Seaman who has been pensioned off but recalled in wartime	°	°	°	°	°	°	°	°	°	°	
Proby mid	Probationary	°	°	°	°	°	°	°	°	°	°	

Surname	First names	Birth and death dates	Rank	R. N/R.N. R/R.NV. R	What happened after	Rescue mode	Any other interesting info	Interned and number given in camp	Description of role	Mentioned in Jørstadmoen camp list 17 July, 1917	Contact with descendants	
	midshipman											
Probtr	Probationer	°	°	°	°	°	°	°	°	°	°	
Tempy mid	Temporary midshipman	°	°	°	°	°	°	°	°	°	°	
Tempy wnt tel	Temporary warrant telegraphist	°	°	°	°	°	°	°	°	°	°	